HARD TO KILL

A hero's tale of surviving Vietnam and the Catholic Church

Published by Hellgate Press
(An imprint of L&R Publishing, LLC)
PO Box 3531
Ashland, OR 97520
email: sales@hellgatepress.com

Editor: Harley B. Patrick
Book design: Michael Campbell
Cover design: L. Redding
Cover photo and authors' photos by Jeff Noble

Cataloging In Publication Data is available
from the publisher upon request.
ISBN: 978-1-55571-906-7

HARD TO KILL

A hero's tale of surviving
Vietnam and the Catholic Church

JOE LADENSACK

with Joseph A. Reaves

For the brave men who were slaughtered
on Black Virgin Mountain
and the far-too-many souls
whose lives were ruined by sexual abuse.

Contents

Introduction

By Joseph A. Reaves

JOSEPH CONRAD LADENSACK was finally ready to talk.

And I was more than ready to listen.

This was twelve years after Ladensack made history by becoming the first priest to voluntarily testify against his peers and superiors in the revolting Roman Catholic sexual abuse scandal, and thirty-five years after an extraordinary tour of duty in Vietnam during which he won two Silver Stars, six Bronze Stars, a Purple Heart and was told he was being nominated for the Congressional Medal of Honor.

I'd tried, without luck, to interview him in 2003 when I was an investigative reporter for the *Arizona Republic* tracking down preda-tor and pedophile priests in the Diocese of Phoenix. I wrote letters that went unanswered. I reached him by phone once and had a very pleasant, totally unproductive conversation. Joe later told me he was impressed how polite and convincing my letters were — and how persuasive I had been on the phone. He said he was on the verge of agreeing to an interview when his wife, Anita, raised her eyebrows and warned him off.

Joe and Anita, who married after he was thrown out of the church, had good reason to be wary. Joe had been receiving death threats, veiled and not-so-veiled, for years since he first reported to police a case of a fellow priest molesting the teenage son of one of his friends in 1984. Those threats only increased in January 2003 after he appeared before a grand jury investigating wholesale sexual abuse by more than fifty priests and church employees in Phoenix — crimes that were covered up for decades by Bishop Thomas J. O'Brien.

Ladensack's testimony led directly to the indictments of six priests and would have led to O'Brien becoming the first Catholic bishop in the United States to be charged with felony obstruction of justice and perjury but for an immunity agreement that stripped him of much of his power and forced him to make an embarrassing public written admission of guilt.

Luckily for me, my newspaper, and our readers, I didn't need to talk to Ladensack directly in 2003. There were enough court records, church documents, courageous victims, relentless investigators, and helpful leaks to piece together the staggering and sickening scope of criminal exploitation by men of feigned faith.

On June 3, 2003, Maricopa County Attorney Rick Romley, a Catholic disabled Vietnam veteran and dogged prosecutor, announced the indictments of six priests and the stunning confession of guilt by O'Brien.

Romley's investigation lasted thirteen months. I covered it from start to finish and paid a huge emotional price.

I sat with grown men who wept when they abandoned long years of silence to tell me how they had been raped as children by priests they once honored.

Each day, I grew angrier and darker as I learned more about the malignancy rotting inside the church I once revered as an altar boy and retreat captain at an all-boys Catholic high school in suburban New Orleans.

I battled regularly with my editors, who were increasingly reluctant to publish stories on the scandal, particularly as we learned how widespread the abuse had been. My chief editor was a devout Catholic, a member of the Knights of Columbus, the church's largest and most prestigious lay organization. He was unabashed in his desire to protect the church. Once, deep into our investigation, he tried to stonewall a story I and another determined reporter, Kelly Ettenborough, had spent weeks piecing together. It chronicled how the worst predator priests in Phoenix had been systematically transferred to Hispanic parishes where their new victims were especially vulnerable and far less likely to report their abuse. O'Brien and his predecessor, Bishop James S. Rausch, not only covered up for their criminal underlings, but actually made it easier for them to prey on children for decades.

The editor grilled me relentlessly daily on every date, fact, allegation, court record, attorney rebuttal, and victim quote in the story. Fair enough. That's what a good editor does — and he was a good editor. But one afternoon, in obvious exasperation, he looked at me and said: "I just don't get it. Why is this a story?"

We were in his glass-walled office just off the newsroom and his door was open.

I was incensed and reacted in a way I regret today, but can't undo. I stood and slammed an open palm on his metal desk with an ear-shattering thud.

"What don't you get?" I screamed. "This is about priests bending little boys over the altar and fucking them up the ass in the name of God!"

That was the last time I spoke to that editor. I worked with another, more objective editor for the rest of the project. The original editor died of cancer in 2010 and was given a full Catholic funeral mass. I slipped into church shortly after the service began and sat alone in the last pew. Seven years had passed and I was still so angry I couldn't find it in my heart to forgive. I'm not sure I ever will.

IN EARLY 2005, eighteen months after the church investigation ended, I took a new, happier job as national baseball writer for the *Republic*. That may sound a strange transition — investigative reporter to sports columnist — but I had a history of similar strange transitions.

In 1991, I was the *Chicago Tribune*'s Warsaw bureau chief covering the heady days of Poland's unexpected conversion from communism to capitalism. I'd been with the *Tribune* since January 1982 when I was hired away from the United Press International bureau in Vienna, Austria, where I was Chief East European Correspondent, chronicling the Solidarity uprising in Poland. In all, I'd been a foreign correspondent since 1979 and, as I told my boss at the *Trib*: "I'm tired of getting shot at, shit on, and never knowing when I'm going to be home."

I had been accepted into a PhD program at the University of Tennessee and planned on getting my degree and teaching journalism the rest of my life.

My boss at the *Trib*, F. Richard Ciccone, a Marine veteran who won a Bronze Star in Vietnam, was the most inspiring leader I came across in a forty-year career. He refused to let me quit. Dick offered me everything until he finally hit on something I couldn't refuse: The Cubs. I came home from Warsaw to Wrigley and eventually wrote a book by that name.

I covered the Cubs and White Sox for the *Tribune* for four years from 1992-95 until my wife, Lynne, was offered a job as vice president of the most prestigious British public relations firm in Hong Kong. From 1995-98, I was the spousal appendage, working on a master's degree at the University of Hong Kong and turning my thesis on the history of baseball in Asia into another book while my wife was the power broker.

In July 1998, we decided to come home to the United States. Lynne is a Texas girl. I am a New Orleans boy. And we had lived around the world — New Orleans, Houston, Dallas, London, Vienna, Chicago, Beijing, Hong Kong, Manila, Rome, Warsaw. We opened a bottle of wine in our beautiful flat overlooking Victoria Harbor and talked about where we should move. I chose Hawaii, where I had done a fellowship at the East-West Center before becoming Beijing bureau chief for the *Tribune*. Lynne chose Arizona, where she reveled in the memory of picture-perfect Spring Training mornings when I covered the Cubs.

We looked at real estate prices and moved to Arizona.

My bizarre career took another twist in 2007 when Los Angeles Dodgers General Manager Ned Colletti, who had been a vice president with the Cubs during my years covering the team, came to Arizona and asked me to work for him. I joined the Dodgers' front office as Director of International Relations and was still there October 28, 2014, when Joe Ladensack found me through an internet search. He mailed a short letter to Dodger Stadium.

> *Hi Mr. Reaves,*
>
> *You contacted me about ten years ago concerning the priest pedophile investigation in Phoenix, AZ. Since all of the cases now have been resolved and the time for appeals exhausted, I am able to talk about my experiences with the Diocese of Phoenix.*
>
> *If you are still interested in this story, I am willing to be interviewed by you.*
>
> *I look forward to hearing from you.*
>
> *Thank you,*
> *Joe Ladensack*

He included his home address, phone number, and e-mail.

Even though I worked for the Los Angeles Dodgers, my main office was in Arizona where the team had its Spring Training headquarters and where I lived. Joe's letter lingered in the L.A. mailroom for weeks. When I finally received it, I was torn. The anger and darkness of the church investigation swelled over me again. Those times had been so emotional, and my feelings so raw, that my wife and I nearly divorced.

I told Lynne about the letter from Ladensack and said I thought I would go see him. She said no. She talked about what she called the "dark spirits" that enveloped us during the investigation and said she didn't want them in our lives again. I understood and agreed. But I knew from my research that Joe Ladensack was an extraordinary man.

Besides being a fearless whistleblower in the priest abuse scandal, he was a Vietnam War hero—an incredibly highly decorated hero. I told Lynne I thought I owed Ladensack the respect of at least a visit.

Reluctantly, Lynne agreed, and on June 9, 2015, as I was preparing to retire from the Dodgers, I drove one-hundred-fifty miles from our home in Scottsdale, Arizona, to Joe and Anita Ladensack's in Tucson. I'd never laid eyes on Joe Ladensack. We had been "partners in crime," but we'd never seen each other. I'd come to pay my respects to a man worthy of respect and planned on leaving as quickly as possible.

I rang the doorbell on a modest white adobe house and stood outside a dark screen door that swung open surprisingly quickly. The transom revealed a bear of a man—no, a cub of a man, because he was burly, but compact; not intimidating like a grown bear, more cuddly like a cub. Joe Ladensack stepped onto the porch and I heard his lovely, infectious, high-pitched laugh for the first time.

"Joe," he said to me in what only could be called a priestly tone. "I'm dying. And like everyone who's dying, I made a bucket list. You're at the top of my bucket list. I wanted to meet you. We did some good stuff together."

That's how this book came to be.

LITTLE DID WE know that our work together was not yet finished. Fourteen years after Ladensack's testimony helped bring down Bishop Thomas J. O'Brien and indict a half-dozen predator priests, a new lawsuit accused the bishop of personally serially molesting an altar boy in the late 1970s and early 1980s. The impressive young lawyers who brought the case—Tim Hale of Santa Barbara, California, and Carlo Mercaldo of Tucson—met Joe and me to review what by then had grown to more than seventy-five cases of priestly abuse in the Phoenix Diocese.

Joe had been battling cancer for little more than ten years by then and his white blood cells, platelets, and red blood cells all were critically low. Any infection almost certainly would be fatal. He rarely left the protective bubble of his home and in the two years we had been working on this book, we'd never been anywhere together other than his house. But when I told Joe about the lawyers, he was determined to meet them. I drove to Tucson to pick him up and found him in a shirt and tie, in his usual good humor, eager to climb into my car for the meeting at Mercaldo's office.

"Let's go, Joe," he said as we stepped into the searing August Arizona sunshine. "We've got more good stuff to do together."

Chapter 1
Tucson, Arizona ~ The End
Father Joe Ladensack

BY THE TIME I got there, Harry Takata was drunk and had a gun.

That's when I should have known my days as a priest were numbered.

Takata, a longtime friend, was in a blind rage. Two hours earlier, he had walked into his son's bedroom where another priest — another longtime family friend — was orally copulating the fifteen-year-old boy.

"I'm going to kill him!" Harry barked when I stepped into the living room of the Takatas' cinder-block home in Chandler, Arizona — then a quiet, but soon-to-be-sprawling, suburb of Phoenix.

Harry's wife, Mary Magdolna Takata, a Hungarian-born World War II bride who immigrated to Arizona from Japan with her husband in 1970, had called me and begged me to come to the house.

"Father Joe, you're the only one we thought might believe us," she wept. "You have to help, please! Harry is going crazy."

It was a Saturday night on Memorial Day weekend in 1984 and I was unpacking at a new assignment in a parish in far West Phoenix. The last thing I wanted to do was drive forty-five minutes across town to calm a hysterical friend. But Magda was as relentless as her namesake, Mary Magdelene, had been at the tomb of Jesus. She implored me in broken English with her heavy Hungarian accent until I finally gave in.

Harry, wearing a tight-fitting "wife beater" sleeveless white cotton tank-top, was seated on a beige and mauve fabric sofa when I arrived.

He was clutching what I later learned was his sixth twelve-ounce can of Coors in less than two hours.

On the arm of the sofa was a loaded pistol.

"Harry, you don't want to do this," I told him when he spat out his threat to kill John Giandelone, the serial pedophile who had just molested Harry Takata Jr. "You kill him and your life is ruined. You'll go to prison and your son will lose a father."

Giandelone had fled as soon as Takata walked in on him. Harry Jr. remained in his bedroom weeping the rest of the night.

I spent more than an hour patiently cajoling Harry Sr. before I convinced him to let me call the police.

The moment I did was the beginning of the end of my life as a priest.

Incredibly, and horribly, I had reported Giandelone to my superiors for an attack on another boy in a different parish five years earlier. Then-Bishop James S. Rausch assured me he would take care of Giandelone. Instead, Rausch, a former general secretary of the National Council of Catholic Bishops who had his own sexual demons, did what church leaders across the world were doing — and continued to do — for decades. He quietly transferred Giandelone to a new parish, hid his crimes, and blindly allowed him to continue preying on children.

I'd reported a half dozen other predator priests in the five years since Giandelone's first molestation and every one of them was handled the same way — first by Rausch, then by his successor Thomas J. O'Brien, who became bishop in 1981 after Rausch died of a heart attack at age fifty-two. They quietly transferred the guilty priests.

Finally, I'd had enough. I wasn't going to let it happen again. The Takatas and I called Chandler Police and filed a formal report. Then I drove to my new rectory and happily let Bishop O'Brien know what we'd done.

I must admit, it felt good on so many levels — not the least of which was knowing I was rubbing O'Brien's nose in his own filth.

A diminutive man who entered the seminary at age thirteen, Thomas J. O'Brien was never in touch with the real world. He hated controversy and confrontation and dealt poorly with all but the most meek priests under his rule.

The bishop had what he called a "Bat Phone" with a private number available only to his priests, who were under orders to use the line judiciously, if at all. I called the "Bat Phone" and knew immediately O'Brien was put out.

"This had better be good," he snapped before I could say a word.

By the time I finished relaying the gory details of John Giandelone and Harry Takata's son, O'Brien was beside himself. He was livid. Sickeningly, not because of what had happened, but because of the complications it would bring. Then, when I told him I'd already reported the incident to the police, O'Brien blew totally out of control.

"Why did you go out there?" he yelled over the Bat Phone. "Why did you call the police? You have to come to me with this immediately. To me first, and only to me.

"You owe me obedience. You took a vow, and I must remind you, young man, that you need to keep your vow."

The bishop ordered me to go back to the Takatas and have them recant the story to the police.

I reminded O'Brien that I was a military veteran and asked him if he remembered the Nuremberg Trials.

To my astonishment, a prince of the Roman Catholic Church, which celebrates intellect and scholarship, said he'd never heard of the Nuremberg Trials.

"No, what are they?" O'Brien said.

When I recovered from the shock, I told the bishop I had been trained as a young officer that there was such a thing as an unlawful order — that I thought what he was telling me to do was immoral and I refused to do it.

THREE DECADES AFTER that painful confrontation, the end is near.

Finally.

It's long overdue.

I've been to the brink, what? Two? Three? Four times?

The truth is, I'm hard to kill. I've always been hard to kill.

But this time, I really am dying. And I'm at peace with it. I've had a good life. I've been a warrior, a Catholic priest, a good husband, and a loving father. I knew how to obey orders and when to ignore them; how to storm in for the kill and when to run and hide.

From May 1969 to April 1970, I served in Vietnam with the 2nd Battalion (Mechanized), 2nd Infantry Regiment of the 1st Infantry Division — the storied Big Red One.

During those eleven months of hell, I was shot in the head, survived dozens of major battles and firefights, and became what my officers called a "highly decorated soldier." I was awarded two Silver Stars, six Bronze Stars with V for valor, a Purple Heart, and Vietnam's Cross of Gallantry with Palm — given by the South Vietnamese government for heroic conduct in combat. I was recommended for the Congressional Medal of Honor — until I made the mistake of telling two *Stars and Stripes* reporters the truth about a bombastic brigadier general who got too many good men killed for no good reason.

Vietnam changed me. War changes everyone, of course. But in my case, the transformation was epic. I morphed from warrior to Catholic priest. Living through hell made me want to be closer to God. Unfortunately, being closer to God eventually drove me from the Catholic Church.

On September 1, 1970, just two weeks after my discharge from the Army, I registered at St. John's Seminary in Camarillo, California, as a third-year undergraduate. I already had my history degree from Arizona State University and had started work on a master's in Oriental history with Mandarin language classes before I went to Vietnam. But the faculty at St. John's didn't know how to handle a twenty-three-year-old newcomer to religious study. Most of my classmates had been in the seminary since they were freshmen in high school. The powers-that-be eventually decided my ASU degree wasn't really the right track for a priest, so they enrolled me as a junior in a four-year program to earn a Bachelor of Arts in Philosophy.

From my first days in the seminary, I was uneasy with the unusually high number of faculty and students I perceived to be — how can I put this? — well, effeminate. Thirty years later, news reports would reveal that St. John's was one of several notorious nesting grounds for would-be priests who went on to become serial pedophiles and sexual predators. The seminarians at St. John's all professed the values of priestly celibacy, but many ignored it in practice.

Less than three years after my ordination, in 1976, I made my first report of child sexual abuse by a fellow priest — the despicable John Maurice Giandelone; the very one who would later attack Harry Takata's son.

During the years that followed, I witnessed an unrelenting muster of monsters who preyed on innocents that was as ghastly — and dangerous — as anything I lived through in Vietnam.

In war, I learned I was hard to kill. I learned it again during the agonizing years it took for the enormity of children abused by clerics to become public. Members of the church, and some of its strongest political allies, threatened to kill me if I spoke to the media. The threats were constant and real.

Two years after the Takata showdown, O'Brien withdrew my priestly privileges and I went into hiding in remote Southern Arizona for nearly two decades. One wonderful blessing of that time was meeting and marrying Anita Cooper, a widow, whose sons became mine.

Anita, John, and Charlie brought me more happiness than I ever could have imagined.

Now, I'm finding I'm still hard to kill.

On Memorial Day 2013, I entered hospice six years after being diagnosed with Hairy Cell Leukemia, a rare cancer of the blood in which my bone marrow makes too many lymphocytes, a type of abnormal white blood cell that destroys the body's natural white blood cells. Doctors gave me six weeks to live. Twenty-five months after I went into hospice, they threw me out. I wasn't dying fast enough for them.

Three years after that, I'm still around, still working to bring Bishop O'Brien and his legions to justice.

The end may be coming, but I'm still hard to kill.

Chapter 2
An Lộc District, Vietnam ~ May 23-24, 1969

2nd Lt. Joe Ladensack

ONE DAY AND I'M DEAD.

That's what I thought as we neared the crest of a hill and I saw a North Vietnamese Army anti-armor squad laying in ambush with a 57-mm recoilless rifle aimed directly at my Armored Personnel Carrier.

I'd been in Vietnam less than twenty-four hours, landing at Fire Support Base Thunder IV in the An Lộc District, 107 kilometers (66 miles) north of Saigon. I was assigned to Alpha Company, 2nd Battalion (Mechanized), 2nd Infantry Regiment of the 1st Infantry Division. My mortar platoon leader, 1st Lt. Mike Mulhern, who, like me, was from Phoenix, Arizona, drove me to the village of Quần Lợi, where a Brigade of the 1st Cav was based. Alpha Company would be spending the night there.

Not long after we arrived at Quần Lợi, Alpha Company roared in from a day-long patrol. The men and their tracks — their M-113 APCs — were covered in the red dust I soon realized oozed unceasingly from the jungles in this part of South Vietnam. I remember thinking: "Is this really an American unit?" They looked ragtag, dirty, disheveled, and undisciplined — something you would have seen a decade later in the *Mad Max* movies. It would take only a few hours for my naïve first impression of these men to change forever.

Once the APCs rumbled to a stop, Mulhern walked me to one of them and introduced me to Capt. Dudley "Pete" Combs, the company commander. Combs quickly dismissed Mulhern and turned to me.

"Do you remember me?" he asked.

I was petrified. This man was intimidating.

"No, sir," I stammered.

"You attended Infantry Officer Basic Course last year, didn't you?" he said. "Well, I was the officer in charge of the map reading committee."

Now, I was more than petrified. I flashed back to my training. Map reading was the hardest part of the Infantry Officer Basic Course and the reason was this man, who was constantly in everybody's face.

"I'm going to Vietnam soon and God help any lieutenant assigned to me who doesn't know how to read a map!" he boomed every day.

Here I was, less than a year later, assigned to Combs.

"Well, I hope you learned because knowing where you are at all times is the most important skill in my company," he said. "You have ten days to show me you can read a map or I'll kick your ass out of Alpha and I don't care where it lands.

"I don't like lieutenants. Sergeants are better leaders than lieutenants. At least they know something. But the Army says I have to have you — so here you are. Let me give you some advice. An infantry platoon is like a street gang. It always chooses a leader. Lieutenant, that had better be you!"

I didn't know it then, but Pete Combs would become one of the most important men in my life — even though we would be together just one month.

THAT FIRST NIGHT, my platoon, the Second, was assigned to establish a mounted ambush about a kilometer from the clearing where Alpha Company was dug in for the night. With our APCs facing outward in a circle, our job was to protect the rest of the company while they slept.

Instead, every one of us in the mounted ambush fell asleep.

I was awakened at 2 AM by popping sounds that reminded me of the fireworks my family used to watch every Fourth of July in our front yard about a mile from the Phoenix Country Club.

These popping sounds, though, came from M-301A1 illumination rounds being fired by friendly mortars over our heads. Capt. Combs had been desperately trying to reach anyone by radio and realized we were all asleep. He ordered the illumination rounds, each of which burned in the night sky for up to seventy-five seconds, drifting down slowly by parachute, lighting an area twelve-hundred yards wide.

"You Sons of Bitches wake up! Wake up! Wake up!" Combs was screaming on the radio three feet from my ear.

I woke the man sleeping next to me, 1st Lt. Dick Mailing, who I'd be replacing as platoon leader later that day.

"Holy Shit!" Mailing said as he saw the night sky lit up. "We're in big trouble!"

He grabbed the radio.

"Alpha Six, this is Two-Six. Over."

A screaming Capt. Combs responded immediately.

"Sorry to wake you, Two-Six. I hope the entire North Vietnamese Army knows where you are now and kills every one of you bastards!

"Any of you still alive report to me at 0745! Over and out!"

The next morning, at precisely 0745, Mailing and I were standing in front of Capt. Combs.

"For this little stunt, Second Platoon will pull 'point' the next ten days and the next ten night ambushes," he yelled.

"Mailing, you sack of shit, I'm glad you're getting the hell out of here! Ladensack, or whatever your name is, watch this lazy S.O.B. today and try to learn from him."

Combs was about to dismiss us when his radio operator sprinted up and said Lt. Col. Jacques Michienzi, the Battalion Commander, wanted to speak to him immediately.

Minutes later, everything was controlled chaos.

Our reconnaissance platoon had been ambushed in the nearby village of Minh Đức.

"Saddle your ponies," Combs barked. "Second Platoon is in the lead followed by Third Platoon, mortars, and First Platoon pulling drag. Let's roll!"

The entire company instantly shrugged off any lingering early morning grogginess and sprang to life. Men climbed up the sides and backs of APCs, pulling on flack vests and helmets, crackling out radio checks, grabbing M-16s. I'd never seen an Army unit move so fast and efficiently. It was a beautiful sight.

AT FIRST LIGHT, the recon platoon had been given the mission of reinforcing a small South Vietnamese outpost that had been attacked by a North Vietnamese Army unit the night before. When recon reached Minh Đức, on the edge of a rubber plantation, one of the APCs was hit by a rocket-propelled grenade. The platoon was scattered up and down the road by the time we reached them.

"Drive through the village and hang an immediate right," Lt. Col. Michienzi yelled. "That's where they are."

Michienzi, a veteran of World War II, Korea, and Vietnam, was right. The NVA were outside the village in force. The next three hours were a blur. I was at Lt. Mailing's side as the company moved from one firefight to another, changing formations, killing scores of NVA soldiers, and scrambling to survive a "dance of death" that seemed as if it would never stop. I realized at one point that this was my one day to learn on the job how to be a platoon leader. It seemed an impossible task. I would need a month, no, six months, with Mailing before I'd be ready. But that wouldn't happen. I had another nine hours or so. Then I'd be on my own to lead this street gang.

Not long after one of the major firefights, Capt. Combs walked up to our track. Mailing and I jumped off the APC — about a six-foot drop. I would take that plunge hundreds of times in the next eleven months. To this day, I don't know how I didn't break an ankle or fall on my face.

Combs was a changed man. Instead of the gruff, screaming captain of the morning, he approached us with an almost fatherly air.

"Big stud," he said affectionately to Mailing — the same guy he'd called a "sack of shit" not more than two hours ago. "We just had a Loach spot a pair of 51 cal anti-aircraft guns on top of that hill."

"Loach" was the military acronym for Light Observation and Control Helicopter, a nimble little, two-seat firefly of an aircraft that provided invaluable battlefield intelligence in Vietnam.

"How do you want to attack them?" Combs asked. "In formation? Or like the Russians?"

I wasn't sure just then what Combs was asking, but I quickly came to understand he was giving Mailing the option of a slow, deliberate attack with our APCs in the customary "Box" formation or a "fast attack" in a single column that would shift to the Box only after making contact with the enemy.

"Russian-style," said Mailing, opting for the fast attack.

We jumped up and Mailing said, "Keep your head low and follow me everywhere. I can't watch out for you."

Mailing barked out orders and his track started to weave up a narrow logging road along the incline of a small hill. As we neared the crest of the hill, trailed by three other APCs, I glimpsed movement out of my left peripheral vision. I turned my head and caught sight of that NVA anti-armor squad with a 57-mm recoilless rifle aimed directly at us. Before I could react, I saw a white cloud of smoke that should have heralded my death on my first full day in Vietnam. Instead, miraculously, the round hit a low-hanging tree and exploded harmlessly.

I "un-assed" myself from Mailing's track and charged the NVA before they could load and fire another round. A short burst from my CAR-15, Colt Automatic Rifle, sent the NVA scrambling into the brush like scared squirrels. I sensed something to my left and turned to see two 51 caliber anti-aircraft guns firing at the Loach that first alerted us to them. Without thinking, I ran forward, spraying the small group of NVA. Two went down and four others raised their arms in surrender.

I glanced behind me expecting Mailing and the rest of the Second Platoon to be close at hand and ready to heap praise on me. Instead, I realized they were a good twenty-five yards behind, still deploying on line.

As I prodded my prisoners to keep their arms up, Capt. Combs and Mailing caught up with me.

"You damn S.O.B.," Combs yelled. "This is going to get you killed real fast."

I ignored the rebuke.

"Sir, I have five KIAs and four POWs for you."

Combs said, "We haven't had any POWs in months."

"Well you have some now," I said proudly.

"You don't understand me," Combs barked back. "We haven't had any POWs in months."

Slowly, it dawned on me what he was saying. Combs was like a mother lion telling her cub to administer the "coup de grace" on some helpless antelope.

I was about to protest — to shout I wouldn't kill an unarmed prisoner — when Michienzi, the battalion commander, appeared out of nowhere.

"Hell of a job, Combs," he said. "These POWs will give us a lot of info on what we are up against here."

Combs accepted a hearty handshake from his commander, shot a scowl at me, and told me to get back to Second Platoon.

My first day as a warrior was over. One day and still alive. So far, so good.

I'm just glad I didn't know what my second day had in store.

THE NEXT MORNING, May 24, 1969, Lt. Mailing handed me his field map and left for his new job as X-O, Executive Officer, of Bravo Company. I was officially a platoon leader and within minutes was dealing with my first problem.

Without consulting me, one of my sergeants started making whole-sale personnel changes — moving men from one track to another. When I asked Staff Sgt. Cantor Hill what he was doing, I got a curt reply: "These changes are necessary. Lt. Mailing okayed them. I'll fill you in later."

Before I could address the situation, Capt. Combs called his platoon leaders to brief us on the day's duties. We would conduct a Reconnais-sance-In-Force through the nearby An Lộc Rubber Plantation.

When the briefing wrapped, Capt. Combs asked me to stay behind.

"I noticed Hill is moving your troops around," Combs said. "He will be your biggest problem. Mailing couldn't control Hill. You have ten days to do the job or I'll kick your ass out of here. Now go back and square your shit. We move out in fifteen minutes and, as promised, Second Platoon pulls the lead."

I went back to my platoon, told Sgt. Hill the mission of the day, and gave the order to saddle up. I knew Capt. Combs would be monitoring my map readings all day, so I told Hill my track would lead the way.

As I climbed into my helicopter seat behind the driver's hatch, I noticed a new driver, a new gunner, and a new squad leader. All three had been banished to my track by Sgt. Hill. All three would have sig-nificant roles in keeping Second Platoon and Alpha Company on "life support" the next six weeks.

We took a left turn out of Fire Base Support Thunder IV and drove through the center of An Lộc city. We hadn't gone more than a kilome-ter when Capt. Combs' voice crackled through my radio.

"Alpha Two-Six, this is Six. Where are you on the map?"

I was Alpha Two-Six... Alpha Company, Second Platoon, and Six signified the unit commander. Many of the men who served with me never knew my name. They just knew me as Two-Six.

I glanced at my map and read off the grid marks for Combs.

"Okay, good. That's correct," he said. "Proceed to grid mark 128816 and turn right."

Whew, I thought. But that was an easy one. I knew Combs was going to pepper me the rest of the day. I needed to focus. A wrong answer would mean hell to pay.

In short order, we rolled into the An Lộc Rubber Plantation, a beautifully landscaped park the French still were operating despite the war swirling around it. The rubber trees were laid out in a such a way that no matter which direction you looked, you saw perfect twelve-foot wide boulevards. Each tree had a bowl attached to collect sap. The plantation building, atop a small hill, was beautiful colonial architecture with arched terraces.

We had made three or four gentle turns when the radio snapped to life.

"Two-Six, this is Six. What is your position?"

After I answered correctly, Combs snapped back.

"What villages are within one click of your position?"

I wasn't expecting the added degree of difficulty, but I quickly searched the map and read out three villages — Cầu Sắc, Ấp Bến Cầu, and Ấp Ba.

Combs sarcastically corrected my pronunciation then asked a question I was completely at a loss to answer.

"Two-Six, where is the next possible ambush site?"

I knew I couldn't answer and knew I'd be humiliated if I read out the wrong coordinates. Everyone in the company was tuned to the same radio frequency. I opted to be honest and told Combs I didn't know.

"When you figure it out let me know," Combs said. "And don't take all day."

Now I really had to pay close attention to the contour marks on the map. My head was swirling as we continued down the road at twenty-five clicks per hour. I felt picked on, but I knew Combs was only trying to keep me and my men alive.

The rest of the morning was spent practicing "battle formations." I was surprised how efficient the company was. On order by Capt. Combs all twenty APCs would whirl into what seemed to me to be a frenzied fur ball until, almost magically, we were arrayed in a tactical formation to address a particular enemy threat from a particular direction. All I had to do was tell my platoon a particular move and all tracks would quickly move into their positions.

Years later, as I looked back at my early days with Capt. Combs, I realized I had been taking a crash course in "mech infantry operations." Nothing in my ROTC instruction at Arizona State University or training at the Infantry Officer Basic Course touched on the topic. I later discovered that all these "tactics" originated with Heinz Wilhelm Guderian, father of the blitzkrieg tactics used by the German army. By the time of the 1st Gulf War, 1990, the U.S. military had mastered its own version of blitzkrieg with the "AirLand Battle Doctrine," which was designed to defeat the enemy using fast, slashing attacks of coordinated, concentrated, and overwhelming land and air forces. Vietnam was the testing ground for the AirLand Doctrine and Capt. Combs was an early master. To keep up, I had to ramp up my learning curve quickly.

AT ABOUT 1300 on my second full day in Vietnam, Alpha Company was alerted that Bravo Company had made contact with an unknown enemy force. We spent the next two hours trailing Bravo at various times moving to protect their right, then left, flank. Capt. Combs was becoming increasingly frustrated and grumbled that "Bravo was chasing ghosts." But then about 1500 we learned the Recon Platoon was heavily engaged with an NVA force in a bunker complex and that Lt. Col. Michienzi, the Battalion Commander, was with them. Michienzi radioed for us to head north by northwest in a double column and follow directions from the Loach flying above us.

As soon as we burst out of the rubber plantation and turned left on to a narrow logging trail, Capt. Combs ordered Lt. Mike Mulhern's Mortar Platoon to drop off, set up its three mortars, and wait for firing instructions. The rest of us roared down the trail at top speed until Combs ordered us into a Box formation with First Platoon in the assault position and Third Platoon, led by Staff Sgt. James Bondsteel, on the left reinforcing the beleaguered Recon Platoon. Bondsteel would be a national hero before the battle was over.

"Two-six, cover our right flank and stay off the radio," Combs radioed me.

I was at the rear of a mile-long line of APCs at the time and had to scramble to get into position. As I neared a stand of rubber trees, I saw the tops explode in a series of scary flashes mixed with green tracer rounds.

Boy, Mulhern is sure working out, I thought.

I was wrong. That wasn't Mulhern's work. We were under heavy enemy fire. Everyone in Second Platoon, except our .50 caliber gunner, clambered off our tracks and took up positions behind the rubber trees facing right. The roar of battle was deafening.

For the next four hours, our APCs sat abandoned, with motors running, as we fought off a battalion-plus size base camp of between six-hundred and eight-hundred NVA. In addition to being outnumbered, thick jungle foliage, highly skilled snipers, and a labyrinth of fortified bunkers and tunnels put us at an overwhelming disadvantage. Our gunners burned out one .50 caliber Browning Machine Gun after another, firing too rapidly and too long for the weapons to hold up.

I trooped the Second Platoon line and quickly realized many of my men were unprepared for battle. They had their M-16s, but most were carrying just one magazine with twenty rounds, no grenades, and no water. Others had a bandolier of bullets, but no loaded magazines. They would have to laboriously reload each magazine by hand.

Besides the relentless roar of gunfire, occasionally a Rocket Propelled Grenade would swoosh overhead and slam into the side of an APC. I was surprised to see how frightened some of my men were. When I ordered several of them to the tracks to bring back more ammo, they refused — frozen in fear. Frustrated, I jumped into the open rear hatch of an APC and started searching for M-16 ammo cans and grenades. Not one of the first ten or twelve ammo cans I opened contained a single magazine. They were all filled with personal gear — shaving cream, razors, mirrors, combs. It was maddening. I threw one after another across the track, slamming them against the opposite wall with loud bangs.

Suddenly, I was overcome with an uncontrollable fear. Nobody would follow my orders. My platoon was quickly running out of ammo. The thunder of battle was deafening. I was surrounded by hell, but here, in the womb of an 11 ½-ton bed of steel, I was safe. If I stayed where I was, my men might find me later cowering in fear, but at least I'd be alive.

I don't know how long I wrestled with my fear, but at some point I opened one more ammo can. The sight of twenty or so loaded magazines jolted me out of my stupor. I closed the can and threw it outside. Then I found some hand grenades still packed in their paper cylinders. Finally, I came across the mother lode — an M-60 machine gun wrapped in a black plastic bag. I threw it outside, as well.

With a renewed sense of hope, I jumped out of the APC to see several soldiers cowering as I just had been. I grabbed the can of magazines and trooped the line, encouraging soldiers to rearm and start firing again. As one soldier after another got back into the fight, I felt my strength gathering — in both body and spirit.

Near the end of the line, I came across Pfc. Robert Tribble, a small, slight man, wandering around in a daze, impervious to the cataclysm around him. I grabbed him and forced him to look me in the eyes.

"Can you fire an M-60?" I yelled.

"Yes, sir!" he said.

"Well, come with me and I'll give you one."

I picked up the M-60 and Tribble followed like a puppy. We ran to the end of the right flank where I set the M-60 down, loaded it with a hundred-round belt, and pushed Tribble down behind it.

"You are the end of the line," I said. "No NVA can get beyond this point. If they do they'll attack us from behind and we'll all die. Do you understand?"

"Yes, sir."

Almost immediately he shouted: "There's one" and fired a quick burst.

"That's the way to do it. Keep it up," I said.

"Yes, sir. No one gets behind this point."

I told him I would be back in a minute with more ammunition.

As I sprinted down the line, I was proud to see the men reinvigorated, aggressively firing their M-16s and throwing the hand grenades I'd liberated from the APC. I grabbed three boxes of 7.62-mm rounds for Tribble's M-60 and raced back to him.

"I've already gotten seven or eight of them," he said, clearly proud and determined to add to the total.

"Good job," I said. "I'll be back again in a bit."

I began to troop the line and asked one of the E-5 buck sergeants if he had seen Staff Sgt. Cantor Hill.

"Yes, sir. He's out there."

"Out where?"

He pointed forward. Twenty to twenty-five yards in front of the firing line was Hill, cowering behind a rubber tree with a blood-stained right leg.

"Let's go get him," I said to the E-5 only to be met with a glazed, empty stare.

Oh, hell, I thought. *Here we go, again.*

I zig-zagged my way to Hill, crouching and darting faster than I ever thought possible.

"You're a damned fool for running out here!" Hill screamed at me when I reached the tree.

"You're the damn fool who ran out here in the first place!" I screamed back. "How bad are you?"

"It didn't hit anything vital," he said, looking down at his bleeding leg.

I saw four empty M-72 Light Anti-Armor Weapon (LAW) tubes scattered on the ground. It was obvious Hill had gone "freelance" bunker busting.

"Where are the gooks?" I screamed.

"The one who got me is two trees over there!" he said, pointing to an area twenty yards or so to his front.

Just then an NVA solider peered around a rubber tree and fired a short burst toward us. It was wide.

I threw a grenade at the soldier's position, but he jumped from behind the tree, picked it up, and threw it back.

Without thinking, I covered Sgt. Hill with my body and waited for the explosion. After what seemed forever, I got up and looked at the grenade. The safety clip was still attached. The pin hadn't been pulled. In the chaos of battle, both of us had flunked grenade-throwing 101. It wouldn't happen again.

I picked up the grenade, flicked off the safety clip, pulled the pin, let the spoon fly off and counted to six. I lobbed it behind the tree with a softball toss.

The NVA jumped out to throw the grenade my way again, but it exploded before he could pick it up.

"Are there any more out there?" I asked Hill.

"I don't think so."

"Okay," I said. "Get up, put your arm around my neck, and let's get back to the perimeter."

Back behind our lines, I asked Hill if he had seen any more bunkers.

"Yes, sir. There's lots of them out there."

"You seem to like LAWs," I said. "If I get you some more, could you start taking bunkers out?"

Hill said, sure, and I headed back to my track to grab five more LAWs. I ran to two other APCs and found two more boxes.

"Get started and I'll get you some more."

My platoon had become a fighting force again and, with Hill's lead taking out bunkers, we began to turn the tide of a long, tough battle.

I checked back in on Tribble, who said he hadn't seen any NVA in ten to fifteen minutes.

"What should I do?" he asked.

"Stay here and fire randomly just to discourage any who might try to escape."

Tribble giggled and let loose a burst of machinegun fire into the trees.

TROOPING THE LINE, I ran into Staff Sgt. Bondsteel, acting Third Platoon leader. Bondsteel was a short, squatty man with a thick torso whose nickname was "Buddha." He'd already personally destroyed four occupied enemy bunkers, been wounded by a grenade, and saved our commander's life by shooting an NVA soldier who was standing over a severely wounded Capt. Combs about to kill him.

"Bondsteel went from bunker-to-bunker diving into them with a grenade and his M-16 blaring," Spec. 4 Donovan "Spike" Kolness of First Platoon recounted years later. "He'd get one and then go on to the next one, blowing these bunkers left and right.

"At one point Bondsteel dove into a bunker head-first and got stuck. I can still see his feet and legs kicking up in the air as he was trying to back out of that small opening. He was barely out when the concussion from a grenade blew him back."

Bondsteel got shrapnel in his face and chest, but refused medical attention and found me a short while later. He told me Combs' track had been hit by four RPGs. The captain and his entire crew had been evacuated.

"First Platoon doesn't exist anymore," he said. "It's you and me. We should go and get some more bunkers. You got any grenades?"

I told him I did and he said, "Okay, let's go!"

Against my better judgment, I went with him. He was fearless. The two of us charged several bunkers and tunnels, most of which were empty. But Bondsteel went into one tunnel and emerged holding an NVA soldier by the scruff of the neck. He pushed a .45 caliber pistol into the soldier's face and screamed what sounded to me like: "Dinky dow crocodile, Mother Fucker."

Bondsteel had spent time in a village working with the Special Forces and spoke Vietnamese fluently. What he actually said was *Dien cai dau croc-a-dao*. *Dien cai dau* means someone who is crazy or loony. *Croc-a-dao* is dead or kill. Bondsteel was roughly saying: "I'm crazy as hell, Mother Fucker, and I'd rather kill you than look at you."

The prisoner, who turned out to be a North Vietnamese colonel, was terrified and became a great source of intelligence.

Just after we captured the colonel, I heard a deafening roar and looked up to see a Box formation of newly arrived APCs. It was Charlie Company riding in to reinforce us. As they drove through our position, their infantry "un-assed" and pushed deep into the bunker complex firing their .50 cal machine guns, M-16s, and tossing a shower of hand grenades.

Charlie Company always had a special place in my heart after that.

After Charlie disappeared farther into the bunker complex and stopped firing, I was overwhelmed by silence. The past four hours had been a non-stop symphony of thunderous explosions and gunfire. Now, in the almost dead silence, I could hear the low rumbling of our APC engines. They had been idling all through the battle when their drivers abandoned them for the fight.

IN THE AFTERMATH of the battle, a slight soldier with a 35 millimeter camera slung over his neck approached me. He was painfully out of place in a crisp uniform with a clean camouflage cover over his helmet and wearing aviator sunglasses.

"Who are you?" I asked.

"Well, who are you?" he snapped back.

"I'm the new lieutenant who started yesterday."

"Well, I'm Lt. Evans, Alpha's X-O. Capt. Combs has been evacuated. Let's clean up this mess, get the men reorganized, pick up the weapons and discarded ammo. Flare ships will guide you back to Thunder IV. Pull the tracks back that don't run."

It took us about an hour to get our convoy ready to roll. We were dragging three or four tracks. We didn't get back to Thunder IV until about 2200. The men got fed and the perimeter manned. We left the disabled tracks on an interior road.

I was done. I sat on the ground and a rather rotund sergeant walked up to me with a plate of food — steak, potatoes, and fresh green beans.

"Lieutenant, I'm the mess sergeant. I thought you might be hungry."

While I was gobbling the unexpected banquet, the sergeant asked what was wrong with my leg. I noticed a small round hole. The sergeant squatted and found another small hole near my ankle.

"Hell, lieutenant. You got shot in the leg," he said. "You're lucky it didn't hit anything. Here, have a swig of this."

That was the first time in my life I'd ever had Jim Beam. I didn't care much for the taste at first, but in a few minutes, I felt a calming warmth. I took another swig.

WE DIDN'T KNOW it at the time, but the enemy who engaged us was later identified as the 141st Regiment of the 7th North Vietnamese Army Division. We would battle them almost continuously for much of the next six weeks, eventually effectively wiping them out, but at great cost to us.

For our actions, the 2nd Battalion (Mechanized), 2nd Infantry Regiment, received a Valorous Unit Award by order of the Secretary of the Army. Staff Sergeant James Bondsteel was awarded the Congressional Medal of Honor — the last recipient of the nation's highest honor to receive his medal from President Richard Nixon. I was awarded the first of my two Silver Stars, the third-highest military decoration for valor behind the Congressional Medal of Honor and the Distinguished Service Cross. The official citation praised me for "unquestionable valor in close combat against numerically superior forces."

I'd been a platoon leader for less than forty hours.

Chapter 3
Little Ranch of the Parakeets

Father Joe Ladensack

IF I HADN'T gone to school with predator priests like John Giandelone, I never would have heard about plethysmography.

And I would have been perfectly fine with that.

Plethysmography, according to the American Medical Association Encyclopedia of Medicine, is "a method of estimating the blood flow in vessels by measuring changes in the size of a body part."

You can probably guess what body part gets measured in a predator priest.

Doctors at the University of New Mexico's Sex Offender Research and Therapy Department used plethysmography in making psycho-physiological assessments of hundreds of priests who were sent to a Roman Catholic retreat outside Albuquerque beginning in 1947. The retreat, since shut down, was run by the Servants of the Paraclete, a religious congregation of men dedicated to helping priests and Brothers going through personal difficulties.

Originally, the overwhelming majority of priests sent to the retreat were dealing with alcohol or substance abuse issues. But almost immediately, sexually active priests began arriving and just one year after the retreat opened, Rev. Gerald Fitzgerald, its founder, announced he would refuse to accept priests dealing with "abnormalities of sex."

The policy was short-lived. By the early 1960s, Father Fitzgerald reported half the priests sent to the retreat were there for sexual reasons. Some were what he called "heart cases"—priests who were having affairs with women. But the majority were homosexuals and, eventually, large numbers of pedophiles.

"When I was ordained, forty-three years ago, homosexuality was a practically unknown rarity. Today it is rampant among men," Fitzgerald wrote in a 1964 letter to a friend, Bishop Joseph Durick of Nashville.

Fitzgerald tried for decades to draw the line at helping pedophile priests, writing repeatedly they should be thrown out of the ministry because their sin was so great and their likelihood of reoffending almost certain.

"This extreme type will never be converted," he wrote to a fellow priest. "Men who sin with little children certainly fall under the classification of those who '*it were better they had not been born.*'"

By the time I was ordained a Catholic priest in June of 1976, the Congregation of the Servants of Paraclete was awash with sexual predators. Dr. Jay Feierman, a psychiatrist formerly associated with the Paraclete Fathers, testified he treated more than six-hundred priests for sexual problems at the New Mexico retreat from 1976 to 1986.

One of those priests was John Maurice Giandelone, who was two years behind me at St. John's Seminary in Camarillo, California.

Giandelone was trouble from the beginning. He had a lot of problems in the seminary. Lots of problems. Drinking problems. Drug problems. He abused prescription drugs and was high more often than not.

I learned years later that Giandelone had a rough upbringing. An only child, he was raped by a sixteen-year-old relative when he was just six years old. He was molested twice more in high school—once by a postal worker and once by a deputy sheriff.

Giandelone's father, Maurice, a stern man of Sicilian descent, had a terrible temper and took it out on John often. His mother, a Cajun with the French name to prove it—Euil "Peachy" Giroir—called her son a "freak" because of his molestations by boys and men.

Giandelone grew up in the offshore drilling support town of Morgan City, Louisiana, and went to three different elementary schools. He graduated from Morgan City High School and enrolled at Nicholls State University in Thibodaux, Louisiana, where he was something of a math whiz. John graduated with a Bachelor's in Math Education and went on to earn a Master's in Secondary Education.

In college, Giandelone said he realized for the first time he wasn't a "freak."

"During my sophomore year, I discovered the existence of other homosexuals and gay bars," he said years later. "I was relieved to know that I was not one-in-a-million. I was stunned and glad at the same time. I rarely went to those bars, but it felt good to know they existed."

Giandelone was engaged to a young woman for several months in college but broke off the relationship. He taught high school math in Morgan City after earning his undergraduate degree and thought that might be his life's vocation. However, school administrators told him they knew of his "gay reputation" and refused to renew his contract.

He was studying computer science in Louisiana when he decided to become a priest. St. Meinrad's Seminary and School of Theology in Indiana accepted Giandelone in 1972, but he lasted just one year and transferred to St. John's.

Giandelone tried hard, at first, to hide his homosexuality at St. John's. He was nervous and afraid he would be expelled. But he soon realized he was surrounded by kindred spirits and became close to several classmates whose careers would be intertwined for decades.

While administrators never condoned it, or even spoke of it, homosexuality was surprisingly prevalent during my years at St. John's. And I believe that furtive culture helped spawn the outbreak of sexual impropriety among priests. Fred Berlin, an associate professor of psychiatry at the Johns Hopkins School of Medicine, told the *Los Angeles Times* in 2005 that if — as I knew, and others believed — a "subculture of permissiveness" had taken hold at St. John's, then students prone to molestation likely found it easier to succumb to their desires.

"We often see that people, when they get into these group situations, will sometimes behave in ways they might not otherwise behave," he told the newspaper.

That same article produced a staggering statistic that corroborated my suspicions about the sexual hypocrisy at St. John's. The *Times* reported that fully one-third of seminarians who graduated from St. John's between 1966 and 1972, were later accused of sexual molestations. *One third!* And those were only the ones who were reported.

It didn't stop with those years, either. Another survey by the John Jay College of Criminal Justice "determined that the quarter-century from 1960 through 1984 was particularly troublesome for alleged abuse by clerics nationwide."

I graduated from St. John's in 1976 after six years of undergraduate and graduate studies. Not once during that time was I propositioned or approached improperly by a fellow seminarian. They knew I was different. Because of my Vietnam experience, and the way I was brought up as the eldest in a family of nine, I was much more aggressive than my fellow seminarians. They thought I was sort of mean — especially on the football field. But, I'd tell them, "Hey, football *is* a contact sport, isn't it? Come on guys."

I was different in another way. I was extremely interested in studies. I already had a degree from Arizona State and had started graduate work there before I went to Vietnam. I liked school. I loved to learn, to teach, to do research. Most of my undergraduate classmates at St. John's didn't study at all. The prevailing sentiment was, "We're going to be priests. Lah-dee-dah. They'll give us a C no matter what."

Guys like me, who enjoyed studying, were called "Bookers." Most Bookers got sent to Rome where they went on to big things at the Vatican. I went to Phoenix, where I did big things in a bit of a backwater.

At St. John's, I was always looking to improve things. One silly example came early on when I realized my superiors needed help organizing the students' duties. Everyone took turns cleaning, serving in the dining room, etc. Well, the school had this really dumb way of doing the rosters where nobody understood when and where they were on duty. So I came up with a system and presented it to the dean, who loved it, implemented it, and asked if I would like to be the dorm monitor next year?

The monitor was the student in charge of organizing everything, including the duty rosters. I loved it. I totally changed everything.

Periodically throughout my early years, I would get these performance reviews and they were, invariably, flattering and frustrating.

"Oh, Joe, you're doing great." Dah-dah-dah-dah. "But you're not pious enough."

"Pious? What does that mean?" I would ask.

"Well, you should know what that means. You're just not pious enough."

I would say: "Can you give me some examples?"

"No, it's awfully hard. You just have this aura about you. You're not pious enough."

Hmmmm.

This was as I was ending my undergraduate studies at St. John's and preparing to enter graduate school. At my final evaluation, the dean again told me he didn't think I was pious enough.

"So, because of that, we're going to let you go on to graduate school, but you'll be on probation. We'll look at it again in a few months and decide whether you stay or don't stay."

I had to laugh — to myself, of course — when I was out of the room. I couldn't help but remember the scene from the movie *Animal House* where Dean Vernon Wormer decides he's going to get John Belushi's fraternity, the Deltas, kicked off campus. Greg Marmalard, the smarmy, straight-laced, suck-up president of the fraternity next door to the Deltas, asks the dean:

"What do you intend to do, sir? Delta's already on probation."

"They are?"

"Yes, sir."

"Oh... Then, as of this moment, they are on *Double Secret Probation!*"

Like the Deltas, I was on double secret probation until, somehow, I became pious enough.

So I started looking around at my classmates. And you know what? Every single seminarian who was considered pious, was what I called back then "queer." Today, I'd use the more politically correct word: gay. But back then, they were queer — and, of course, pious.

Once I got into graduate school, however, I excelled. Being a Booker turned out to be a primo thing. All of a sudden, my teachers appreciated a guy who got A's in all his courses. I was a scholar. I tutored my classmates to help them pass and I taught a few classes. And on my entrepreneurial side, I got to implement some programs.

I took a little course in psychology and loved it. My professor, a guy from UCLA by the name of Dr. Hansen, came to me one day.

"Joe, I've been trying to get a program going for years," he said. "I haven't been able to find anyone to do it, but would you be interested in doing a psychiatric internship down at the Brentwood VA?"

Wow! Would I!

What a fabulous experience. Suddenly I was a psychiatric intern working with disabled vets from Vietnam I could identify with. Man, what a rewarding time.

My professor was impressed with my work and gave rave reviews to my superiors at the seminary.

"Ah, Joe's fabulous" and all this stuff.

I was also doing well in student government and various other areas. Suddenly, I realized my piety wasn't being questioned.

At the end of four years, I was ready to go into the priesthood. We had eighteen seminarians in our class and there was this process called "clips." If the administrators didn't think you were ready, they would clip you, which meant you didn't go on to the next step. You stayed an extra few months or a year or so. Well, I must have been pious enough because I didn't get clipped. Father John Grindel, the rector of St. John's, called me in and said: "Joe, you were the first one to be approved. Congratulations."

I felt great.

"However," Father John added, "let me say one thing."

I was thinking, *Oh, no. What now?*

But I just said: "Sure."

"There's something about you I don't understand," the rector said and paused searching for the right words.

"Um, you don't really buy into this obedience thing, do you?"

I had to laugh. Truth is I did buy in — for the most part, anyway.

But unquestioned obedience isn't always the best moral path.

IN MARCH 1978, twenty-one months after I was ordained, John Giandelone was preparing to graduate with his class at St. John's Seminary when I learned it wouldn't happen. He got clipped.

No one outside the rector ever knows exactly why a seminarian is held back. But in this case, the decision was brilliant. Giandelone *never* should have become a priest.

When he got clipped, Giandelone was sent to Chandler, Arizona, a bedroom community outside Phoenix, to serve as a deacon. Amazingly, he stayed out of trouble for six months — long enough to be ordained a priest in the Diocese of Phoenix on September 23, 1978.

The day of Giandelone's ordination, Father John Grindel, the St. John's rector who wondered about my attitude toward authority two years earlier, made a special trip to Phoenix. He confronted Bishop James Rausch about Giandelone. Father Grindel made it brutally clear he opposed making Giandelone a priest.

I was working closely with Rausch by that time and was in the room to witness what proved to be a brief, but interesting and ugly showdown.

Rausch was offended by Grindel's interference.

"Father Grindel," he said, his face reddening. "I am the bishop and I will ordain who I want to ordain."

Grindel's face reddened, as well.

"Have you seen my most recent evaluation of this guy?"

Rausch admitted he hadn't, but said his Director of Religious Vocations had and told the bishop he "highly recommended" Giandelone.

I wasn't surprised to hear it. That particular Director of Religious Vocations had a reputation for recruiting problem seminarians. He sought out young men who had been rejected elsewhere or who had jumped from one seminary to another.

Father Grindel, on the other hand, was flabbergasted.

"Well, don't blame me when this disaster blows up on you," he said, and stomped out of the room.

The rector got in his car and drove back to California without attending the ordination service.

Giandelone was a mess that day. He was practically falling down drunk. And he wasn't happy to see me. He knew I knew he was trouble. At St. John's, I tried to push Giandelone to clean up his act — so much so that one day one of his closest classmates, Charlie Schultz, confronted me and warned if I didn't get off Giandelone's case, he would see to it that I came to a "bad end."

I learned years later that Schultz probably wasn't a man to mess with. He was removed from two positions — as pastor in California and as chaplain at Luke Air Force Base outside Phoenix — after parishioners and colleagues filed at least five complaints of physical and verbal abuse against him. Once, more than one-hundred members of his congregation in California gathered to angrily accuse him of creating a hostile work environment and using force against teens in the community.

I could have come to a bad end if Charlie Schultz had put his mind to it.

FATHER JOHN MAURICE Giandelone molested his first juvenile just thirty-three weeks after he became a priest and vowed, at his ordination mass, to "strive to lead a holy and devout life, and to please almighty God."

I didn't find out about that first attack for another year and a half — and all the while Giandelone continued to molest the young man. I was Director of Religious Education for the Phoenix Diocese at the time. Bishop Rausch, who came to Phoenix in 1977, asked me to take the post in early 1978. I had spent the first two years of my priesthood as an associate pastor at St. Mary's Parish in Chandler, Arizona, then a still-small, but steadily growing suburb southeast of Phoenix bounded on two sides by the Gila Bend Indian Reservation. I loved my time in Chandler. In addition to regular pastoral duties, I taught at the elementary school. I taught religion to juniors and seniors at a nearby Catholic high school. And I taught adult education. I got to know, and become close to, quite a few families there — relationships that would change my life and John Giandelone's life in the years to come.

In late 1980, Rausch promoted me for the second time in two years from Director of Religious Education to Vicar of Christian Formation. My new job meant I directed fourteen departments associated with religious education in the diocese — the Department of Religious Education, Youth Ministry, Family Life, all the high schools, all the elementary schools. It was a monumental administrative position. Right up my alley.

I was barely in the job when we faced a scandal in the Youth Department. At the time, about the only thing the Youth Department did was organize retreats. And the layman who ran the retreats got a young girl pregnant. So, of course, we fired him and began restructuring the Youth Department. One of the first things I did was hire two new youth ministers out of Denver. They were young hotshots in the field — the most sought-after youth leaders in the country. We immediately changed the methodology of the Youth Department. Instead of having retreats directed by a layman, my two new hires fanned out to the parishes and taught our people how to run retreats.

Before I sent the two new youth ministers out, I pulled them aside and gave them a warning.

"Now, you guys are laymen and you might run into problems out there," I said. "Since you're not priests, they are going to just run over you. So when you find a problem, come to me and I will see if I can help you. I'm a priest. They can't run over me."

Not long after that, John Farnsworth, one of the new youth ministers, walked into my office.

"Remember you told us to come to you if we ran into any problems?" he said.

"Yep."

"Well, I've got a problem, but I don't want to tell you about it. I need to talk to Bishop Rausch."

I asked Farnsworth if he was sure there was a real problem — and one so big he needed to go directly to the bishop?

"Joe, I've done my homework," he said. "I'm a pro. I need to see the bishop."

I told Farnsworth I'd get him in.

Bishop Rausch and I got along pretty well. I'd been working down the hall from him for two years and, just then, I happened to be living at his residence because his chancellor had left and Rausch needed someone to help with his day-to-day affairs.

Normally, to get to see the bishop, you had to go through his chancellor, book an appointment, jump through hoops, and wait and wait. But I was in a position where I could simply walk down to his office, go through a back door, and say, "I gotta talk to you." So that's what I did.

"The new youth ministers I hired…"

And before I could get to the point, Rausch interrupted to say how impressed he was with Farnsworth and his associate, Michael Keefe — how great they were.

"Yeah, they're doing a fine job," I said. "but they need to see you. They need to see you fast. They've got a problem and I think you really should talk to them."

Rausch told me to send them down to his office in a half hour.

An hour later, Rausch summoned me to his office. He was livid.

"Joe, do you know what they wanted to talk to me about?"

I told him no. All I knew was they had a problem they thought was big enough to bring to the top.

"Well, there's some little pedophile boy, or something like that, who's accused one of our priests of molesting him," the bishop said. "I don't believe a word of it and I don't want to hear any of this."

Then he started in on me. He was angry at me for having abused my privilege to get the youth ministers into his office.

"You said yourself what a fine job these guys are doing," I said. "They're not rookies. They've worked in Denver a number of years and I think they really needed you to hear what they had to say. I think you need to act on whatever this is."

After Rausch calmed down a bit, he said someone needed to meet with the boy's family.

"Yeah, that's why the guys came to you, isn't it?"

"Yes, the family wants to meet with me," the bishop said. "I'm not gonna do it, so who can we get?"

I suggested Monsignor Thomas O'Brien, the vicar general, second-in-command—the man who would eventually succeed Rausch and change my life and scores of others.

"Yeah. Yeah. Let's have him meet with them. I'll take care of it."

Little did I know I'd just heard the anthem of bishops everywhere in what would turn out to be a worldwide sexual abuse scandal.

"I'll take care of it."

A couple nights later, at dinner in the residence, Rausch told me he was sorry he had exploded at me for helping the youth ministers get in to see him.

"I really have to apologize because Monsignor O'Brien has met with the family and there really is abuse here," he said. "The young boy is the son of a Lutheran minister. And being a fellow clergyman in trouble, he just wants to have the priest removed from the situation.

"The minister said his son is very confused sexually and he just wants to get him away from Father Giandelone."

Giandelone!

My mind flashed back to our years at St. John's and then to Father Grindel's words to Bishop Rausch the day Giandelone was ordained.

"Don't blame me when this disaster blows up on you!"

THE LYING STARTED then and didn't stop for decades.

Bishop Rausch lied.

Monsignor O'Brien lied.

John Giandelone's victim wasn't the sexually muddled son of a Lutheran minister. He was a good Catholic, an altar boy, who would survive his molestations, go on to become a police lieutenant, and work with a dogged investigator twenty-three years later and half a continent away to get Giandelone to admit what he had done.

I didn't know Rausch had lied to me until March 6, 2003, when I read an article in the *Arizona Republic* that revealed the victim's true identity. I thought the article, by Joseph A. Reaves, a veteran reporter who spent much of his career at the *Chicago Tribune*, was especially poignant.

> *After nearly a quarter century, the roles were reversed.*
>
> *This time the priest was helpless.*
>
> *And the altar boy was in control.*
>
> *The emotional turnaround came in a packed 12th-floor downtown courtroom Wednesday when John Maurice Giandelone was sentenced to 22 months in prison for molesting a former altar boy who now is one of Mesa's top street police officers.*

The victim, Lt. Ben Kulina, issued a statement that was read in court:

"I have waited a very long time for this day. Nearly twenty-five years ago this man was placed in a position of trust and authority over me as a child. He betrayed that trust. This was God's representative that was doing these horrible things to me."

Kulina was just one of thousands worldwide who were betrayed by God's representatives. But he wasn't Giandelone's only victim.

Not long after Monsignor O'Brien met with Ben Kulina's family and convinced them to remain silent, Giandelone disappeared from St. Joseph's Parish, where the abuse had taken place. No one seemed to know what happened to him. Then I spotted a little notice in the Diocesan newspaper that Giandelone had been transferred to my original parish, St. Mary's in Chandler. I was furious. I was still close to many of the families there. I loved them. So I went to Bishop Rausch.

"How could this happen?" I asked the bishop. "This guy has already molested one boy and from what I know from my psychology background, he'll probably continue to prey on young boys."

Rausch was firm.

"You're absolutely wrong," he said. "He's okay and I'm the bishop. I've made my decision."

That was that. And then, six months later, on May 18, 1981, Rausch died of a heart attack suffered in a car while riding with an aide headed to a meeting in northern Arizona. He was fifty-two years old and died before his own horrid sexual history became known.

For years, Rausch had traveled regularly to Tucson, ostensibly to meet with fellow Bishop Francis J. Green, whose diocese was having serious financial troubles. Green's business manager had been extorting money for a decade or longer and Rausch told me he was giving Green advice on how to straighten things out.

That probably was partially true, but while he was in Tucson, Rausch was paying a heroin-addicted teenage male prostitute for sex. Details of the bishop's trysts with then seventeen-year-old Brian O'Connor didn't become public until 2002 — twenty-one years after Rausch's death — when the church settled a lawsuit filed by crusading Tucson attorney Lynne Cadigan. In the suit, O'Connor testified Rausch picked him up on a street corner in Tucson in June 1979 and gave him fifty-dollars to allow the bishop to perform oral sex on him in the bishop's car. Rausch identified himself as "Paul" and continued to meet O'Connor on his Tucson trips until his death. O'Connor said he learned the bishop's real name several months into their affair by rifling through a glove compartment while Rausch was registering for a motel room.

"He (Rausch) explained that he was only relieving stress and any number of other excuses for acting out his libido," O'Connor wrote in a court document.

Before Rausch's death, O'Connor said the bishop passed him on to two other Tucson priests — Monsignor Robert C. Trupia and Rev. William T. Byrne — who had sex with him for years. Trupia preyed on young men and children so often, and openly, that his fellow priests dubbed him "chicken hawk." Court records show he was known to bring young sexual partners to St. John's Seminary in Camarillo, California, for unauthorized weekend encounters.

Shortly after Rausch died, Trupia gave O'Connor a job at the Tucson Diocese chancery, where Trupia was in charge of the marriage tribunal. Byrne also worked there.

In 1992, Trupia was confronted by his superiors with an accusation he sexually molested an altar boy. Sealed court records obtained by the *Boston Globe* allege Trupia responded by threatening to reveal he had a sexual relationship with Rausch — and that he, the bishop, and Byrne all had ongoing sex with O'Connor, who was given the chancery job to ensure his silence.

As close as I was to Rausch, I never had an inkling of his sexual appetite. No sign whatsoever. But others did. A.W. Richard Sipe, a nationally recognized expert on pedophile priests, who attended seminary with Rausch, was one of them.

"There is no question that Bishop Rausch was a man who was sexually active," Sipe told Reaves of the *Arizona Republic* in 2003. "He was certainly a good man and he did many very good things, but he was also sexually active, which set the tone for the diocese through easy forgiveness and understanding, and too great an acceptance of violations by other priests."

That attitude of acceptance, that indifference to the sins of fellow priests, continued when Rausch was succeeded as bishop by his henchman, Thomas J. O'Brien.

O'Brien knew Giandelone was a predator and made it possible for him to find other victims. Just four months after Rausch died, Giandelone began molesting a thirteen-year-old boy in my old parish, St. Mary's. I didn't know about it at the time, but I was beside myself two years later, in January 1984, when I learned Bishop O'Brien had transferred Giandelone again, this time to the faculty of Bourgade High School.

I went to Bishop O'Brien.

"You know this guy's past better than anyone," I said. "You know what he's done and now you're putting him in a high school! This isn't right."

O'Brien gave me the same answer Rausch had given me four years earlier. He'd made his decision. He was the bishop. And I had no choice but to accept it.

Just four months later, on Memorial Day Weekend 1984, Giandelone was caught giving oral sex to the teenager he'd been abusing in St. Mary's Parish since 1981. The boy's father, a friend of mine since the early days of my priesthood, walked in on the scene and was beside himself. He wanted to kill Giandelone.

The boy's mother called and begged me in tears to help.

I talked Harry Takata Sr. out of murdering Giandelone. "You'll go to jail for the rest of your life for something he did," I told him. "Let's just call the police."

That, of course, wasn't the way predator priests were handled — in Arizona or anywhere else. For decades, these things were kept under wraps. But, for me, the Takata molestation changed everything. This was the perfect storm. I'd known Giandelone since our days in the seminary. I knew he was a bad guy. I knew he had abused kids in other parishes. And now, here he was victimizing the son of a family I knew and loved. If I went to the bishop, I knew he'd just cover this up. Going to the police was the only way to put an end to this ugly madness.

In keeping with the perfect storm, the officer who responded to our call, was another longtime friend, Richard Felix. I had a very close relationship with Dick. Very close. He was a first cousin of the most famous lay Catholic in Phoenix, Eddie Basha, owner of what then was the most popular grocery chain in Arizona.

Dick interviewed the Takatas, got the information he needed, and I walked him to his car.

"Joe, are you sure you want to do this?" he asked in a friendly voice.

"Why?" I asked.

"You don't know how much pain this is going to cause us both. Are you sure?"

"Yeah," I said.

"Fine. If you want to go through with it, I'll go through it with you."

AFTER OFFICER FELIX left, I got on the "Bat Phone" and had my showdown with O'Brien — the one where he ordered me to convince the Takatas to recant and I schooled him on the Nuremberg Trials and immoral orders.

Dick Felix and the Chandler Police Department were great. Giandelone was charged with four felony counts of sexual conduct with a minor — all involving Harry Takata Jr. from October 1, 1981 through Memorial Day 1984. Under a plea bargain agreement, two counts were dropped and one was reduced to a misdemeanor. Giandelone pled guilty to the misdemeanor and one felony count and was sentenced to one year in prison.

At the time of his sentencing for the Takata incident, Giandelone was in residence at the Servants of the Paraclete retreat outside Albuquerque. O'Brien sent him there. I called the place The Little Ranch of the Parakeets. Treatment at the facility was a joke — nothing but a bunch of psycho-babble, as far as I was concerned. And hearing about the plethysmography tests that measured "changes in [Giandelone's] penile circumference" only underscored my feelings.

Michael J. Dougher and Randal J. Garland, the director and assistant director of the University of New Mexico Sex Offender and Treatment Program, administered the test. They hooked up Giandelone, showed him a series of pornographic slides, and measured his erections. One set of slides showed nude adult men and women engaging heterosexual intercourse. One set showed men ranging in age from the late teens to mid-twenties engaged in masturbation, fellatio, and homosexual intercourse. And the final set showed nude boys ranging in age from eight to eleven.

Dougher and Garland sent a typewritten report to the Phoenix Diocese.

> *The following conclusions and recommendations can be made. Mr. Giandelone experiences problematic sexual arousal in regard to males in the mid to late teens. He does not appear to become sexually aroused by prepubescent boys. Furthermore, he reports no deviant sexual urges for prepubescent boys. Mr. Giandelone appeared frank during the assessment procedure and was aware of the problematic nature of his attraction to teen-aged males. Furthermore, he seemed motivated to work therapeutically on this deviant attraction to teen-age males.*
>
> *Given Mr. Giandelone's intellectual abilities and motivation, he stands to benefit considerably from therapy. Behavior modification techniques could be implemented to reduce his deviant attraction to teen-aged males. This could be followed by intensive verbal psychotherapy to help Mr. Giandelone adjust to his homosexual orientation and, perhaps, to develop appropriate sexual outlets.*

That was good enough for Bishop O'Brien. He was convinced Gian-delone was "fixed." Citing the report's promise that Giandelone "stands to benefit considerably from therapy," he wrote letters appealing for leniency. The letters worked. A judge eventually allowed Giandelone to spend his year-long sentence working for the bishop in the diocesan library instead of serving time in prison.

All thanks to plethysmography and the Little Ranch of the Parakeets.

Chapter 4
Black Virgin Mountain ~ July 12, 1969
2nd Lt. Joe Ladensack

THE DISASTROUS BATTLE of Black Virgin Mountain was all-but over when I was shot in the head. It was the third time I'd been wounded in five hours. And I was one of the lucky ones.

When the shooting stopped, I was the only line officer remaining on the field of battle. Sixty-eight of the seventy soldiers in Company A, 2nd Mechanized Battalion of the famed Big Red One Infantry Division, were dead or wounded. All because of one colossal clusterfuck after another. We were sent into an ambush, in a place we never should have been, full of false hope and bad intelligence, and forced to fight out of our element — on foot instead of riding the Armored Personnel Carriers we were trained on and only used later to haul away our casualties.

Our mission that day was to assess the damage a B-52 bombing raid had done to dislodge a force of regular North Vietnamese Army dug in on a massive granite mountain named Núi Bà Đen, eighteen miles east of the Cambodian border and fifty-five miles northwest of Saigon. Núi Bà Đen is Vietnamese for Black Lady Mountain. One of many legends has it that in the Ninth Century, the maidens of a village leapt to their deaths off the mountain rather than submit to a horde of Chinese invaders. Since then, Black Lady Mountain has been known as Black Virgin Mountain.

Capt. Donald G. Cook, the first U.S. Marine captured in Vietnam on New Year's Eve 1964, was held near Núi Bà Đen for a time before being shuttled to a string of primitive jungle camps. Cook is the only Marine in history to win the Congressional Medal of Honor while a POW for his heroic actions leading and protecting a group of ten other prisoners with him during his three years of captivity. He died of malaria in the highlands of South Vietnam near the Cambodian border on or about December 8, 1967, and was promoted posthumously to colonel.

We could have used Col. Cook at Núi Bà Đen.

BLACK VIRGIN MOUNTAIN is an extinct volcano rising 3,268 feet above a vast plain of jungles and flat farmlands. It is riddled with deep caves and dense basalt boulders formed from the lava flow of Núi Bà Đen's last eruption in the Pleistocene Epoch, more than twelve-thousand years ago.

The mountain became part of my life beginning the morning of July 7, 1969, when Capt. Richard L. Buckles, our company commander, called his platoon leaders together and told us we were being temporarily assigned to the 25th Infantry Division, home-based out of Hawaii and known as "Tropic Lightning." We were to reinforce the 25th because military intelligence believed two divisions of North Vietnamese Army troops were about to cross the Cambodian border. The NVA goal, we were told, was to capture a base camp near the city of Tây Ninh, in the shadow of Black Virgin Mountain, in hopes of gaining leverage at the Paris Peace Talks, which had begun fourteen months earlier and — unknown to us then, of course — would drag on another four years.

None of us were particularly pleased being assigned to the 25th, a regular infantry division. We were mechanized. And experience long proved the leaders of "leg" infantry units rarely understood how "mech" units operated. Regular supply and maintenance was disrupted. Often, the leg units failed to consider the kinds of fuel, ammunition, and mechanical support needed for a mechanized unit. Too often, a mech unit placed under Operational Control of the leg unit would be assigned foolish and unnecessarily dangerous missions.

The practice of "OpCon-ing" units sometimes had its advantages, however. Six weeks earlier, shortly after I arrived in Vietnam, the 2/2 Mech of the 1st Division — my unit — was put under Operational Control of the 1st Cavalry Division during two weeks of battles around An Lộc, fifty-five miles north of Saigon. The First Cav gave 2/2 its own area of operations and very little control or direction. We were free to kick ass. And we did.

But things would be different at Núi Bà Đen.

SHORTLY AFTER CAPT. Buckles notified us we were being assigned to the 25th Division, two of our three companies rolled out of a base station south of the Dầu Tiếng reservoir and headed forty miles west-northwest to our new position at Fire Support Base Buell, squat in the middle of an open plain between Black Virgin Mountain and the city of Tây Ninh. I was impressed. FSB Buell was a work of art compared to the dump we left at Dầu Tiếng. Capt. Buckles told us that during the Tet Offensive, eighteen months earlier, Buell was nearly overrun by two regiments of NVA. Since then, the place had been fortified, and fortified again. It looked like a model you would have found back at Fort Benning. If we were going to have to hold off the NVA, Fire Support Base Buell was as good a place as any — better than most.

We settled in to Buell and spent the next three days doing RIF — Reconnaissance-In-Force — both north and south of Black Virgin Mountain. We saw steady, unmistakable signs of enemy activity. Trampled elephant grass. Smoldering fires. Trails leading toward the mountain.

All three afternoons, Capt. Buckles suspended our missions briefly so we could watch sorties of F-4 Phantom jets conduct bombing runs against the side of Núi Bà Đen. The sudden whoosh and roar of the silver jets and the colossal explosions and billowing black smoke they rained was staggering. Seeing the might of the American military

machine was spine-tingling. It impressed upon us the somber reality
of what we might be up against.

THE MORNING OF July 11, 1969, we went on recon again, but this time
on foot. No one in our company could remember ever conducting
a dismounted operation. We scoured a thick jungle northeast of the
mountain. And we had all kinds of problems. One platoon got lost, ran
out of water, and several troops were overcome by heat. Capt. Buckles,
a career Army officer and the son of a retired lieutenant colonel, was
not pleased. But we had only just begun to kindle his wrath.

When we got back to camp, we found it overrun with Vietnamese
civilian vehicles and personnel. Villagers were selling Cokes, ice, and
haircuts outside the perimeter. Inside, was worse. G.I.'s were having
sex with prostitutes in the APCs.

First Lt. Mike Mulhern, my friend from Phoenix, had been left in
charge of the base camp. When Capt. Buckles went looking for him,
he found Mulhern asleep. That was the last straw. Buckles ran around
yelling at G.I.'s and the locals. He became so enraged, he fired his pistol in the air, which, of course, scattered the civilians. After about ten
minutes all the Vietnamese had been driven off and Buckles called a
company formation. He chewed us out for nearly twenty minutes. It
wasn't pretty.

About an hour later, Buckles summoned all his platoon leaders.
We assumed he was going to continue dressing us down for the day's
debacles. Instead, he told us he had just received new orders from battalion headquarters.

"At 2330 tonight, the Air Force will launch an 'Arc Light' strike
against a concentration of NVA on the Black Virgin," he said, letting
us know that for the first time in the war, giant U.S. B-52 Stratofortress
bombers would be used against the mountain.

"We are going to have to move our positions to the north. The
Arc Light will be conducted by radar and we need to be at least

kilometer-and-a-half from the mountain for our safety. We'll be moving as soon as this briefing ends."

Buckles told us the Arc Light strike was a prelude to an attack on Núi Bà Đen that would begin in the morning with a company of regular infantry being dropped by helicopter to the top of the mountain. Their mission was to sweep down the mountain, doing bomb damage assessment, and driving any NVA survivors to the bottom. Our company was to cordon off the base of the mountain with our APCs and kill or capture any NVA the infantry might drive down.

"Be ready to move out at first light," Capt. Buckles said. "But we only move on orders from battalion. They'll be coordinating everything by air.

"Try to get some rest, men."

JUST BEFORE MIDNIGHT on July 11, 1969, I sat spellbound as I watched a scene so beautiful and horrific it defied imagination. We were hunkered down in our positions about a mile north of Núi Bà Đen when six B-52D "Big Belly" bombers from U-Tapao Royal Thai Navy Airfield in Thailand turned night into day and silent stillness into thunderous tumult.

The B-52s flew so high in the stratosphere they could neither be seen nor heard from the ground. The brutish eight-engine behemoths, flying in two arrowhead formations of three planes each, swept over the mountain and spat a staggering three-hundred-sixty-thousand pounds of explosives in less than thirty minutes.

Years later, when I saw the movie *Apocalypse Now*, I was reminded of how shocked the NVA on Núi Bà Đen must have been to have the tranquility of a near-noiseless night instantly transformed into Dante's Sixth Circle of Hell, where heretics are condemned to eternity trapped in flaming tombs. In the 1979 movie, the character Mr. Clean, played by Laurence Fishburne, perfectly describes an Arc Light raid on the Viet Cong:

"Charlie don't ever see 'em or hear 'em, but it'll suck the air out of your damn lungs."

What I saw that night was beyond belief. The ground shook as if we were living through an earthquake. Our ears ached from the concussions. And debris rained on the perimeter of our dug-in positions a mile from the nearest impact. It was spectacular.

"Those poor bastards on that mountain," I thought.

Little did I know.

PRIVATE FIRST CLASS Richard England, the Second Platoon medic, was roused out of bed with the rest of us just before o-five-hundred July 12, 1969. It was his twenty-first birthday — and the last day of his life.

He wouldn't die alone that day.

Since the NVA had a habit of attacking Fire Base Stations at dawn, normal procedure was to hold a "Mad Minute" every morning. The history of the Mad Minute dates to pre-World War I when the British Army required its riflemen to reel off fifteen rounds in a minute or less at a four-foot target three-hundred yards away with bolt-action Lee-Enfield rifles.

In Vietnam, a Mad Minute consisted of the rapid, random firing of all perimeter weapons to discourage any infiltration by the enemy.

The morning of July 12th, there was no Mad Minute at the positions we'd dug in overnight. Instead, at 5:15 AM, we were given the order to "stand down" and have breakfast. The atmosphere wasn't particularly tense — no more-so than usual. After the Arc Light strike a few hours earlier, most of us assumed the day would be spent doing BDA — bomb damage assessment; counting craters and hauling the charred and mangled remains of Vietnamese soldiers off Black Virgin Mountain.

At 6 AM, we received orders to "mount up," which meant we were to board our Armored Personnel Carriers in full battle dress — helmets, flak jackets, and ammo pouches — awaiting the order to "move out." I doubted the order would come any time soon because we were enveloped in fog so thick I couldn't see more than fifty yards. And I was right. About 6:45 Capt. Buckles radioed that the leg infantry was having some problems and we should "stand down," but be ready to move out at a moment's notice.

Around 8:30, we finally started moving toward the base of the mountain. When we got there, an hour later, we found bomb craters, punji pits, and booby traps, but no NVA. So we moved on to a position about a kilometer away. Capt. Buckles summoned the platoon leaders to his APC and told us about a change in plans. The helicopters that were supposed to airlift the regular infantry to the top of Núi Bà Đen had waited as long as they could for the fog to lift. But when it didn't, the choppers were called away on another mission. No infantry would be coming down the mountain from the top. And we weren't going anywhere for the time being. Buckles ordered us to re-establish an overnight defensive position, which meant putting up screens to protect against rocket-propelled grenades, re-digging fighting positions, and conducting routine maintenance of the APCs and our weapons. All pretty routine stuff.

About 10:30 AM, with everything in a holding pattern and our defensive position re-established, I asked Capt. Buckles if the guys in my platoon could toss a football around. He said, okay. Seemed innocent enough at the time. But that football game wound up playing a role in one of many twists of a deadly day.

A WEEK EARLIER, on the Fourth of July, we'd had an officers-versus-enlisted men volleyball game at our old base in Dầu Tiếng. The guys who weren't playing all were cheering for the enlisted men. It seemed great for morale. Capt. Buckles agreed. I wanted to take things a step further and start a flag football team in my platoon and challenge other platoons to regular games. Tossing the football around during that down time in the shadow of Black Virgin Mountain was as close as we ever came.

We had only been playing about ten minutes when trouble arrived in the guise of a UH-1 "Huey" helicopter with 25th Division markings that hovered over us briefly then landed just outside our site.

"We were kinda relaxed," Spec. 4 James A. Hale, one of our APC drivers, remembered decades later. "When I saw a helicopter overhead, I thought to myself: 'This is gonna piss someone off. We don't look professional.'"

I didn't hear Hale's prescient words, but learned of them from an oral history of survivors of the battle compiled by Bill Sly, our company historian, who later self-published those memoirs in a paperback entitled: *No Place to Hide: A Company at Núi Bà Đen.*

Aboard the helicopter hovering over us that fateful morning was Brig. Gen. David S. Henderson, the 25th Division's newly appointed assistant commander for support. When Henderson landed, Capt. Buckles met him and escorted the general and two of his aides to the captain's track.

No one alive today heard the conversation, but the general's voice was loud — very loud — and he was waving his arms wildly. The group huddled for about ten minutes, then Gen. Henderson and his aides took off and Capt. Buckles called the platoon leaders to his track.

The captain was flushed and spoke emotionally. He said the general was upset that we were "running around like a bunch of wild Indians."

Buckles said he would take the blame for that, but now we had a new mission. Since the regular infantry couldn't come down Black Virgin, we were going to go up the mountain to do bomb damage assessment. We would move out in about ten minutes with my platoon, the Second, on point.

All of us were shocked that we were being ordered to leave our APCs behind and walk up a mountain held by NVA troops who were dug in. Buckles tried to reassure us — and probably himself — by saying what we all hoped: that the NVA probably had been wiped out by the midnight B-52 strikes.

What was really happening was we were about to be massacred because an egotistical brigadier general was pissed off that we had been playing football instead of cringing and waiting for orders.

Before we moved out, I asked about bringing the tracks with us. Buckles said the foot of Black Virgin Mountain was swampy land that wouldn't support the weight of an APC.

"Besides, after the screw-ups we had yesterday, maybe a nice walk in the sun will teach the troops not to break discipline," Buckles said.

The captain did hold out one ray of hope, though. He said he had put in a radio call to Lt. Col. Newell E. Vinson, battalion commander, about the mission change.

"Maybe he won't think walking up a mountain is such a good idea and he'll give us another mission," Buckles said.

The captain was right. Lt. Col. Vinson clearly thought sending his mechanized units on foot up a mountain that hadn't been scouted was a bad idea. He confronted one of Brig. Gen. Henderson's aides.

"I'm not going to send any of my people up there when I don't think the objective is worth it," Vinson told the aide. "I'm not going to risk people like that."

The general's aide was adamant. He told Lt. Col. Vinson that his men were going to do a bomb damage assessment and were going on foot.

"I don't accept that," Vinson argued. "Call Col. Hayward and tell him I don't want to do that. I refuse to do that without a direct order to do so."

Col. Hayward was Col. Charles W. Hayward, a West Point graduate who had been named commander of the 25th Division's 1st Brigade just three months earlier and later would serve for a time as acting chief negotiator at the Paris Peace Talks. He stood by the orders.

"Col. Hayward gives you a direct order to dismount and go up that hill," Hayward's aide told Vinson, who passed the disheartening news to Capt. Buckles.

I assembled my platoon and told them how we would go up the mountain. Each man was to carry four-hundred rounds — twenty magazines — of M-16 ammunition, at least one field dressing, and at least two canteens of water. The temperature that afternoon would only reach ninety-three degrees, but with humidity ranging from sixty percent to ninety percent, the heat index would top one-hundred-twenty-five degrees.

"I don't think we'll be gone long enough to need food, but carry one C-ration meal if you want a snack. But only one," I told the men.

Since none of us were used to moving on foot, I explained how I wanted the men organized. Sgt. Calvin Maguire, who had leg experience during a prior tour with the 1st Cavalry Division, would lead the left element with six troops. I would lead the middle with my radio operator and the platoon medic, Pfc. Richard England. The right element would be led by Staff Sgt. Cantor Hill, another veteran on his second tour, with eight troops.

Including myself, Second Platoon set out for Black Virgin Mountain, with nineteen men. The First and Third Platoons, which would follow, each had a few more men. And Capt. Buckles' command group, which fell in between us and the First Platoon, included two radio operators, a company medic, the company forward observer, and his radio operator.

In all, seventy officers and men set out for an ambush on Núi Bà Đen. Sixty-eight would be killed or wounded in the next few hours.

THE LEAD ELEMENTS of Alpha Company started toward the mountain just after noon on July 12, 1969. We marched a mile through two separate wooded areas, one denser than the other, and across a dirt road, before reaching a large rice paddy. This was the swampy ground Capt. Buckles had worried wouldn't support our APCs. I tested the ground and judged our tracks easily could have crossed.

After the rice paddy, we hit one more thick of woods in the middle of which was a huge bomb crater, probably twenty-five yards wide and thirty feet deep — obviously from the B-52 raid.

As we reached the edge of the woods, we could see the base of the mountain lined with a ring of elephant grass about four or five feet tall. And just before the elephant grass: a small berm, about three feet high, frayed at both ends by bomb craters.

I halted the platoon at the edge of the woods and ordered Sgt. Maguire to rush the berm with his six troops. The rest of the platoon would provide cover. Maguire and his men reached the berm without drawing any fire. Staff Sgt. Hill's element quickly followed and I went last with my men. Everything was quiet.

From behind the berm, we got our first up-close look at the Black Virgin. I was taken aback by the size of boulders on the mountainside. An average boulder was as big as our Armored Personnel Carriers.

The mountain was covered with thick, dark woods, except for large swaths where the 500-pound bombs had struck. I radioed Capt. Buckles and reported the bare area was about one-hundred-fifty yards wide and rose from the base to half-way up the steep mountain. Buckles told us to head up the mountain on the left side of the bare area.

I ordered Sgt. Maguire and his men to move out and almost immediately lost sight of them. The mountain was so steep and the boulders so huge that it was impossible to maintain visual contact with the men working their way up. I looked down, though, and could see, in plain view, First Platoon starting to climb.

Just about then, Sgt. Maguire yelled that his element had found a tunnel. I let Buckles know and climbed to Maguire's position. The tunnel entrance was about three feet in diameter and located at the edge of an especially large boulder. A rope ladder dangled into the darkness. I dropped a grenade into the opening and heard it explode before hitting bottom. That was the first ominous sign that, maybe, the awesome Arc Light strike hadn't been as deadly as we assumed.

Seconds later, the nightmare began.

I WAS A poor judge of time whenever I was in combat. Once an operation started, I rarely looked at my watch. Some minutes under fire seemed like hours and some hours seemed like seconds. But an official after-action report later confirmed the shooting started at 1305 — 1:05 PM.

The "swoosh" of a rocket-propelled grenade came from above and to my right. I picked up the flight of the rocket, followed it down the mountain, and saw it hit near the elephant grass at the base where the First and Third Platoons were just beginning their unprotected climb. Clearly, the NVA let us pass and waited until the last of our men started up the mountain before opening fire. A perfect ambush.

"I was sitting inside a crater, near the right side of it when the round flew past my head, missing me by only a couple of feet," remembers Spec. 4 Donovan "Spike" Kolness of First Platoon. "The RPG landed in the soft, light-colored, clay-like dirt created by a B-52 blast. It landed right between (Sgt.) Bob Hall's legs and exploded.

"The soft dirt helped shield the blast, but that wasn't enough. The explosion literally blew the pants off Hall. He took shrapnel in his left calf."

Capt. Buckles radioed everyone to stay in position until we could get Hall evacuated.

About then Sgt. Maguire found three more tunnels, also under massive boulders. These had even larger openings with cooking fires near the entrances and pots of fresh rice strewn around. I threw grenades down all three and, again, they exploded long before hitting bottom. I could hear long, ill-omened echoes rumbling inside the bowels of the mountain.

The last of the grenade explosions had just faded when we started receiving small arms fire from the area where the RPG had been launched minutes before. We never saw a single NVA soldier, but the fire was heavy. I estimated somewhere between fifteen and twenty AK-47s and two light machines guns were concentrated on us. We had good protection from the boulders and when I radioed Capt. Buckles to report our situation, he told me First Platoon was under fire, as well.

"Stay put," he ordered.

We had been taking heavy fire on and off for ten minutes when Capt. Buckles called back to say a tank company from the 2nd Battalion, 34th Armor Regiment was on its way to reinforce us. They arrived about a half hour later, set up on the dirt road we had crossed earlier in the day, and began launching 90-mm, high-explosive rounds over our heads into the boulders where the AK-47 fire was coming from. If a storm of five-hundred-pound bombs dropped from the stratosphere didn't do anything to dislodge the NVA, these tanks couldn't be expected to do much. And they didn't. The 90-mm tank rounds hit the boulders and bounced back like ping pong balls. They had absolutely no effect. Small arms fire continued to pepper us as we hunkered down.

While the tanks were trying in vain to help us, most of the men were having the same thoughts as Spec. 4 Ron Pilgrim.

"We felt like the stupidest sons-of-bitches in the world," he remembers. "Here we were up on a mountain with everybody shooting over the top of our rock and nothing for us to shoot back at. I mean, I never saw an enemy that entire day.

"You know it's strange. Things were so confused, I didn't know the other two men who were up there with me. One was a sergeant, but that's all I can remember. And three of us spent a long time up there. We would look at each other every few minutes and say: 'What the hell are we supposed to shoot at? We can't see anything.'"

ABOUT 1345, FORTY minutes after the ambush started, Capt. Buckles radioed that we needed to get off the mountain. He told us to maneuver down the same way we had come up and to keep a sharp eye for any possible counter-attack from the NVA.

I called Maguire and Hill to my location and told them everyone had been ordered off the mountain. Since Second Platoon was first up, we'd be last off. I told them I expected we'd catch a helluva lot of fire and if there was a counter-attack, we'd bear the brunt. I wanted them to move only one or two men at a time and use everyone else to provide cover fire. I told them I would be the last man off the mountain and when I was safely down, we'd withdraw across the elephant grass by two's and three's, past the berm, and into the wooded area.

The retreat went exactly as planned — at least for Second Platoon. Enemy fire was heavy, but with only a few of our guys moving at a time, and supported by cover fire from the rest of us, the NVA had a difficult time aiming at their targets.

I was the last man down and when I made my break for the berm, the covering fire from Second Platoon was a roar. I was proud of my guys — and incredibly thankful for them.

When I got behind the berm I found everyone in the platoon was accounted for, ammunition was holding out well, and we still had water.

Just then Capt. Buckles came to my position with his medic, Spec. 5 Elmer Dehaven, a practicing Seventh Day Adventist who had been drafted as a conscientious objector and assigned to the Medical Corps. Buckles was in a rage. He started yelling that I'd left some of my platoon on the mountain. He'd had a radio transmission from two soldiers who were trapped. I told him I was the last man off the mountain and the radio transmission was wrong.

"You think you're a real smart ass, don't you?" the captain screamed at me. "Well, I'm going to prove you're not so smart, and when I do..."

With that, Capt. Buckles sprinted toward the mountain, tailed closely by the company medic.

I was muddled. I knew all my men were off the mountain. What I didn't know was what was happening to First and Third Platoons. I'd soon learn both platoons had lost their leaders and were in disarray. Buckles was yelling that I'd left two of my men behind and even though I knew it wasn't true, I knew he needed support if he was going back into an ambush. I told Sgt. Hill I was going forward with the captain and to keep the platoon where it was and give us covering fire.

"Don't withdraw until I get back," I said as I jumped in front of the berm and raced to follow Capt. Buckles.

By the time I caught Buckles and Medic Dehaven, we were drawing concentrated small-arms fire. All three of us dove head-first into a bomb crater at the base of the mountain and lay face down for several minutes.

Finally, Capt. Buckles decided to scout the enemy positions. The second he did, he was shot between the eyes.

"Doc D" cradled Buckles in his arms, but the captain died instantly. The first fatality of a dreadful afternoon. The first of too many.

I ordered Dehaven to head back to the berm and find Staff Sgt. Hill. He was to tell Hill that Buckles was dead and inform 1st Lt. Mike Williams he was now in command of the company. Hill should send three men forward to help carry Buckles' body back.

I was alone in the crater with Capt. Buckles' body, taking heavy fire, for about twenty minutes before Dehaven came back with Sgt. Gerald Wullenweber, Pfc. Johnny King, and Pfc. George S. Kimmel. Dehaven, Wullenweber, and King carried the C.O.'s body back while Kimmel and I gave them cover. I then covered Kimmel's retreat and made a mad dash of my own down the mountain.

WHEN I GOT back to the berm, I found my radio operator, Pfc. Bob Oether. He was wounded in the thigh and was crying. I gave him first aid and tried to calm him. He told me the radio had been hit and was out of commission. I told him to stay put and I would get him evacuated as soon as possible.

I then crawled behind the berm where Staff Sgt. Hill was supposed to be and found a horrible sight. Spec. 4 Alberto Colon-Coto was guarding the bodies of Sgts. Calvin Maguire and Calvin Harris.

Colon-Coto was wounded in several places, including one shot that went through the back of his leg and out his foot. He said Pfc. Richard England, the platoon medic, had patched him up and he was doing okay.

"Take a look," Colon-Coto said, motioning with undisguised disgust and empathy at the two bodies. "I think we have snipers with scopes up there."

Like Capt. Buckles, both Maguire and Harris died of head shots, though I later learned from our company historian Bill Sly that both brave sergeants had been wounded several times before their kill shots.

"I noticed a man about twenty-five yards from me," First Platoon Spec. 4 David Anderson told Sly after the battle. "It was Sgt. Maguire. He was hit pretty bad. He was almost dead if he wasn't dead already. I grabbed him and tried to pull him toward me when I was shot in the foot.

"More bullets hit the curve of my helmet. One hit the elastic band and ripped the canvas cover right off the helmet. I didn't realize how close I came to death until later, but I had to drop Maguire and roll back into the grass for cover. That's when a sniper honed in on Maguire and shot him… and shot him again, and again."

Anderson, whose nickname was Popcorn because his hair was white and curled liked fresh kernels, was with Spec. 4 Donald "Spike" Kolness when Harris was massacred.

"Sgt. Harris lay to our left with a severe wound to the arm near the elbow," Kolness remembers. "Harris was yelling and hollering in pain and we tried to calm him down.

"Popcorn tried to reach over and comfort him, but even the slightest movement drew more fire. Finally, Harris' cries turned to a whimper and he calmed down a bit. Then we heard a loud yell and Harris was silent. A sniper got him."

In the horror, Anderson and Kolness decided to pray.

"We started reciting the Lord's prayer," Anderson said. "'Our Father who art in Heaven…' I was positive then I was going to die that day.

"Spike joined in: 'Hallowed by Thy name…'

"We got about half way through the prayer and neither of us could remember the rest. We were convinced that when we died, we were going to hell for not remembering. It scared the piss out of us."

THE BODIES OF Sgts. Maguire and Harris were spread before me like sacrifices on an altar. I was afraid I would break down. I looked at

Spec. 4 Colon-Coto and told him to stay put. I promised I would get help and crawled away — only to find more death. It was everywhere that unforgiveable afternoon.

Within minutes, I found Sgt. Wullenweber with the body of Pfc. Daniel L. Wagenaar. Another brave young man shot through the head. Then "Wully" told me Staff Sgt. Hill and 1st Lt. Williams both had been badly wounded and evacuated.

With Williams out of the picture, I was now the only line officer forward. I found a radio and called 1st Lt. Mike Mulhern back at the base camp. I filled him in on Buckles and Williams. Mulhern was now in command of the company.

"We need to bring the tracks up to cover our withdrawal and evacuate the dead and wounded," I told Mulhern.

"Negative. They'll get stuck," he said.

"I walked the ground this morning. It's okay. The APCs can handle it."

Mulhern was hesitant. When I continued to press, he said he needed to get orders from battalion headquarters.

Frustrated, I started back down to the berm and was almost immediately hit in the arm. It hurt like hell, but it wasn't bad. I put a field dressing on it and went looking for my wounded radio operator, Pfc. Oether. He was doing okay.

I crawled past him and a few yards away came across yet another horrific scene — maybe the most ghastly of a bloodcurdling day. Sprawled on the ground, in a contorted, bloody jumble, were three of my men — Privates George Kimmel, Johnny King, and Richard England.

Kimmel, twenty-one years old from Cumberland, Maryland, had just joined Alpha Company the day before. He was still alive — barely. He'd been shot in the chest. I held him in my arms as he cried for his mother before dying.

King, who had helped carry Capt. Buckles' body off the mountain not more than an hour earlier, was an eighteen-year-old strong-jawed soldier from North Carolina. He'd been shot in the head and died instantly.

Slumped over Kimmel and King was Pfc. Richard England, my platoon medic, who died trying to give life to two brothers on his twenty-first birthday.

"I wanted to take care of England," remembers Doc Dehaven. "That boy wasn't in country no time, God love him. He was young and brand new and didn't even know what it was all about yet. He never lived long enough to learn."

Another fairly new arrival, Sgt. Steven T. Cummins, who I had trained at Fort McClellan, Alabama, before going to Vietnam, carried Kimmel's body down the mountain, placed it on a track for evacuation, and returned to the battlefield. Minutes later, he, too, was killed. Another clean head shot.

We discovered later that Kimmel's body was missing. It had fallen off in the high grass. We searched for weeks and finally found the remains in early August.

Months later, I received a letter from Kimmel's mother thanking me for helping to recover her son's body. This time, it was my turn to weep.

After the gruesome discovery of King, Kimmel, and England, my head was spinning. I realized my platoon was gone.

Just then, I was shot in the leg.

AS I WAS putting a bandage on my leg, a soldier from Third Platoon crawled over to help. He said his acting platoon leader had been wounded and was evacuated along with Lt. Williams' sergeant from First Platoon. We were being massacred.

I told the soldier to stay low and began to crawl to where I thought First Platoon might be. Yet another gruesome find: the body of twenty-year-old Pfc. Robert Sires, First Platoon medic, shot in the head as he selflessly, and courageously, rendered aid to a wounded soldier. Every medic in Alpha Company — all three platoon medics and the company medic — now had been wounded or killed.

At that moment, I heard the beautiful roar of engines and saw nine APCs breaking out of the wooded area behind us. I spotted my Second Platoon command track and climbed on from behind as it passed. I grabbed the gunner and told him to fire at the mountain, then stood in the back hatch and signaled the other tracks to do the same. They did, immediately.

I got on the radio and told all the tracks to continue firing at the mountain and to drop their ramps so we could load our dead and wounded. Small groups of soldiers began rushing behind the APCs. Some were carrying wounded. Most were wounded themselves.

Lt. Mulhern had set up a Medevac Zone in the small clearing we had spotted on our way in and I told the APC drivers to head there as soon as they had a full load.

IN THE MIDST of misery and chaos, whimsy and farce sometimes find root. That happened that afternoon when Sgt. "Wully" came up behind the Second Platoon command track and told me one of our APCs had fallen into a bomb crater. The driver and gunner were trapped.

I asked him to take me to the scene and, sure enough, an APC was at the bottom of huge crater, belly up. Its driver and gunner inside yelling for help.

"Wully, get those guys out," I said. "It's your job."

Sgt. Gary Wullenweber simply said, "Yes, sir" and started digging through the soft dirt with his hands and helmet.

"When you get them out, send them my way," I said. "We're gonna need all the help we can get with the wounded."

"Yes, sir. Will do."

When I got back to the APCs I found several of the gunners had been wounded and three of the APCs had taken off for the Medevac Zone. I called Lt. Mulhern to confirm they'd arrived and he said many of the wounded already were being airlifted to the 25th Infantry Division's' base camp at Củ Chi, forty miles southeast, which had a hospital.

I organized small groups of soldiers to search the high elephant grass for dead and wounded when, about an hour later, I spotted Sgt. Wullenweber walking up with the two very dirty, but obviously unharmed, privates he had dug out of the overturned APC.

Wully was smiling from ear to ear.

"You know you guys owe Sgt. Wully a beer and you have to name your first born after him," I said.

"We will. We will," they said in unison.

LATE IN THE afternoon, I had no idea what time, but after-action reports later indicated it was around 4:40 PM, I was aboard the Second Platoon command track, the only APC left. The rest had taken the dead and wounded to Mulhern's Medevac Zone. I decided to make one last quick search of the berm for any missing men when I came across a small bomb crater occupied by 1st Lt. Toney Mathews, the company forward observer who had done a brilliant and valiant job all day calling in air strikes and artillery that kept us from being completely wiped out.

Toney, a 1968 graduate of West Point who would remain a friend for life, also had been firing his M-16 all day and was one of the few who actually saw the NVA who were slaughtering us.

"I know for sure I killed four or five of the little rascals," he told me.

"Glad to hear it, Toney. But it's time to get out of here. We're the last party forward."

Toney popped up and said: "Let's go!"

I was on foot guiding my APC toward the Medevac Zone and had just turned my back to the mountain when Spec. 4 Don Weber, the .50 caliber gunner on the track, was hit. The bullet broke Weber's arm in two and hit me in the head. I'd lost my helmet in the battle and my first reaction to the sharp sting of the bullet was anger. I was mad. Real mad.

The next thing I remember was seeing myself in the air looking at my body on the ground.

"I must be dead," I thought.

I turned around and saw my grandfather, Carl August Ladensack, who died when I was only four years old. I remember him quite well because I was the oldest grandson and he used to let me get under the covers with him as he was dying of leukemia. With him were two young men, who I somehow recognized as brothers of my mother. Both had died as infants.

My grandfather and the two boys said to me: "Don't be afraid."

As strange as that may sound, what followed was even more bizarre.

I found myself at the entrance of a tunnel with a dim light at the end. I entered the tunnel and the light got brighter and brighter. It drew me to it. I began running toward the light, but just as I got close, a voice told me to go back. It was not my time.

I was angry, again, because I didn't want to go back.

Then the voice said: "I have work for you to do and I love you."

The next thing I knew, I was on the ground with a horrible headache. I reached to the back of my head and pulled out of piece of metal, a bullet fragment.

I never told anyone the story until years later when I read *Life After Life*, a moving book about near-death experiences by Dr. Raymond Moody that touched my soul.

My own out-of-body experience would change the direction of my life after Vietnam. It would lead me to the priesthood.

THE FOLLOWING SPRING, when I returned home from Vietnam, my mother pointed to a 1969 calendar with the date July 12 circled. She said she had a dream about me being in great danger that day and the curtains had fluttered in her bedroom.

She asked me what happened that day.

I told her about the near-death experience and she said she knew it.

"That's what I dreamt," she said.

Chapter 5
Village People

Father Joe Ladensack

WHEN I JOINED the priesthood, I was looking for a Band of Brothers. Instead, I found the Village People.

In the 1970s and '80s, the Phoenix Diocese was like a raging river full of sewage. I was swimming in it, trying to keep my head above the muck, but the waves just kept getting bigger and bigger.

The criminal prosecutions that created national and international headlines decades later were just a tea cup, a tiny scoop, from the surge of excrement that surrounded me in my years as a seminarian and priest from 1970-86.

John Giandelone was the first predator priest I reported to Bishop Rausch in August 1979, only to watch him go unpunished for years until I finally called the cops in 1984. But in those five years — and for another two before I was thrown out of the church by Rausch's successor, Bishop Thomas J. O'Brien — I reported a half dozen troubled clergy.

Most of the scores of victims were boys, but a few were young girls. One I remember, in particular, was Kathleen McCabe, a beautiful young woman who had gotten entangled in a complicated and ugly relationship with her parish priest. She originally sought counseling from Father Patrick Colleary in late 1974, when she was a seventeen-year-old high school senior. A friend of her brother's had exposed himself to her and she was, understandably, upset.

I was still in the seminary in California at the time, but Kathleen later explained how her relationship with "Father Pat" began.

"I was coming to him with a problem of a sexual nature — something I had never told anyone — and he responded with his own sexual desires," she said. "He was very charismatic and manipulated my emotions."

Kathleen became active in the church youth ministry and worked closely with Colleary in group programs for the mentally handicapped. She said she often met Colleary for dinners, movies, and retreats. The day she graduated from high school, Colleary said the graduation Mass and she went to dinner with him instead of joining her classmates at a party. That night, she said, Father Pat took her hand and put it on his crotch.

Colleary was a bad guy from the beginning. In the 1970s, a teacher in one of our schools complained to church officials three times about Colleary's "outrageous behavior." One of the officials who fielded those complaints was the Rev. Michael O'Grady, pastor of the parish where Colleary was assigned. O'Grady admitted "Father Pat was out of control" and that he couldn't keep Colleary from "sneaking out and partying all night." Still, O'Grady did nothing.

In 1976, the year I was ordained, nineteen-year-old Kathleen McCabe moved to Idaho to get away from Patrick Colleary, but he tracked her down and begged her to come back to Phoenix. She did. When he molested her, Kathleen came to me. I tried to get her to go to the police. She refused and eventually began a consensual affair with Colleary that continued for two years before I convinced her to end the unhealthy relationship and move from Phoenix for good.

Colleary was an equal opportunity predator. He preyed on little boys as well as young women. In 1978, the year Kathleen broke off her affair, Colleary fathered a child with another woman and, at the same time, began molesting a ten-year-old altar boy.

The altar boy, Mark Kennedy, went on to become a U.S. Marine and a top paramedic in Mesa, Arizona, but repressed the memories of his serial molestations for years. His parents, Doris and Jack Kennedy, tried stubbornly to hold Colleary accountable, pleading with Bishops Rausch and O'Brien and going to the police after Mark's older brother, Dominic, walked in on Colleary fondling Mark in the family home. Police questioned Colleary, listened to his denial, and never interviewed Mark or Dominic.

Business as usual.

IN 2002, WHEN the *Arizona Republic* began reporting extensively on clergy sexual abuse in the Phoenix Diocese, Mark Kennedy and Kathleen McCabe both went public with their stories. So did Sharon Roy, the woman who bore Colleary's daughter.

A grand jury indicted Colleary on three counts of child molestation in December 2002, but prosecutors determined the statute of limitations had lapsed and he was released one month later.

Colleary went to Ireland on vacation after his release and was there when three new felony charges of "sodomy with a boy under fifteen" were filed. He refused to return to the United States.

Maricopa County Attorney Rick Romley worked to bring Colleary home to face justice. He collaborated with the U.S. State Department to arrange an extradition hearing in Ireland. But just days before the 2005 hearing a publicity stunt by Maricopa County Sheriff Joe Arpaio — the self-proclaimed Toughest Sheriff in America who later would be convicted of criminal contempt of court only to be pardoned by President Donald Trump — ruined any chance of Colleary's return. Arpaio marched seven-hundred prisoners clad only in pink underwear, pink handcuffs, and pink flip-flops through the streets of Phoenix from an old detention facility, where Colleary had once been held, to a new jail. The humiliating parade made television newscasts around the world, including Ireland, where Judge Philip O'Sullivan of the Irish High Court cited the display in his decision to block Colleary's extradition to a jurisdiction that brazenly demeaned its prisoners.

Colleary left the priesthood in 2002 and lives in his native County Sligo, Ireland.

BY 1980, I had a reputation for reporting predator priests and Bishop Rausch was getting tired of it. So were more than a few of my fellow priests. But I couldn't ignore what was going on around me.

I was in my second year as Director of Religious Education and living in the rectory of St. Paul's Parish in north-central Phoenix. Father Harold Graf was pastor and we were assigned a deacon, Joseph Marcel Lessard, who basically was doing an internship before his ordination.

One March afternoon, I came home early from my office at the Diocesan Center and found Lessard and two young boys — brothers, aged eight and ten — running around the rectory, giggling. All three were wearing nothing but white cotton briefs.

I told the boys to put their clothes on and called their mother to pick them up. I sent Lessard to his room and told him I was going to find Father Graf.

When Graf arrived, Lessard was, amazingly, belligerent. He insisted he'd done nothing wrong. He and the boys were just having fun. Besides, Lessard said, he had a Ph.D. in psychology and he thought Graf and I were "homophobic."

Dishearteningly for me, since I respected him, Graf would be banned from the priesthood years later for "sexual misconduct with a minor" that occurred in 1978. The diocese never disclosed the nature of the misconduct, claiming the victim did not want details revealed, and noting the incident was the lone complaint against Graf in more than three decades of service.

I had no idea about the 1978 offense. Graf hid it well and behaved appropriately, I thought, when he confronted Lessard. He castigated his young deacon and ordered him to stay away from young boys. Graf said he was going to report the incident to Bishop Rausch and recommend Lessard's ordination be called off.

When Rausch heard Graf's description of the man-boy panty party, he dismissed it as "innocent horseplay" and personally presided over Lessard's ordination weeks later.

Business as usual. The bishop had handled it.

LESSARD'S PREFERRED METHOD of stalking his prey was to ingratiate himself with the young boy's family. He did it over and over again, going to a family's home for dinner, helping with odd jobs around the house, lavishing attention on the children.

Horribly, and almost unimaginably, one of his early targets was the son of a man I fought alongside in Vietnam — 1st Lt. Mike Mulhern, leader of Alpha Company's Mortar Platoon. Mulhern was the one who had been in charge and fallen asleep while Vietnamese prostitutes and vendors milled about our base camp on the eve of the Battle of Black Virgin Mountain. And he was the one who originally balked at my request to bring up the APCs to cover our withdrawal when we were being massacred the next day.

Despite those incidents, Mulhern and I remained friendly long after Vietnam. He and his wife, Maureen, lived in Mesa, Arizona. They had three children and I had known Michael Jr., the oldest, since he was born in September 1970, just as I was beginning my studies at St. John's Seminary.

Michael Jr. was ten when Maureen called me one afternoon.

"Joe, I gotta talk to you," she said.

"Sure, Maureen."

"This is really hard for me to say."

I told her we'd known each other for a long time. She could tell me anything.

"Well, Father Joe Lessard has been coming over to the house and he's been showing a lot of interest in Michael," she said. "Joe, I feel very uneasy about this and Mike really thinks I'm just weird or something, but I just gotta talk to you. What should I do?"

I told Maureen she made the right decision to call me. I didn't tell her I knew how dangerous Lessard was, but I had a plan to get rid of him — a plan that would take advantage of my reputation within the diocese as a whistleblower.

A year or so earlier, I'd given the Mulhern boys some models I made of tanks and Armored Personnel Carriers from the Vietnam era.

"Here's what you do, Maureen," I told her. "You take those little tanks out and you put them on the dining room table next time Father Lessard is coming to the house. When he's there, you have Michael Jr. say something like: 'This tank is one of my favorite things. It was given to me by a very good friend of mine.'

"Father Lessard will probably say something like: 'Oh, that's nice.' And you have Mike say, 'Yeah, his name is Father Joe Ladensack.'"

I didn't hear back from Maureen for a while, but she finally called and said Michael Jr. had done exactly what I suggested.

"You know what?" she said. "We ain't seen Father Lessard in months."

A quarter century later, after the *Arizona Republic*, the Phoenix *New Times,* and other media outlets revealed my role in uncovering whole-sale sex abuse by priests in the Phoenix Diocese, I got a phone call from Maureen Mulhern.

"Joe, hi. I just read everything," she said. "Hold on, Michael wants to say something."

Thirty-five-year-old Michael Mulhern, Jr., got on the phone.

"Father Joe," he said. "Thanks for taking a bullet for me all those years ago. You saved me."

I MAY HAVE helped save Mulhern's son from Lessard, but it was only a matter of time until some other young boy fell victim.

Several months after Maureen's phone call, I happened to visit Rev. Dick Moyer, pastor at St. Jerome's Parish in west Phoenix, where Lessard was assigned.

"How is Joe Lessard doing?" I asked.

Moyer read the tone of my seemingly innocuous question and asked me what I meant?

"Well, you know Harold and I were his supervisors at St. Paul's and we had some real concerns that we thought should block his ordination," I said. "We brought them to the bishop, but he didn't listen to us."

Moyer surprised me.

"I'm aware of what went on at St. Paul's and I've already noticed some warning signs here," he said. "I've forbidden him to go anywhere near children."

Moyer said he, too, had gone to the Bishop Rausch with his worries about Lessard.

"The bishop didn't want to hear it," he said. "He called me on the carpet and told me to stop being such a hard-ass with Lessard."

When Thomas O'Brien became bishop in 1981, he followed Rausch's lead protecting Lessard and more than fifty clergy who were accused of sexual misconduct in the diocese. He routinely, and aggressively, protected his predator priests, even when complaints escalated to civil or criminal proceedings.

In August 1985, Lessard was arrested and charged with two felonies: sexual misconduct with a minor and dangerous crimes against children — specifically performing oral sex on a thirteen-year-old boy.

The victim, John Starkey, a slender, blond boy, laid out Lessard's familiar pattern for police.

"My parents invited Father Lessard over for dinner, and a friendship grew out of that," he said. "We were always together, like five out of seven days a week, usually at my house. We even joined a health club together.

"Every day he was buying me lunch at expensive restaurants. Then we started taking trips together. After a while, he was spending pretty much every waking moment with me. My parents didn't think there was anything strange about it."

Starkey said he and Father Lessard planned a trip to the Grand Canyon and the priest stayed overnight so they could get an early start in the morning. Lessard had stayed at the Starkey home several times before, but usually slept on the couch. That night, he went up to Starkey's bedroom to see the boy's new waterbed.

With John's parents sleeping in the next room, Lessard pinned Starkey down and performed fellatio on him.

"Finally, he finished with me and, at that point I could get up, and I did," Starkey remembered. "I found my underwear and told him I was going to the bathroom. I walked right into my parents' room and told them what had happened.

"'Mom, Dad. Father Joe is sucking on my dick.' Those were my exact words. I was a little kid. I didn't know how else to express it."

Starkey's father confronted Lessard, who shrugged off the allegation.

"It must have been a dream. He must have been sleeping," Lessard said. "I'm gonna go home. I'll come back tomorrow and we'll work this out."

As soon as Lessard left, the Starkeys called police. Lessard went directly to Bishop O'Brien's residence and told him a young boy was accusing him of sexual misconduct.

Under a tough law passed just that year, Lessard faced up to twenty-five years in prison for the two felonies. But O'Brien intervened. He and Lessard were close friends.

O'Brien refused to help investigators. He told police he and Lessard had a "confessional conversation" and he was forbidden from cooperating with them. But he did write a personal letter to Maricopa County Superior Court Judge Michael D. Ryan requesting leniency for Lessard, saying the priest had expressed "extreme remorse."

A pre-sentencing report labeled Lessard a "regressive pedophile" and warned "the defendant poses a severe threat to the safety and welfare of children within the community and will maintain a propensity to reoffend."

Despite those blunt assessments, Ryan accepted a plea bargain in March 1986 that reduced Lessard's felonies to a single misdemeanor.

Instead of the possible twenty-five-year sentence, Lessard was given three years' probation and fined one hundred dollars. In all, he spent six hours in jail for his crime before O'Brien had him bailed out and Judge Ryan let him off the hook.

Lessard underwent counseling and was transferred later that year to the Diocese of Rockford, Illinois, where he worked as a hospital chaplain until 2002 when new allegations led to his removal from the priesthood. The last I heard, he had moved to Thailand.

MOST OF THE long line of predator and pedophile priests I knew in the Phoenix Diocese were unabashedly gay. Some were off kilter enough to fit in nicely with the Village People, the legendary disco group known for their costumes openly playing to gay fantasy stereotypes — the hunky construction worker, hot cop, exotic Indian chief, strapping cowboy, sexy sailor, and leather-chapped biker. The real Village People are all incredibly fit. Not so with one of the creepiest predator priests who came to Phoenix when I was there.

Father George Bredemann was crude, flabby, and disheveled — a mess of a man. At least he became that way. The night of his ordination, May 19, 1983, Bredemann was still crude and flabby, but he was scrubbed clean and smiling — looking positively priestly in his brilliant white surplice. I had tried hard to stop that night from ever happening. Too bad I failed.

When George Bredemann applied to become a priest in Phoenix, I was Vicar of Christian Formation, overseeing fourteen departments in the diocese. One of those departments was religious vocations, whose director was responsible for recruiting and screening potential priests, sending them to seminaries, then recommending whether or not they should be ordained.

One particular Director of Religious Vocations I dealt with was notorious for finding candidates who would never be accepted anywhere else. That was troubling, so I had his department begin administering psychological tests to all applicants.

"This is just a bunch of crap that Ladensack is imposing on us," the director told one of his staffers.

The psychological tests were supervised and evaluated by Catholic Charities, which had a well-trained staff of social workers. One day the head of Catholic Charities came to me and asked if I knew George Bredemann?

"Yeah, I know who he is," I said.

"Well, take a look at his test."

I did and was mortified.

"This guy is unbelievable," I said. "It's horrible. He looks like an underachieving Neanderthal."

Turns out, I wasn't off much.

I took the test and went to see the Director of Religious Vocations. I told him we couldn't possibly accept Bredemann.

"Too late," he said. "He's already been accepted. I'm sending him to Meinrad."

Meinrad is St. Meinrad's Seminary and School of Theology — a Benedictine institution in Meinrad, Indiana. Some schools have reputations for not being particularly good. Meinrad was one of them. Not coincidentally, it was where Bishop O'Brien went.

The director was farming out candidates to seminaries across the country because St. John's in Camarillo, California, where I went and where many of the Phoenix diocesan priests went, had begun administering tough psychological tests — rejecting more and more applicants or sending them out for further evaluation and counseling.

This particular director was trouble from the beginning. Early on, I asked him to show me how he was spending his funds. In the paperwork he submitted was a receipt for a dinner he had hosted for a group of seminarians. The receipt included a *Five-Hundred-Dollar tip!*

I asked him about it and he smiled.

"Yeah, [the waiter] gave us excellent service," the director said. "Besides, he was real cute."

He gave me a mischievous wink and went back about his business.

I worked hard to rein in that director. Implementing the psycho-logical testing was an important step. But I also set up a system that included screening boards with lay experts to vet potential seminar-ians, combing through their personal records and interviewing them extensively.

Not long after Bredemann was approved for the seminary, I went to Bishop Rausch and told him I intended to fire the troublesome Direc-tor of Religious Vocations.

"You can't," Rausch said.

"Sure I can," I said. "I'm the vicar. He's under me. I'm going to give you all the reasons why I want to fire him and you tell me why I can't."

I laid out everything from the five-hundred-dollar tip to the unfor-givably poor choices on seminarians.

Rausch listened and asked a bizarre question:

"Are you sure you aren't jealous of him?"

I was flabbergasted.

"I don't know why you would say anything like that," I told the bishop. "I've dealt with you very up-front, very professionally. Where would a comment like that come from?"

"I just wondered," Rausch said, then relented and agreed to let me fire the director. Rausch gave him a parish.

A few weeks later, I ran into the still-angry ex-director.

"Joe, you know who you remind me of?" he asked curtly.

"Who would that be?"

"Serpico," he said, invoking the whistleblower New York cop whose colleagues turned on him when he exposed their corruption.

"And you know what happened to Serpico."

GEORGE BREDEMANN NEVER made it through St. Meinrad. He shuttled among three schools before finally graduating from St. Pius X Seminary in Dubuque, Iowa. That tangled and troubled journey was typical. Before becoming a Catholic priest at age forty-one, Brede-mann experimented being a Lutheran and a Baptist. He had been a carnival barker, a teacher, and an executive with the Boy Scouts of America in Chicago.

All of that, coupled with his disturbing psychological test results, should have been enough to warn, first, Bishop Rausch, then his successor, Bishop O'Brien, off Bredemann. But there was more, far more. Bredemann admitted molesting at least fifteen minors before applying to the priesthood and, years later, investigators suspected O'Brien almost certainly knew about those attacks before Bredemann was ordained. Incredible.

Bredemann's first assignment was to St. Theresa's Parish in east Phoenix. Almost immediately, I started hearing rumors of trouble. Three years later, he was transferred to St. Catherine of Siena, a predominantly Hispanic parish in south-central Phoenix, where he almost seemed to flaunt his predilection for young boys. He would spend nearly every weekend at a twenty-acre ranch in a remote part of the desert an hour's drive northwest of Phoenix. Bredemann called the place his "Castle" and, in his mind, it was just that — the heart of his personal kingdom where he ruled over his loyal subjects, all of whom were young boys.

The Castle was a two-story ramshackle building with a kitchen, living room, and a "medical room," complete with a doctor's examining table, on the first floor. The only bathroom was a closet off the living room without a door and a five-gallon plastic bucket topped with a toilet seat.

Bredemann's bedroom was on the second floor, accessible by a single staircase, and designed to be private from the rest of the shack.

For years, Bredemann would drive a beat-up old van to the Castle, accompanied by two or three young boys who spent the weekend in "counseling." He called the boys his "critters."

As soon as he arrived at the Castle, which was accessible only by a long, poorly maintained dirt road, Bredemann would strip and run around naked, his flabby belly bobbing up and down. He'd encourage the boys to undress, as well, telling them it was only natural.

Details of his escapades became public in December 1988 when Bredemann was charged with three counts of child molestation and six counts of indecent exposure. Phoenix *New Times* reporter Terry Greene, whom I worked with as an anonymous source on several stories about the church over the years, wrote a wonderfully detailed account of Bredemann's romps at the Castle several months after he was arrested.

Bredemann brought a large group of his parishioners to the Castle shortly before he was to be sentenced and instructed them how to write letters to the judge begging for leniency and saying what a terrific priest Bredemann was. More than one-hundred appeals poured into Maricopa County Superior Court Judge Robert Hertzberg.

Only four letters were written on the victims' behalf. One was a poorly spelled plea from an eight-year-old boy Bredemann molested.

> "I hope you give fouther Gorge 15 years in jail and so dose my bruother... plese plese put him in jail for that long because he did something rong and god sed not to do that sruff he's not a post to do that stuff because he is a preast."

As he had done with Joe Lessard, Bishop O'Brien personally wrote the judge appealing for leniency and, this time, flat out lied.

"There was nothing in [Bredemann's] past to indicate that he had any problems of this nature," O'Brien wrote.

Bredemann faced life in prison for the felony child sex charges. He struck a plea deal with prosecutors, who dropped the indecent exposure charges and reduced the sex charges to attempted child molestation. Even with the lesser charges, Bredemann faced up to twenty years in prison and Cindi Nannetti, an incredibly dogged prosecutor, pleaded passionately for fifteen years.

Judge Hertzberg ignored Nannetti's arguments and sentenced Bredemann to one year in jail, lifetime probation, and ordered him to never again have unsupervised contact with minors. Nannetti, who was friends with Hertzberg's wife, Janis, and knew she was such a devout Catholic that she once thought seriously about becoming a nun, was stunned at the injustice of the judge's ruling.

The unfathomably light sentence drew public outrage. The *Phoenix Gazette* ran a pair of editorial cartoons days later in its morning and afternoon editions. The morning cartoon depicted Bishop O'Brien using an oversized crucifix on a chain to batter a statue of Lady Justice while an ugly figure labeled "Child Molester" looked on. Above the molester, the paper's cartoonist scrawled the words: "Don't worry Father Bredemann, we won't let the lady molest you." The afternoon editions of the *Gazette* that same day carried a cartoon showing O'Brien, seated on his episcopal throne beside a huddle of youngsters labeled victims of sexual molestation. O'Brien is saying to them: "Oh, stop that whining. We've got to check with our lawyers first."

Bredemann, who later admitted he molested at least twenty-three boys over the course of two decades, served his prison sentence, but violated probation and was re-arrested. A sympathetic nun had driven him to Florida, where he was trying to flee to Rio de Janeiro, Brazil — on a ticket he bought from a con artist for $60,000 — when police caught up with him. He was sent back to prison for forty-five years and died there of apparently natural causes on March 31, 2012. Arizona Department of Corrections Inmate #83222 was sixty-nine years old. His oldest victims were in their forties.

MARK STRIBLING, PROBABLY the best criminal investigator in Arizona for four decades, spent years chasing predator priests. He once told me the Phoenix Diocese reminded him of a kitchen at midnight.

"You turn on the light and you see cockroaches everywhere," he said. "All you can do is get the big ones."

One of the big ones in my time was Rev. Wilputte Alanson "Lan" Sherwood — Lan the Man.

In 1984, my last year as Vicar of Christian Formation, Sherwood was arrested for masturbating in public. He pleaded guilty and was fined three-hundred dollars.

That was the first inkling we had of how seriously sick Lan the Man was. It would take years for the ugly truth to come out, but we eventually learned Sherwood was an insatiable sex maniac, who preyed on young hitchhikers. He was a self-described "statistical fanatic" and kept a calendar log of one-thousand-eight-hundred-forty homosexual encounters, including twenty-two juveniles, he had from 1984-93. The log included a one-to-ten rating system that Sherwood used to grade each partner on body, face, sexual ability, and personality.

In 1985, less than a year after Sherwood's first public masturbation arrest — there would be another in 1986 — Bishop O'Brien sent him to St. Benedict's Church in the Phoenix suburb of Chandler, where Sherwood oversaw, among other things, its youth programs and altar boys.

That year, Sherwood bought a camcorder and added video highlights to his comprehensive logs.

I was gone from the priesthood in 1993 when Sherwood's diary and the enormity of his sexual activities became public. Detectives served a search warrant and seized his log books and recordings after Sherwood was arrested March 11, 1993, for exposing himself to a seventeen-year-old hitchhiker.

He pleaded guilty to attempted sexual misconduct with a minor and attempted sexual exploitation of a minor, both for an encounter with a fourteen-year-old boy that he documented on Sept. 22, 1987. Judge Cheryl Hendrix watched Sherwood's own videotape of his tryst with the boy before sentencing him to ten years in prison.

Sherwood served all ten years and was re-arrested by U.S. marshals in 2008 for violating probation, moving to California, and failing to register as a sex-offender. At the time, Sherwood was listed as the "Most Wanted Sex Offender" by the Maricopa County Adult Probation Department. He was extradited back to Arizona and given another twelve-and-a-half-year sentence in May of 2014. Sherwood is scheduled to be released on April 9, 2025 — two months before his eightieth birthday.

O'Brien. Giandelone. Lessard. Bredemann. Sherwood.

They were supposed to be my Band of Brothers. Instead, they were more like the Village People.

Chapter 6
"You're Gonna Learn the Hard Way"

2nd Lt. Joe Ladensack

TWO DAYS AFTER the unforgiveable massacre on Black Virgin Mountain, the military newspaper *Stars and Stripes* published an article under the headline: "GIs Batter Reds in Battle of Mount."

Datelined Saigon, the story, by staff correspondent Spec. 4 Ron Minnix, began:

"At least 32 North Vietnamese Soldiers died Saturday when American GIs and U.S. jets ripped into the rugged slopes of Black Virgin Mountain near Tây Ninh City, fifty-five miles northwest of Saigon.

"The mountain, called Núi Bà Đen by the Vietnamese, has been a Communist stronghold. A small group of American and South Vietnamese are on top with other allied soldiers positioned at the base, but the Communists have holed up between the two units."

I understand Minnix, who had graduated just twenty-five months earlier from the University of Oklahoma with a journalism degree, was only working with information fed him by the military brass in Saigon — that he never was anywhere near the battle. But the amount of wrong information he "reported" in just those two opening paragraphs was staggering.

And it didn't stop there.

Minnix wrote that "Communist troops fled their caves and bunkers in an attempt to escape the heavy cannon fire and bombs and ran into the 'Big Red One' troops." He listed U.S. casualties as four killed and eighteen wounded.

To say those of us involved in the fighting were incredulous when we read the article would be a knee-buckling understatement. I honestly don't think it's hyperbolism to argue the *Stars and Stripes* story was propaganda worthy of the best efforts of Joseph Goebbels — Adolph Hitler's Reichsminister for Propaganda and National Enlightenment.

The reality was:

- Our casualties were three times greater than Minnix reported.
- We had no idea how many enemy troops had been killed, but there could be no doubt it was nowhere near thirty-two.
- We didn't have any troops on the top of Núi Bà Đen.
- The NVA weren't trapped between us.
- They hadn't fled their caves and bunkers and run into us. They remained so well hidden most of us never saw the enemy that day.
- They sat in those caves and bunkers and picked us off one-by-one.
- We were the troops who were battered. Not the "Reds."

The only quote in Minnix's story was from Maj. Carmen Cavezza, who would go on to retire as a three-star general in 1994 after thirty-three years in the Army, including stints as commander of Fort Benning, Georgia, and Fort Ord in Monterrey, California. After retiring from the military, the Citadel graduate became president of Columbus State University in Columbus, Georgia, and a founding director of the National Infantry Museum and Soldier Center in Columbus.

Minnix wrote that Cavezza watched the battle from "a small U.S. outpost on top of the mountain," which was impossible, though, giving him the benefit of doubt, he may have seen some of the fighting from an adjacent mountain called Núi Cầu, a little less than half the size of Núi Bà Đen at 1,679 feet, where a few dozen troops of the 25th Infantry Division were stationed.

"It was just like sitting in the front row at a war movie," Cavezza told the newspaper.

A war movie, indeed. More like a horror movie for those of us who were actually doing the fighting — not just watching.

Our battalion commander, Lt. Col. Newell Vinson, was as incensed as any of us by the *Stars and Stripes* story. In a letter to his wife that Vinson shared years later, he told her:

"The media must be covering a different war. We were continually engaged and the coverage was obviously of us, but it was so inaccurate that I could barely recognize the activity. When reporters rely on press briefings given in Saigon, they are reporting on news that has been reviewed and altered a number of times."

He then told his wife how the inflated enemy casualty figures came to be.

"The 25th Division contacted me on body count, telling me I could pick any number I wanted (up to a few hundred)," he wrote. "We had reports of choppers counting thirty-two bodies from the air and that was the number we selected."

When he finished writing his wife, Vinson wrote another letter — this one complaining about the story to the editors of *Stars and Stripes*.

"The only thing you got correct in the article was the year, the unit, and what country the battle was in."

Vinson was born to lead. His father, Capt. Thomas Newcome Vinson, graduated from the U.S. Naval Academy in 1914, just two months before the outbreak of World War I. He was a star pitcher and football player as a Midshipman at the academy and later became a popular instructor at Annapolis.

Newell Elliott Vinson chose an Army career over the Navy and had little trouble getting into West Point, in part because of his father's stellar military background, but more so on his own merit. He scored a perfect eight-hundred on the math section of his SAT exams.

Vinson graduated from West Point in 1954, served as a tank commander in Korea, earned a Master's degree in Geography from Columbia University, and became head of the Geography Department at West Point before taking command of the 2nd Battalion (Mechanized), 2nd Infantry, of the 1st Infantry Division June 9, 1969 — two weeks after I arrived in Vietnam and a month before the Battle of Black Virgin Mountain.

The day of that battle, Vinson fought the chain of command, trying desperately to rescind orders that led our mechanized company on foot into a bloody ambush. He lost and was visibly shaken when he learned the horror of the day. One of the first things he did early on the evening of July 12 was to order Spec. 4 Bill Sly, the company's awards and decorations clerk, to begin interviewing survivors of Alpha Company to determine who should receive medals, and which medals they deserved.

Before any citations were announced, two days after the battle, Vinson came to me and said he'd spoken with Sly and a number of soldiers and he wanted me to know, personally, how proud he was of what I had done on Núi Bà Đen.

"I'm going to promote you to captain," he told me.

Hmmmm, I thought. Second lieutenant to captain. That's pretty amazing. You know how much money that means? I'd been dreaming of buying a Dodge Charger when I left Vietnam. Now, I might think about a Corvette.

Even with a field promotion to captain, though, I knew I was still a junior grade officer. Vinson couldn't give me command of a company, yet.

"Well, Colonel, what are you going to do with me?" I asked.

"Joe, I'm putting you in for the Medal of Honor," he said.

The Medal of Honor!

Alpha Company already had one Medal of Honor pending. Staff Sgt. James Bondsteel, "Buddha," had been nominated for the Congressional Medal of Honor after the battle of An Lộc, where he destroyed a half-dozen enemy bunkers before I joined him charging another that led to the capture of an NVA colonel on my second day in Vietnam.

"We already have Bondsteel in confinement," Lt. Col. Vinson said with a chuckle. "What we'll do is simply put you in confinement, too. You and Bondsteel can sweep the floor. You're already buddies so you guys can just stay in the dock because we're not going in any way to put you guys at risk."

Wow!

And Vinson had more.

"I hear you are interested in an RA commission," he said, meaning a Regular Army commission, which is vital to career advancement. As a ROTC graduate, I was considered a "reserve" officer, not "regular," and would always be at a disadvantage if I stayed in the Army.

"Yes, I'm very interested in an RA," I said.

"Well, we are going to make it happen," he said. "You know I'm head of the Geography Department at West Point. When I get done here in Vietnam, I'm going back to West Point and I'd like you to be in my department. Are you interested?"

Man, oh, man. Captain's bars. More money. West Point. Medal of Honor.

My head was spinning.

And still Vinson wasn't finished.

"I know you have a background in Chinese," he said. "So, we're going to make you an FAS."

FAS was a military acronym for Foreign Area Specialist — commissioned officers who concentrate on military, political, cultural, sociological, economic, and geographic awareness of specific countries and regions. They must be fluent in at least one language in their region.

"We'll either send you to Stanford or the University of Hawaii to focus on Chinese," Vinson said.

I thought: "Stanford! I'm just a kid from the boonies and I might be going to Stanford! This is all surreal."

Turned out it *was* all surreal.

TWO DAYS AFTER Lt. Col. Vinson's nasty note to the editors of *Stars and Stripes* about the bogus story on the Battle of Black Virgin Mountain — and one day after he pulled me aside and promised me the moon — a pair of young, enlisted reporters showed up at our base camp. They said they were there to find out what was wrong with the original story and to "set the record straight."

The two reporters had learned I was the only line officer in the field at the end of the battle and wanted to talk to me. I said sure.

Looking back, I can't believe how incredibly naïve I was. I didn't realize *Stars and Stripes* was — at least during the Vietnam War — a carefully controlled trumpet for military disinformation. Sure, Minnix's original story should have been a powerful clue. But I was kind of busy. I had work to do fighting a war and trying to save the lives of my men. I didn't have time to critique reporters or newspapers or their motives.

I spent nearly an hour talking to the two reporters, telling them everything about the battle. I told them about Brig. Gen. David Henderson landing his helicopter after seeing us playing football and about the obviously angry confrontation he had with Capt. Buckles. I told them Capt. Buckles said Henderson was upset that we were "running around like a bunch of wild Indians" and ordered us to leave our APCs behind and move out immediately, on foot, up the mountain. I told them how Lt. Col. Vinson had tried desperately to get Henderson's order rescinded. And I talked about the brave men, including Buckles, who were picked off one-by-one in a bloody ambush that never should have happened.

The reporters looked genuinely stunned. When we finished, each had a nearly full notebook. They thanked me and promised, again, to "set the record straight."

I never saw either of them again.

More importantly, the record never got straight.

ABOUT A WEEK after I spoke with the *Stars and Stripes* reporters, I was in the field when a helicopter landed nearby. I had been given command of the battalion's Recon Platoon and we were in an area surrounded by five-foot-high elephant grass, expecting contact with the enemy any moment. I thought the helicopter was landing to give me intelligence about NVA movement in my area.

With the chopper's blades still whirring, a full bird colonel popped out, strode over briskly, pulled me aside, and spoke in an angry, disciplinarian tone.

"We don't like young officers who talk to the press the way you talked to the press," he said. "We don't like that at all. You're gonna learn the hard way, that's not done."

I was dumbfounded even before he added a not-so-veiled threat.

"As a matter of fact," he said. "You have a pretty high-risk job here. It probably would be best for you if you didn't make it home."

Message delivered, he turned on his heels, climbed into his helicopter, and flew off.

It all happened so quickly, I didn't even get his name. I never knew what unit he was with. All I remember is the black spread-wing eagle embroidered on the right collar of his combat fatigues and the unwavering, unnerving tone of his warning and threat.

I shook it off immediately. That's my personality. I had a job to do. I was in charge of men's lives. I couldn't afford to let my ego or anger cloud my judgment.

The fact that a full bird dressed me down and threatened me meant that what I told the two young reporters had gone from their desks in Saigon up through the chain of command. The "real" story of Black Virgin Mountain wasn't published for nearly half a century — never in *Stars and Stripes* or in the yearbooks of either the 1st or 25th Infantry Divisions. The yearbooks record combat operations for history. Since we had been op-conned briefly to the 25th, their historians could easily ignore the botched battle. Alpha Company's historian in the 2nd Battalion (Mechanized), 2nd Infantry Regiment of the 1st Infantry

Division — Spec. 4 Bill Sly — admitted in 2016 that he intentionally failed to write up the misery of July 12-13, 1969.

"When I wrote up the history of the battalion, I didn't put those two days in it simply because the last person I knew who told the truth about the battle got into a problem," Sly confided to former *Chicago Tribune* and *Arizona Republic* reporter Joseph A. Reaves in June 2016. "I remember the story of a *Stars and Stripes* reporter talking to a lieutenant after the battle and that the lieutenant had gotten into trouble because he told the truth.

"I was writing up the histories in early November and was leaving the Army in January. I wasn't about to do something that would get me into trouble with that little time left to serve our country. So the battle does not exist in history."

Sly spent decades gathering facts about the Battle of Black Virgin Mountain and tried to make amends for his failure to write it up in the Division yearbook by self-publishing a detailed account in a book entitled: "*No Place to Hide: A Company at Núi Bà Đen.*" My wife, Anita, and I helped Sly for years. We were happy when his book came out in August 2016, as I was writing this account, but continue to regret it took so long for the truth to come out and still regret those selfless warriors of that dark day never truly received the recognition they deserved.

Early in the process of producing Sly's book, he said he wanted to tell the story of how he was ordered to stop his preliminary interviews and write-ups for my Medal of Honor. He hoped doing so would convince the Army to re-open the request. I asked him not to bring up the Medal of Honor. His book was about a battle that never officially happened. How could the Army ask Congress for a Medal of Honor for someone in a battle that never happened? Sly's book is all about the bravery of the men who fought at Núi Bà Đen. I didn't want take any of the spotlight away from them. They were my men and they were heroes.

THE COLONEL WHO confronted me in the field was right. I learned the hard way that you don't tell the truth about a bungled battle to reporters for the military newspaper. I paid a steep price.

My field promotion to captain never happened. The paperwork for my Medal of Honor was stopped. Lt. Col. Newell Vinson never again spoke to me about his promises. His offers to join him at West Point and study at Stanford to become a Foreign Area Specialist simply faded into the fog of war. I don't hold it against Vinson. He was a good man, a good soldier, a great leader. He knew how to give orders and take them. He did his best to stop the massacre at Núi Bà Đen. Those above him ordered him to stand down. And when I made myself a pariah to the chain of command by telling the truth, he knew he couldn't deliver on the promises he'd made to me in good faith. His hands were tied.

But, apparently Vinson quietly did what he could. In August 1969, less than a month after I talked to *Stars and Stripes*, I was promoted to First Lieutenant. My RA commission was eventually approved by the Army, as well. But to be official, Regular Army commissions must be ratified by Congress. Before that happened, I left the military and enrolled in St. John's Seminary.

In a recorded conversation with Bill Sly, our company historian, while he was doing interviews for his book on the Battle of Black Virgin Mountain in April 1995, Vinson singled me out and was effusive in his praise.

"Incidentally, there's a Lt. Ladensack, who, I guess you talked to," Vinson said. "He's got to be my favorite soldier of Vietnam. I think he may have about four Silver Stars."

Sly told the colonel I had two Silver Stars.

"I pinned at least two of those on him and maybe more, but, well, he's my favorite soldier," Vinson said.

Vinson retired as a full colonel in 1984, died March 20, 2004, and is buried alongside his first wife, Patricia Whelan Vinson, in Arlington National Cemetery. In a tribute published by the West Point Association of Graduates, Vinson's son, Mark, a graduate of the U.S. Army

War College, said his father's "deep pride in his unit was only matched by his deep regret at the loss of some of his soldiers."

Another son, Doug, who graduated from West Point thirty-five years after his dad, said the Battle of Black Virgin Mountain had a "significant impact" on his father's life, "which is how it made it into the eulogy."

"He knew it was a bad tactical decision to walk up a fortified mountain," Vinson wrote of his father in an email exchange with Reaves in January 2016. "The men of Alpha Company were sitting ducks.

"He told me he argued to use another means for the BDA (Bomb Damage Assessment) and was eventually threatened by the brigadier general with being fired on the spot and replaced if he didn't comply."

Doug Vinson said his father told him he didn't sleep for two days after the battle and only finally got some rest on the third day after the battalion chaplain comforted him.

"I don't think he ever recovered from those two days," Doug Vinson wrote. "I believe the loss of so many men, and the casualties of the platoon leaders and company commanders that were under his leadership haunted him.

"He was a loving man, and cared deeply for them all."

I know that was true.

In March 2005, Vinson's daughter, Patricia, herself a Lieutenant Colonel, came to Sierra Vista, Arizona, where Anita and I were living, to receive the Knowlton Award for lifetime achievement from the Military Intelligence Corps Association at Fort Huachuca. She tracked us down and took Anita and me to dinner where she talked movingly about her father. Patricia said she knew I had been at Núi Bà Đen in July 1969 and hoped I could tell her about the battle. She, too, said it haunted her father for years and his grief and remorse worsened dramatically as he approached death. Patricia said Lt. Col. Vinson seemed especially emotional about the death of Capt. Richard L. Buckles, the man he had been ordered to lead the leg assault on Black Virgin Mountain.

I assured Patricia Vinson that her father was one of the most noble men I knew and had done the best he could. He should have never had any regrets, I told her. His lingering remorse was testimony to his heart and the bravery of those who were killed and wounded.

Like me, Lt. Col. Newell Vinson learned the hard way what it cost to try to fight foolish orders from short-sighted commanders. Sadly, it hung over him the rest of his life.

Mine, too.

90

Chapter 7
"You've Lost Your Faith"

Father Joe Ladensack

THE SEXUAL ABUSE scandal that polluted the Roman Catholic Diocese of Phoenix for four decades was Bishop Thomas J. O'Brien's Vietnam.

No one ever fired a rocket-propelled grenade at the bishop. He never clambered aboard a fragile helicopter to get a bird's-eye view of men dying. And he certainly wouldn't have lasted an hour crawling through waves of five-foot-high, razor-sharp elephant grass carrying sixty pounds of gear and an M-16 in one-hundred-twenty degree heat.

O'Brien was a creased-slacks, starched-shirt, silver-cufflinks kind of Catholic — most comfortable behind his polished desk or standing in a high, ornate pulpit basking in the adoring eyes of the faithful.

But, like the generals and politicians who ran the Vietnam War, O'Brien changed the world by trying to stop change. He ruined lives, not with bullets or bombs, but with silence and shame.

The day I called O'Brien on his "Bat Phone" and refused his demands to get Harry Takata's family to withdraw their police report on John Giandelone's molestation of their son was the beginning of the end of my life as a priest. I managed to last another twenty-nine months, but I knew something had to give eventually.

That day I had just moved across Phoenix, preparing for a new assignment on the west side of town that would officially begin the following Friday. Long disgusted by the way O'Brien — and before him,

Rausch — covered up for pedophile priests, I had resigned as Vicar of Christian Formation, a high-profile, high-powered position. I had hoped to go back into the military as a full-time chaplain, but O'Brien refused to release me. He and Rausch were both adamantly anti-military. I mean adamantly anti-military.

Ironically, Rausch had been duped into allowing me to become a part-time chaplain with the U.S. Army Reserves several years before.

One November afternoon in 1979 an Army lieutenant colonel knocked on my door at the Diocesan Center in Phoenix. He introduced himself as Lt. Col. Robert Bentley and asked if I were Father Joe Ladensack. I noticed he was in the transportation corps and wore the big yellow 1st Cav patch on his right shoulder. Surely he was a Vietnam vet.

Lt. Col. Bentley said he was the active duty advisor to the local Army reserve center and had heard I was interested in becoming a chaplain. I told him, indeed, I was interested, but that Bishop Rausch was anti-military and I doubted he would allow it to happen. Bentley, who would become a good friend and play an important role in my life more than once, said he thought he could convince the bishop to give me permission.

I wished him good luck and asked him to let me know how it went.

Ninety minutes went by. I was working and almost forgot about Bentley when he walked back into my office — face flushed red, but smiling.

"Well, you're right," he said. "The bishop is anti-military, for sure. But I convinced him to let you apply."

He handed me a thick manila envelope packed with paperwork.

"The faster you can fill these out and get them in, the better we'll both be."

I was amazed, but delighted.

"Can you come down to the reserve center and celebrate mass for the unit?" he asked.

"Of course, I'd love to. Thanks."

It took more than six months for me to get my commission, but in July 1980 I officially joined the Army reserve as a chaplain — a position I was proud to hold for four years, but one I never technically should have held. It seems Bob Bentley pulled a fast one on Bishop Rausch. Years later, long after I left the priesthood, I came across the letter of permission the bishop had signed. It only gave his consent for me to work with the "inactive" reserve, whose members muster once a year. They don't get paid, they don't drill, and they cannot apply for retirement benefits. But instead of assigning me to the inactive reserve, Lt. Col. Bentley simply pushed ahead with my commission in the active reserve and Rausch never knew the difference.

I wish the bedeviled bishop had lived long enough to learn how Bob Bentley snookered him.

IN MAY 1984, just weeks before my "Bat Phone" showdown with O'Brien, I decided to resign as Vicar of Christian Formation and went to see the bishop about my next assignment. I told him I really wanted go into full-time chaplaincy in the Army.

"No, absolutely not," he said.

"Well, what do you want me to do?" I asked.

O'Brien said he was going to make me an associate pastor and was looking for a parish to place me.

Wow! What a demotion. Here I was a vicar traveling across the country, wining and dining other church officials, and going to conferences. I was a big shot. Now, I'm going to be an associate pastor under what most likely would be some young, jerk priest.

As I did when the colonel landed his helicopter in the field in Vietnam and basically told me my Medal of Honor, promotion to captain, and any future at West Point and Stanford would vanish, I quickly and quietly accepted reality.

Okay, Joe, I said to myself. *You became a priest because you wanted to help folks. So let's get over this ego crap.*

Besides, I thought with a grin, nobody's gonna want me as their associate with my reputation for turning in the bad guys.

I did know one young pastor I thought I could work with. To my surprise, he hemmed and hawed.

"Come on," I told him. "You and I have gotten along fine. You know what I can do. Your parish is poor. It's disorganized. It's a real mess. I can help you bring this place up to speed."

He reluctantly agreed and I became an associate pastor at St. Augustine Parish in the gang-infested west side of Phoenix on June 1, 1984. Less than a year later, the pastor left the priesthood to marry a parishioner. That's how it went in the Wild, Wild West those days.

NO MATTER WHAT job I had or where I went, people would come to me with reports of bad priests. St. Augustine's was no exception. The reports poured in, but I had nowhere to go with them.

When Bishop Rausch died in May 1981, his chancellor — basically his aide de camp, gate keeper, and recording secretary — was Father Jack Spaulding. I knew Jack well and thought he was a good priest. He was known for his special ministry to the deaf. It wasn't till years later that I learned he was a serial molester of little boys. In 2011, he was removed from priestly duties after a church review board determined that four claims filed against him for sexual abuse of minor boys in the 1970s and '80s were credible.

But in 1981, Jack was in good stead with the church hierarchy. Considering what we know now, maybe it isn't surprising he was so close to both bishops. In any case, O'Brien kept Spaulding on as chancellor when he succeeded Rausch. One day in 1981, I needed to talk to Spaulding and found he wasn't in the diocesan offices. I asked a colleague, who looked surprised at my question.

"Don't you know? he asked. "Jack's the new pastor at St. Maria Goretti."

St. Maria Goretti in Scottsdale was the primo parish of the Phoenix Diocese. We called it the Taj Mahal. Overnight, Spaulding went from chancellor to keeper of the Taj Mahal.

We learned later that several counts of sexual abuse stemmed from his years at St. Maria Goretti. But while those tragic events were secret, Spaulding still managed to raise eyebrows during his time in Scottsdale. He made headlines when he told parishioners that Jesus and Mary had spoken to him directly. At some of his prayer services, Spaulding would speak in a slow, monotone voice, saying that Jesus and/or Mary were using him as a microphone.

Spaulding's replacement as chancellor was the Rev. James McFadden, a sixty-eight-year-old priest O'Brien summoned from retirement. At first, McFadden was a godsend for me. When Kathleen McCabe came to me for help after she was molested by Rev. Patrick Colleary, I'd already become such a nuisance to Bishop O'Brien that he refused to hear any more from me. So I asked McCabe if she would tell her story to McFadden. She said yes and told me later the meeting helped. She said McFadden assured her Colleary would be dealt with and offered what to her seemed genuine empathy at the pain she was suffering.

But McFadden quickly went out of his way to make clear to me what I already knew.

"The bishop is concerned about all this pedophile stuff and he doesn't want to talk to you any more about it," McFadden told me. "Okay? So anything you want to talk about, you come to me."

My direct line of communication to the bishop was officially cut off, but at least McFadden held out the possibility of going through him. I could still report to someone in the church hierarchy and hope against hope something would be done.

But even that faint hope faded when I reported yet another priest to McFadden. He shrugged his shoulders and sighed.

"I've talked to the bishop, Joe, and the bishop and I think you have a problem," McFadden said. "We really think you have a problem. You are obsessing on this stuff. We think you have a psychological problem and we're discussing some type of counseling for you."

I was dumbfounded. Counseling?! For *me*? What about the priests who are doing all this stuff?

"These are facts — these complaints I've brought to you," I told him. "Isn't it true? Aren't these all facts?"

"Let's not talk about the facts," he said. "Let's talk about you. We just think you're tired. We think you're burned out."

I said: "Well, you've seen my work. You think I'm tired and burned out?"

McFadden assured me my work and work ethic were fine, but said I should think about not creating any unnecessary stress in my life. He told me I could still bring any complaints to him, but to try to take it easy.

Then, out of the blue, McFadden made an unsolicited, unnerving confession that has stayed with me for decades.

"Joe, listen. You need to understand. I've had some young lovers in my time myself," he said. "I see nothing wrong with it."

Oh, my God!

The diocese really was raging river full of sewage. How was I supposed to keep my head above the muck?

WHEN THE YOUNG pastor at St. Augustine's left to get married, I asked the bishop to let me take over. He was reluctant, but agreed to have a personnel review board make the decision. I was already in the parish and, frankly, nobody else in the diocese wanted the position. So I became pastor of St. Augustine's and started what would be my last year as a priest.

That year was agony. I learned about several more cases of priests molesting young boys and knew nothing would be done. The horror of it was weighing on me daily. I needed to clear my head. I took some time off and hiked the Grand Canyon alone. I went from the North Rim to the South and back — a majestic trek, twenty-two miles each way along two trails one of which begins fifty-eight-hundred feet above the canyon floor; the other forty-five-hundred feet above.

For two days, I marveled at God's splendor and prayed. I asked God for direction. The hike was a journey, but so was my life and I didn't have a road map. I didn't even know where the roads were or where the end point might be. I was lost.

I hiked the Grand Canyon a lot in my youth. You can get lost real quick. You've got your maps and there are plenty of signs. But you can walk down a ways and all of a sudden there's nothing — nothing but wide open space and cacti. Sometimes it looks as if the Colorado River is right there, but it's not. And you don't even know how to get to it. All you can do is walk here and walk there until you find your way.

That's how my life was that year.

So I walked and I prayed for direction.

My prayers were answered.

I came back to Phoenix and asked to see Bishop O'Brien. It was Friday, October 24, 1986 — my fortieth birthday and thirty-two years to the day since President Dwight D. Eisenhower formally pledged to support the government of South Vietnam in its "hour of trial" against communism. To my surprise, O'Brien said he had some time that afternoon. He'd meet me in his office at the Diocesan Center.

O'Brien had known me for sixteen years, since I entered St. John's Seminary in the fall of 1970 after coming home from Vietnam. I never considered the bishop a friend — I don't know how anyone could consider that lost soul a friend — but we had more than a decade and half of at least semi-shared experience.

When I sat down that Friday morning, the bishop began what he clearly assumed would be a collegial conversation by addressing me as he always did.

"Hey, Joe Babes, how are you doing?"

We chatted casually about our years together for a while before I brought up what I'd really come to discuss.

I was blunt. I told the bishop I couldn't live with the rampant sexual abuse any longer.

"I can't take it anymore," I said. "The only way out is to go to the police directly about the whole thing. I know they're probably not going to believe me and I know you're not going to help me. So I'm stuck."

For the past half hour, O'Brien and I had been sitting side-by-side in a pair of leather chairs in front of the bishop's desk—his small, pasty white hand dangling just inches from my black slacks. He was dressed as he always dressed in his office—Bishop Casual, which is to say semi-formal: a brilliant white Romani, the Roman collar, made even brighter by the stark contrast of an expensive black sport coat and a glistening gold cross. Silver cuff links peaked from beneath the sleeves of his sport coat.

The casual shoulder-to-shoulder conversation ended abruptly and the bishop's mood turned dark when I mentioned the police. He stood up and marched behind his desk, a move clearly intended to assert his authority and end what had passed for camaraderie. His face reddened and he licked his lips before sputtering:

"Young man, you have lost your faith. You are relieved of your duties right now. Your faculties are suspended."

Faculties, in the Roman Catholic Church, are what allow you to be a priest.

"You are no longer the pastor at St. Augustine's," O'Brien said. "I will give you twenty-four hours to get your stuff out of the rectory and then the best thing for you is to get out of Phoenix."

I knew going in this wasn't going to be a good conversation, but I didn't expect this. I thought the bishop would give me, maybe, six months' leave. You know, go someplace and chill. Think things over. Then come back and we'll deal with the problem.

But this dramatic dismissal came out of the blue. One second, I was a priest looking for justice. The next I was banned from preaching and practicing my religious duties. I had twenty-four hours to get out of Dodge.

The moment was harsh, but—at the same time—cathartic. I had prayed for direction. Now, at least, I knew I was going. Where? I didn't know. But I was going.

I'VE ALWAYS LIKED flashy little cars. When I was at St. Augustine's I had a red Chrysler Laser with a louvered back windshield. I stuffed everything I owned in that car and headed south the day after my showdown with O'Brien.

I'd been doing some consulting work for my brother-in-law, an OB/GYN doctor in Sierra Vista, Arizona, for years. I called him and told him I'd been thrown out of the priesthood.

"Oh no, Joe, that's terrible" he said. "Come on down and help me out. I'll pay you exactly what you were making as a priest and we'll see how things work out."

Great. Exactly what I was making as a priest. Let's see: two-hundred-fifty bucks a month. Okay, here we go.

I thought I was doing fine with everything until about a half-hour into the drive out of Phoenix, when I suddenly started shaking. The enormity of everything — the endless sexual abuse, all the pain, losing my vocation, my identity, my mission — it all hit me.

The movie *Terms of Endearment*, which had come out in 1983, was one of my favorites. I had the soundtrack on a cassette tape and loved the main theme, a piano melody by Michael Gore. It was incredibly soothing. I looped it over and over. Then I prayed.

"Dear God, I don't know what you want me to do. I don't know. Right now, I'm just one hop from being homeless. I'm sure you're going to do something. I don't know what it is, but all I can say is I trust you."

The prayer and the music calmed me. And I drove on to start a new life.

Chapter 8
Thunder Road

1st Lt. Joe Ladensack

THE M-132 Flame Thrower Armored Personnel Carriers were some of the most terrifying killing machines ever used in combat.

They also happened to be great at trimming grass — an abstruse ability that nearly cost me and my men our lives.

My first experience with the "Flames" came one week after the horrid Battle of Black Virgin Mountain. On July 20, 1969, Lt. Col. Newell Vinson put me in charge of three platoons — two Reconnaissance Platoons, which had been without officers since late May, and a Flame Platoon, which, as far as I knew, never had a platoon leader.

Vinson told me he wanted to meld the platoons into a provisional company to replace Bravo Company, which was being detached from the 2nd Battalion and assigned a different mission. The new unit was designated Echo Company.

A normal mechanized line company in Vietnam consisted of twenty APCs and about one-hundred-forty men, including infantry and mortars. Echo Company would have fifteen APCs and seventy men; no infantry or mortar support.

From the start, it was clear my job was going to be tough. The men of the two Recon Platoons had become lackadaisical after six weeks without officers. Their discipline was dubious; their training lax.

The Flame Platoon was worse. I didn't even *know* we *had* a Flame Platoon until Vinson told me. The men had never been in the field.

They were assigned to large base camps where their sole job was to burn grass to make the place look clean.

Maj. George G. Forrest, the battalion's S-3 in charge of operations and training, called me in for a briefing before I met my men. Forrest had been a hero at the bloody Battle of Landing Zone X-Ray in the valley of the Ia Drang River. That battle, memorialized in a CBS Television special by Morley Safer and the wonderful book *We Were Soldiers Once… and Young* by Joseph L. Galloway and retired Lt. Gen. Harold G. Moore, marked the first major full-scale engagement between U.S. forces and the North Vietnamese Army in November 1965. Seventy-nine soldiers of the 7th Cavalry were killed and more than one-hundred-twenty wounded in an ambush that, at times, degenerated into hand-to-hand fighting.

Forrest was six-foot-five and a ripped two-hundred pounds. He looked every bit the soldier's soldier with the biggest hands I'd ever seen and a calm, soft, melodic voice that only intensified his commanding charisma. He told me Vinson was extremely disappointed in the state of the three platoons and wanted them to spend two weeks in the field training. We would set up in the nearby Michelin Rubber Plantation, bunk in an old barracks near the perimeter the first night, then R.O.N. — remain overnight — in the field the rest of the time.

As soon as Forrest finished briefing me, I walked over and introduced myself to the two E-7 Sergeants who had been acting leaders of the Recon Platoons. I told them about the training mission, asked them to have the men ready to move out at 0800 the next morning, and ordered them to procure concertina wire and cyclone fencing to be made into RPG screens for our overnight defenses.

"Excuse me, sir," one of the E-7s said. "We are Recon. We don't carry that shit like the line companies."

"Well, were are going to be R.O.N.-ing in the field just like the line companies," I said. "So we are going to need it!"

A few minutes later, I addressed my new company for the first time. I heard loud groans when I mentioned we'd be R.O.N.-ing. Then I told them Lt. Col. Vinson wanted me to train them in "dismounted ambushes" — leaving our APCs for ground attacks. That drew even louder groans.

"That's what the colonel wanted," I told them. "But I convinced him that mounted patrols would be more effective. If we pop a few bad guys in the next two weeks, I think he'll let us stay mounted. So let's make it happen."

Once we got in the field, I realized that Lt. Col. Vinson's low opinion of these troops was generous. They were woeful. First, they had no concept of battle drill. All they did was get on line and charge the enemy. That is how 1st Lt. Gary Tucker had been severely wounded on May 24 and 2nd Lt. James Clark killed May 27.

The Recon Platoons would have to be trained how to fight in a modified Box formation, which I knew well. They also needed to be taught to fire their .50 caliber machine guns in short bursts rather than long, unbroken salvos. In the battle on May 24, Tucker's platoon members burned out every one of their .50 caliber machine guns in the first ten minutes by firing continuously.

I paired each track with another to establish "wing man" teams. That would allow one of the two M-60 machine gunners manning either side of the main .50 caliber machine gun to leave his post and haul ammo to his wing APC, making sure we never got in a situation where all six guns on the two APCs were out of ammunition at the same time. Pretty basic stuff, but all unfamiliar to my new company.

The training was slow and tough at first. I had to relieve both E-7s who had been acting platoon leaders when I discovered they were calling in false ambush locations, just to undermine me. The moment they were gone, the rest of the men began accepting my leadership. I pushed them hard and they responded. On the fifth night in the field, we ambushed a platoon-sized NVA force. We did it mounted and the next morning Lt. Col. Vinson and two of his superiors — 1st Brigade Commander Col. Everett O. Post and Maj. Gen. Herbert E. Wolff, the 1st Division Assistant Commander — came into the field to see the devastation we'd wrought. I recapped the ambush for the visitors and Gen. Wolff, who I later learned was born in Germany and fled the Nazi regime in 1939 before being drafted into the U.S. Army during World War II. He was visibly impressed and congratulated Lt. Col. Vinson on the "new, innovative mounted ambush techniques" we had used. Those five words from a high-ranking officer buoyed the men of Echo Company, at once assuring them that mounted ambushes would remain the order of the day and, in the process, elevating their opinions of me. I was winning their confidence and trust. And they were becoming an effective fighting machine.

THE LAST DAY of our training exercise, August 10, 1969, we were operating with an infantry company from the Army of the Republic of Vietnam (ARVN). I was thinking how well things were going when I got a radio call about 1600 from Major Forrest, who told me to return to Dầu Tiếng Base Camp and report immediately to the Tactical Operations Center for new orders. When I got there, I realized I was moving up the pecking order. I sat in on a briefing that included the commanding officers of two other companies — Alpha and Charlie. As new C.O. of Echo Company, I was finally sitting at the grown-ups table.

Maj. Forrest told us we would conduct a night movement to our old base camp at Lai Khê, astride Thunder Road — Route 13, which ran north out of Saigon and then northwest to the Cambodian border. Division G-2, the intelligence staff, believed the NVA were planning to cut the road to strand a major U.S./South Vietnamese military base near the Cambodian border. We would leave one of the Recon platoons at Dầu Tiếng as a Ready Reaction Force for the brigade and take the other with us. I planned to use Lt. Clark's old platoon because it was the weaker of the two and needed more field training. But two of that platoon's APCs were down, so I chose Lt. Tucker's platoon. I also made what turned out to be a fateful move by asking one of the tracks from the Flame Platoon to volunteer to join us.

We only had seventy miles to travel, but the route was winding and muddy, the night was pitch black, the monsoon was in full force, and the constant threat of ambush made the journey unnerving and painfully slow. We rolled into Lai Khê around 1 AM exhausted. I put the men up in an old barracks that, until a few weeks ago, had been our battalion rear.

The next morning we refueled and took on a new load of ammunition. That was in addition to the double supply we'd laid in before leaving Dầu Tiếng. We were loaded for bear and well-rested two days later when we received orders to move up Route 13 to Fire Support Base Thunder III, twenty-eight kilometers (sixteen miles) north of Lai Khê.

The Thunders, as they were known, were a string of oval-shaped Fire Support Bases. Ringed with concertina wire and berms, they were designed to protect supply convoys traveling Thunder Road, Route 13, from Saigon to Quần Lợi, just east of An Lộc, less than fifteen miles from the Cambodian border. The 1st Air Cav Division with three infantry battalions was based at Quần Lợi — more than twenty-four-hundred men, scores of helicopters, and artillery batteries; a huge base. By August 1969, the convoys resupplying Quần Lợi had grown massive. Some were up to five kilometers (three miles) long with more than one-hundred trucks shuttling fuel, ammunition, food, water — everything needed to keep the base operational. A parade of trucks that long made an inviting target for the NVA and they began attacking the convoys relentlessly with a battalion-sized force of about eight-hundred men.

Thunder Road was a narrow red dirt drag that morphed into a rutted, swampy quagmire during the monsoon season. Years before, jungle bordered the highway closely. But as the war progressed, U.S. forces had used Agent Orange, creating a clear zone of about three-hundred yards on each side of the road to prevent enemy soldiers from crawling close for ambushes.

With our call up, FSB Thunder III would be manned by Alpha Company, my Recon Platoon, the one Flame track I had managed to pull away, a tank platoon from Bravo 2/34 Armor, and two artillery batteries — Charlie battery of the 1st Battalion, 7th Field Artillery I1-7FA) and a New Hampshire Army National Guard unit, the 3rd Battalion, 197th Field Artillery (3-197 FA).

Charlie Company of the 2/2 Mech was sent to establish a new Fire Support Base, FSB Hartman, about ten kilometers (six miles) north.

Our plan of action was to divide fifteen kilometers of Route 13 into three sections. Alpha Company, Recon, and Charlie Company each would be responsible for protecting a five-kilometer stretch.

Our first day full day at Thunder III, August 13, 1969, we came under heavy mortar fire, while up the highway, Charlie Company was ambushed and fought a tough three-hour battle. The tone was set. Nearly every day for the next four weeks, we were engaged in heavy fighting.

IT DIDN'T TAKE long for me to realize I'd made a good decision bringing along one of the Flame tracks. I'd been fascinated with flame-throwers since I was a kid. I remember when I was young seeing a documentary about the World War II Battle of Okinawa where the narrator said flamethrowers saved the lives of scores of Marines and G.I.s by destroying Japanese bunkers that otherwise would have had to be stormed on foot. That made a huge impression on me and the first time I had an M-132 Flame APC under my command on Thunder Road I was eager to put it to use.

The M-132s carried two-hundred gallons of compressed napalm and could spew a stream of hellish flame six-hundred-fifty feet. They were the sophisticated, uber-sized descendants of the portable back-pack flamethrowers the U.S. Army first used in World War II. The igniters on those early backpack models had a tendency to fail and soldiers often had to use cigarette lighters to fire them up. GIs started calling the early models, Zippos — a clever sobriquet spawned by the aluminum flip-open cigarette lighters that were all-but standard issue to troops both in World War II and Vietnam. Since then, all flame-throwers, even the APC models, have been known as Zippos.

Our first day at FSB Thunder III, while we were under a mortar barrage, a long line of supply trucks bound for An Lộc was attacked north of us. It took Charlie Company three hours to drive off the NVA. By the time the convoy reached its destination and the supplies were unloaded, darkness had set in and the drivers were forced to spend the night. Unfortunately, another convoy was scheduled the next day. That created a logistical and security nightmare since Route 13 was only wide enough to accommodate heavy truck traffic in one direction at a time.

A decision was made the next day to have the fully loaded northbound convoy pull over near the town of Chơn Thành, about twenty-eight kilometers (seventeen miles) short of Quần Lợi, and let the empty southbound convoy pass on its way back to Saigon. My assignment was to protect the northbound supply train, but everything changed when the empty southbound convoy was ambushed. Rocket-propelled grenades tore through two five-thousand-gallon fuel trucks, which were mostly empty, but still contained enough residual petrol to set off a blaze spewing thick black smoke. My unit was ordered north to attack the ambushing force.

When we reached the site, the only APC to be found belonged to Alpha Company's commander, Capt. David L. Smith. To this day, I have no idea where the rest of his company was and I never had time to ask. Smith hurriedly told me to have my men dismount and advance toward a large thicket of bamboo where the ambushers were holed up.

"I've got a better idea," I told the captain.

I ordered my lone Zippo forward. The gunner unleashed a stream of napalm, but nothing happened. Instead of a rush of deadly flames, all we got was a long line of reddish gel stretching toward the bamboo thicket. The spark box had failed, as so often happened. But where there's a will, there's a way. And we found it. I had my gunner fire .50 caliber tracer rounds into the napalm gel and we instantly had a raging pool of fire.

As soon as the bamboo lit up, I jumped off my APC and was going from one track to another directing my men when I spotted an NVA soldier aiming an RPG. I eliminated him with a burst from my CAR-15 automatic rifle and turned to see another baby-faced Vietnamese fighter, who quickly raised his arms and surrendered to me. Lt. Col. Vinson had recently told us capturing prisoners was a high priority and, now, thanks to my Zippo, we had one. In the next month, we would capture twenty more in the battles along Thunder Road.

IN LATE AUGUST, Lt. Col. Vinson informed me I would receive a Bronze Star — my second — for "courageous initiative and intrepid determination" in the August 14 ambush. The new division commander, Maj. Gen. Albert "Ernie" Milloy, was coming the next day to personally present the award. The general, a square-jawed Mississippi native, was a veteran of World War II and Korea. He had been a paratrooper at the Battle of the Bulge and led troops against the Chinese during the month-long battle of Heartbreak Ridge in the hills of North Korea.

In the morning, before Gen. Milloy arrived, Lt. Col. Vinson told me I should take the afternoon off and not go out on regular patrol with the Recon Platoon. I told him I didn't think that was a good idea. I wanted to go out with my men.

"You've been working pretty hard," Vinson said. "You need a day off. Take it."

Gen. Milloy arrived for the medal ceremony accompanied by his aide, Capt. Dudley "Pete" Combs, my company commander when I first arrived in Vietnam in May — the man who had been the hard-assed map-reading instructor from my Infantry Officer Basic Course in the States. At the end of my first days in Vietnam, after I had charged an NVA bunker and emerged with four POWs, Combs had called me an S.O.B. and told me my bravado was going to get me killed. After Gen. Milloy pinned my second Bronze Star on me, Combs pulled me aside and said again: "You keep this up and you're going to be dead soon."

I laughed it off and looked Combs up and down. He was in a clean, starched uniform that was so different from my battle fatigues he might as well have been dressed in top hat and tails.

"How's it feel to be a kept man?" I asked him.

Combs couldn't help himself. He let out a loud laugh and slapped my shoulder.

As Combs and Milloy were preparing to leave, the general handed me a cigar and asked if he could do anything for me. With Lt. Col. Vinson standing next to me, I said: "Yes, sir. You could give me a ride in your helicopter out to my platoon on Route 13."

Vinson was none-too-pleased, but what could he do? The general made an offer and I cashed it in. Little did I know I was about to land in another mess that would give Combs a chance to tell me again how I was going to get myself killed.

LOOKING DOWN FROM Gen. Milloy's helicopter, I spotted Alpha Company's APCs and a platoon from 1st Squadron, 4th Cavalry — the "Quarter Horse," one of the oldest and most decorated cavalry units in the United States Army.

Then, just as we were descending, I noticed two isolated APCs — their rear ramps down and their crews busily occupied with Vietnamese prostitutes in nearby bushes. The general, grim-faced, was taking in the scene as well.

Oh, man, I thought. *These poor guys are going to be in big trouble.*

I assumed Gen. Milloy was going to storm off the helicopter and lash out at the men. If not him, then surely Combs. Instead, the captain turned to me and smiled.

"Get out lieutenant. This is your platoon."

I was dumfounded and livid when I realized one of the two APCs was mine. The other was commanded by Staff Sgt. William C. Britton, who had won the first of his two Silver Stars the same day I'd won my first, on May 24, outside An Lộc.

As I bolted from the helicopter, I was yelling at my men. The convoy they were supposed to protect was in sight rolling up Thunder Road.

"Battle stations!" I screamed. "Get those ramps up! Let's move."

Looking back, the scene was pretty comical. Men were running and trying to pull their pants up at the same time. The prostitutes were scrambling half-naked in different directions.

But any hint of humor quickly evaporated. Just as I jumped into the armored "helicopter" seat on my track, a loud explosion rocketed off the wooden trim vane of my APC directly in front of me. Several mortar shells landed between me and Britton's track, which still had its rear ramp lowered. We were being ambushed and we were anything but ready.

I told our gunners to fire immediately to our front and ordered both APCs to charge the wood line directly to our front. I figured the mortar observers probably were in front of us and if we could kill them or run them off, the shelling would stop. I was right. Guns blazing, we had gone only about fifty yards when the mortar fire ceased. I ordered both APCs to swing around and head back toward Route 13.

As we approached the highway, I saw about one-hundred North Vietnamese troops advancing toward the trucks in the convoy firing their AK-47s and RPGs. *Out of the frying pan and into the fire*, I thought. *Here we go.*

I wanted to get my APCs between the unarmed convoy and the NVA, but I was on the east side of Route 13, which ran north-south. The NVA were on the west side. As we sped toward the highway, I ordered my gunners to fire between the trucks racing by. I can still see the startled faces of the drivers as .50 caliber tracers whizzed by their windshields. When we reached Route 13 and crossed over to the west side, our two APCs immediately came under intense fire. Suddenly, my head jerked backward. A North Vietnamese bullet had struck my helmet just above the left temple and exited near my left ear. I was incredibly lucky. Maybe Capt. Combs was right. I seemed to keep cheating death. Maybe I really was hard to kill.

My head was ringing, but I knew if we couldn't keep the four machine guns on our two APCs firing we'd be overrun. I ordered my left side M-60 machine gunner to move over and I took his place.

"Grab some ammo and get it to the other gunners," I told him. "Cover them with your M-16 while they reload."

I radioed Sgt. Britton and wanted him to do the same, but one of his men took the radio call. Sgt. Britton and the platoon medic had gone back to the highway to give first aid to a truck driver who'd been shot in the neck, he said.

"Okay," I replied. "Then pull your APC next to mine."

When he did, I had one of my men jump on Britton's APC and take over the gun Britton had abandoned. Now, we were back to four machine guns blazing. I hoped the men would remember how I trained them to fire in short bursts, not long salvos. If any of our guns burned out, we were dead.

In the midst of the battle, I radioed Lt. Col. Vinson's Tactical Operations Center to ask for reinforcements. I was told to get off the radio. A major battle was taking place somewhere else and I'd have to make do with what I had.

Just then, I heard bullets bouncing off the back of my APC and turned around to see a North Vietnamese soldier firing at me from a spider hole on the very edge of the highway. He was raising himself to throw a grenade when I cut him nearly in two with a burst from my .50 cal machine gun.

After about fifteen minutes of heavy fighting, the attack died down. I asked my main gunner where the rest of the platoon was. He said Lt. Col. Vinson had given them several other missions up and down Thunder Road. About that time, Sgt. Britton and his medic came back to our location. Britton said they'd saved the truck driver's life and he had just been evacuated on a helicopter. I told the sergeant to square away his track and send my gunner back to me.

No sooner had the gunner returned than we started receiving heavy fire again. About fifty NVA troops were advancing toward our APCs on foot, on line, and blasting away. They were close to flanking us on the left and right when I got on the radio and called for help.

"All Recon elements come to my position at coordinates x x x... Again, all Daring Recon elements disregard existing orders and come to my position immediately. I am in danger of being overrun."

We continued to hold off the advancing NVA for several minutes until three Recon tracks joined us from the north and four more from the south. We formed a line and sent the enemy fleeing to a wood line three-hundred yards west of Route 13.

I formed the newly reunited platoon into a defensive position and radioed the Tactical Operations Center that we had encountered and destroyed an NVA company. Maj. Forrest took the call and apologized, saying he'd had bad information earlier when he told me to get off the line because a major action was taking place elsewhere. The major attack was really the one against me. In any case, now that the battle was over, he told me my mission was to search the area for enemy dead and wounded, equipment, and documents. When I was finished, I was to return to Fire Support Base Thunder III and explain to Lt. Col. Vinson why I had disobeyed his orders by not taking the afternoon off and then summoning the Recon Platoon tracks he had pulled away.

As I was closing down the communication, I felt a sharp burning on the left side of my mouth. My first thought was I'd been shot. But when I put my hand to my face, I felt a still smoldering cigar stump.

I'd been smoking and chomping on Maj. Gen. Milloy's cigar through the entire battle.

DURING THE SWEEP of the area after the battle, I had yet another near-death experience. Seemingly out of nowhere, I came face to face with an NVA soldier who had his AK-47 raised. "I'm dead," I thought, as I dropped and rolled and fired two shots that killed him instead.

Searching the soldier's backpack for enemy battle plans, I learned he was a captain and made two other gut-wrenching discoveries — a Catholic rosary and a touching photo of the man I had just killed, smiling, surrounded by his family. My heart sank. Nothing the good Jesuit priests who taught me at Brophy College Prep in Phoenix prepared me for that moment. It still haunts me.

When I got back to Thunder III, Lt. Col. Vinson was waiting for me at the gate. He was hot, and ready to chew me out. But before he could start on me, Maj. Gen. Milloy's helicopter landed on Route 13 and the general jumped out.

"Vinson, I just saw the most outstanding armor attack I have ever seen," he yelled. "That lieutenant of yours really knows how to fight."

Milloy then led Vinson to the Tactical Operations Center and Major Forrest sidled up to me and smiled.

"Well, lieutenant, it looks like you'll live to fight another day."

Later in his report of the battle, Milloy recounted how he had flown above the highway and watched the entire battle. He ended his report by writing:

"This was the most effective use of armor I had ever seen."

Despite the glowing report, I never received a medal for that day's action. Lt. Col. Vinson was still upset I had disobeyed orders. He wouldn't sign off on an award.

Years later, after I had been thrown out of the priesthood, I was in hiding in Southern Arizona because of death threats I received for turning in pedophile priests. But my old friend, Capt. Combs — by then retired Col. Combs — managed to find me and came to visit. Among other things, we talked about the day Gen. Milloy pinned the Bronze Star on me and then gave me a lift to my platoon on Thunder Road. I asked him why Gen. Milloy had hovered over the battle?

"Alpha Company was being attacked south of your position and Lt. Col. Vinson had called in airstrikes and artillery," he said. "The general's helicopter couldn't fly into that air space so he decided to watch you."

Combs said the general thought I was winning the battle from the start.

"Where did you learn to maneuver like that?" Combs asked me.

"From you, sir."

We both had a good laugh.

EVERY MORNING FROM mid-August through early September, the two line companies — Alpha and Charlie — and my Recon Platoon would outpost to cover our fifteen-kilometer stretch of Route 13. Recon was responsible for the middle five clicks. Alpha Company to the south, and Charlie Company to the north, were fighting at full strength — twenty APCs with seventy to eighty infantry. My platoon had just six APCs, though, usually, I was assigned two or three M-48A3 "Patton" tanks in support. The NVA were quick to spot the undersized unit and my sector became the focus of most of the ambushes. After a couple weeks, I decided I needed to even things up a bit so I asked the headquarters company commander back at Dầu Tiếng to send me two more Zippos.

"Happy to do it," the C.O. said. "All they're doing here is burning grass. About time they did some real work."

I used the Flame tracks mostly to cover assaults by the Recon APCs along Thunder Road. A favorite tactic of the NVA was to let an advancing APC pass and then pop up from a spider hole to fire Rocket Propelled Grenades at the more-vulnerable rear of the APC. I put the Flame tracks behind our advancing APCs where they were poised to fire .50 caliber machine guns at any NVA popping up behind us. The only time they fired napalm was when we came across enemy hiding in bamboo stands or bunkers.

The Flames were especially effective, and reassuring, at night when we were hunkered down behind the berms and concertina wire at Fire Support Base Thunder III. We used them to provide cover for wide swaths of the perimeter, a tactic that would save us from being overrun in an especially aggressive attack the early morning of September 5, 1969.

That attack came three days after North Vietnam's revered leader, Hồ Chí Minh, died of a heart attack at age seventy-nine. Hồ was a key founder of the Indochinese Communist Party in 1929 and the embodiment of Vietnamese Communism for the next four decades. Although he had been in ill health for years, we knew his death was bound to provoke a strong emotional reaction and increased military action across the country. Our nightly intelligence briefings warned us we would be hit soon.

To strengthen our positions at Thunder III, I sent out daylight details to set booby traps and trip wires around the perimeter. Those would prove important to our survival.

Thunder III was an oval-shaped garrison along the east side of Thunder Road, which ran north-south. Behind a ring of concertina wire, Alpha Company's APCs and infantry were staggered, facing outward, from six o'clock to ten o'clock. The six APCs of my Recon Platoon faced outward from eleven o'clock to five o'clock, with my command APC facing due east at three o'clock. Next to me was one of the Flame tracks. Another was to my left, at one-thirty and the third at twelve o'clock, facing due north. Staggered among our APCs and flames were five "Patton" tanks from the 2nd Battalion.

Behind the APCs, Zippos, and tanks, Thunder III had an interior road that mirrored the oval shape of the concertina wire. Alpha Platoon's mortar tracks were positioned there, facing south. The Tactical Operations Center — the command post — was inside the inner oval, along with an observation tower, latrine, maintenance shed, mess tent, and a little barbershop, which we would discover was a ridiculously reckless amenity. The barbershop was nothing more than a rough-hewn wooden table with a chair — pretty much like a kid's lemonade stand. It belonged to a friendly, elderly, soft-spoken Vietnamese man who used mechanical clippers and charged two dollars a haircut. His only customers were officers. Regular GIs couldn't afford two bucks so they cut each other's hair.

Despite the threat of imminent attack, Lt. Col. Vinson called me in the afternoon of September 4 and ordered me to send the Zippos back to Dầu Tiếng.

"Joe, you have Flame tracks up here?" he asked.

"Yes, sir."

"How many?"

"Three, sir."

"I didn't tell you you could bring the Flame tracks up here. Send them back."

I tried to convince Lt. Col. Vinson he should let me keep them.

"I've been using them and they are very effective," I said. "They're helping me an awful lot."

Vinson was adamant.

"There's an engineer back at Dầu Tiếng who's really mad because it's his job to keep all the grass mowed and the Flame Tracks are gone," Vinson said. "He can't stay on top of the grass and now his brigade commander is yelling and screaming at him and me. You've got to get those Zippos back."

I felt like screaming and yelling myself, but it wouldn't do any good.

"Fine," I said. "I'll send them back tomorrow."

Thank goodness we got that overnight reprieve.

ABOUT 10:30 THAT night, incoming 60-mm mortar rounds began landing in our perimeter—a dozen or so rounds; relatively light and only for a few seconds. Then, suddenly, they stopped. From what we could determine in the after-action report, the brief barrage came from a local Viet Cong unit that was supposed to support the full-fledged NVA assault, but had gotten its signals crossed and started firing a couple hours early.

The real assault began a little after 1 AM, Friday, September 5. Regular NVA forces opened fire from every direction, completely surrounding FSB Thunder III, but the main thrust came from a swampy area directly in front of my sector. We had been in our APCs since the first mortars landed ninety minutes earlier and we were ready. Several of the trip flares we had laid down just days ago alerted us the assault was under way. Otherwise, we might have been overrun immediately.

The night was so dark you couldn't see your hand if you stretched your arm in front of you. In the glow of the first trip flares, I got a quick glimpse of a half dozen water buffalo grazing peacefully in front of my position. I never bothered to see if they stuck around or got caught in the crossfire. I had bigger things to worry about.

FSB Thunder III was a miserable, muddy bog the early morning of the battle. My position, on the far east side of the oval, was five or six feet lower than Thunder Road. Water drained from the highway in my direction. Just off Thunder Road, the west side of the firebase was merely sloppy. But at my position, the mud was calf deep.

The difficult conditions did nothing to stop the NVA sappers who were coming at us from every direction. Using thick rubber bands, they disabled many of our trip flares. Not all, but many. The sappers wore loin clothes or nothing at all. They oiled their bodies so they could slither through the razor-sharp concertina wire with alarming speed and agility. Clearly, we were up against some amazing, formidable fighters.

Once the battle began, the sound and light show was overwhelming. The rumbling roar of fire from APCs, artillery, and mortars was so ear-splitting we could barely hear the radios in our helmets. Illumination rounds fired by our artillery turned pitch night into flickering day. Long trails of red and green tracers streaked in opposite directions. Our weapons left a wake of red tracers. The enemy's AK-47s spat green. If the streaks weren't bringing death, or sending death, they would have been beautiful.

With NVA everywhere, we laid down what we called "lawn mower" fire. We would shoot directly to our front, then walk our machine guns left, back to the right, and back again. Lawn mower fusillades were effective when NVA were dug into spider holes. If they tried to pop up, they were bound to get hit sooner or later.

Shortly after fighting began, an NVA Rocket Propelled Grenade tore through the shell of an Alpha Company APC at the southern end of the firebase setting its fuel tank on fire. Sgt. Jonathan Bortle, a mortar man from Rochester, New York, who had celebrated his twenty-third birthday eleven days earlier, raced to the flaming vehicle. Quickly realizing the blaze was out of control and the APC was loaded with tons of ammunition, Bortle hustled several soldiers away seconds before the vehicle exploded. The massive blast created a gap in our perimeter, which Bortle and his men rushed to defend. In the fighting, Bortle was killed by an NVA grenade.

Nearly two dozen enemy sappers stormed through the breach and reached the interior road where they were massing to attack the artillery and command bunkers when Staff Sgt. Charles Botsford opened fire with a .50 caliber machine gun on the rear of his APC. I was busy with the NVA on my front and wasn't sure what was happening to the south, but I could tell friendly fire was whistling across the interior of the base. It was unnerving. Within minutes, I got a radio call from Lt. Col. Vinson.

"The enemy has breached the perimeter," I screamed to the colonel. "You better tell everyone to button up."

THE FLAME TRACK next to my APC was a godsend during the battle. Once the fighting began, I ordered its crew to maneuver nearly halfway around the inner road to a new position at ten-thirty, facing northwest onto Thunder Road, and flanking the Flame at twelve o'clock, which faced due north. Between the two, NVA sappers were using wire cutters and explosives to clear a path through the concertina wire. Private First Class Robert Affolder, a crew member on an M-48 tank between the Flames, noticed the Zippo next to him wasn't firing at the enemy. In a 2006 article about the Battle for Thunder III in *Vietnam* magazine, Affolder said he made radio contact with the Flame and was told the igniter had failed. Affolder knew someone had to light the napalm and told his commander, Sgt. Larry Knippel, he was going to do it. With Knippel shining the tank's searchlight into the eyes of enemy and simultaneously firing his .50 caliber machine-gun, Affolder sprinted twenty yards to the Flame and used a chunk of burning C-4 explosive to set off the napalm. Instantly, the Zippos hosed one-hundred meters of wire and brush with a holocaust of fire. At the same time, the Flame I had sent away from my side unleashed its napalm and the two Zippos set up a crossfire of nightmare flames.

"It was a scene from hell," Affolder remembered in the magazine. "I saw two dozen NVA running away engulfed by fire. Some exploded when the charges they were carrying cooked off, and others tore off their packs and gear running back across the road."

Affolder made it back to his tank safely and fighting continued for another hour or so, but the enemy never made another attempt to breach the perimeter.

The battle ended just before dawn when a "Spooky" gunship arrived to drive off the enemy force. The Spookies were great. They were specially outfitted C-47 aircraft, military versions of the old, reliable DC-3 passenger planes. Former fighter pilot Col. Ron Terry came up with the idea of mounting three General Electric miniguns, capable of firing three-thousand rounds a minute, in the left-side windows of the C-47. Flying in a continuous hard left-hand bank turn, a Spooky could rain down gunfire and flares on enemy forces. I loved them.

In the Spring of 1965, a *Stars and Stripes* reporter saw one of the first Spookies in action and wrote the tracers streaming to the ground could have been a dragon's breath following the roar of the miniguns echoing from the plane's open door. An officer of the 1st Air Command Squadron read the account and reportedly said: "Well, I'll be damned. Puff the Magic Dragon."

The reference to Peter, Paul and Mary's 1962 hit song stuck. From then on, the C-47s, re-designated AC-47s, were known as Puffs.

The Viet Cong and NVA apparently knew the planes were dubbed Puffs. Captured documents often referred to the plane and warned against attacking a Puff since weapons were useless against it and would only anger the dragon.

AFTER DAYBREAK, RECON Platoon was assigned to sweep the perimeter for NVA bodies and wounded. I hated that duty. Seemed to me it was a job the leg guys — the infantry — should be doing. But I saluted and said, "Yes, sir."

We pulled out of the gate and I decided to check the firebase dump first. It seemed to me a dump would be a perfect place to set up a command post for an ambush. Turned out I was right. As we pulled up to the area, we spotted three Vietnamese, a colonel and two severely wounded soldiers. The colonel quickly stood up and saluted me.

"Congratulations, you put up a tremendous defense of this firebase," he said in English better than mine. "I'm colonel so-and-so. We've attacked many bases and overrun them. But yours was so well-defended we could not destroy it. I want to congratulate you."

I was stunned.

"Sir, you speak extremely good English."

The colonel smiled.

"Of course. I'm an Oxford graduate."

I chuckled and told him to come with me. As we were walking back to Lt. Col. Vinson's bunker, I asked our new prisoner about the fight.

"You said we had a tremendous defense. If you can name one thing, what is it we did best?"

"Oh, those flamethrowers," the Oxford colonel said. "We had no idea you had those things. We were preparing to attack you en masse and wipe you out when all of a sudden we were engulfed in flames."

I gave out a long, hearty laugh that puzzled my prisoner.

"Make sure you tell that to my colonel," I told him. "Make sure you tell him."

WHEN WE RESUMED our search outside the perimeter a short while later, I saw the NVA colonel was right. His troops had been about to wipe us out. Just opposite the spot where the Zippo malfunctioned and Pfc. Affolder risked his life to touch off the napalm, was a gap in the concertina wire wide enough to drive a jeep through. The triple ring of wire had been cut through before the Zippo melted away what was left. A half dozen charred NVA bodies already were reeking in the hot morning sun. On the far south side of Thunder III, we recovered twenty-three NVA bodies inside the base where Sgt. Botsford mowed them down with his .50 cal after they breached the perimeter.

Miraculously, our only fatality was Sgt. Bortle, who was awarded a Silver Star posthumously for "unquestionable valor in close combat against numerically superior hostile forces."

Six other men from Fire Support Base Thunder III were wounded and one went missing. Our friendly Vietnamese barber never returned.

You don't suppose he was working with the bad guys, do you? Guess we'll never know for sure.

One thing I do know, though: Those Zippos saved us from being overrun. Lt. Col. Vinson eventually agreed. After interviewing my Oxford-educated prisoner, Vinson called me in and said the Flames could stay at Thunder III.

"Those guys burning grass are just going to have to make other plans," he said.

Black Virgin Mountain

*Captain Joe Ladensack discharged from
Fort Lewis, Washington, August 1970
(photo by Jeff Noble)*

Two Joes — Ladensack and Reaves (photo by Jeff Noble)

Joe and Anita Ladensack (photo by Jeff Noble)

*Father Joe hikes the Grand Canyon,
contemplating his future in 1986*

*Ladensack (front left) on command
APC with Vietnamese prisoner*

Fuel tanker ambushed on Thunder Road

Father Joe with Mike and Maureen Mulhern,
whose son was the target of a predator priest.

Joe with his impressive array of medals, including two
Silver Stars and six Bronze Stars (photo by Jeff Noble)

*Joe with the chaplain's uniform he once wore despite the
objections of Bishop Rausch (photo by jeff Noble)*

*The chalice Joe's parents gave him when he was ordained
resting atop his medals (photo by Jeff Noble)*

Killed in Action at Núi Bà Đen 12 July 1969

Capt. Richard T. Buckles, Pfc. Robert J. Sires,
Pfc. Johnny L. King, Sgt. Steven T. Cummins, Pfc. Daniel Wagenaar,
Pfc. Richard England, Sgt. Calvin G. Maguire

Not pictured: Sgt. Calvin Harris and Pfc. George S. Kimmel

Chapter 9
I'm Gonna Be a Regular Person

Joe Ladensack

ALMOST EVERY DAY, for four years at all-boys Brophy College Prep high school in Phoenix, the Jesuit priests hammered home two themes: Mission and Integrity.

Each of you young men has a mission, they would tell us over and over again. You have something to do in this world and you had better do it or you will never be happy. Don't run away from your mission. God will help you complete the mission.

They preached endlessly: Always be a man of integrity. You must be a man of integrity. Go forward no matter what obstacles you face. Go forward with integrity.

My freshman year, a guest speaker at a school-wide student assembly, drove both themes home for me in a way none of the determined and devoted Jesuits could.

The speaker was Tom Dooley. No, not the "Hang Down Your Head, Tom Dooley" that most people remember from the 1958 hit record by the Kingston Trio. That Tom Dooley was actually Tom Dula, a Confederate veteran from North Carolina who was hanged in 1868 for the murder of his lover Laura Foster. In Appalachia, names ending with an "a" are pronounced with a "y" — hence Duly, or Dooley.

Foster's murder was especially brutal. She was stabbed repeatedly with a large knife and the viciousness of the crime helped create widespread interest in Dula's trial. A local poet, Tom Land, wrote the song that became a chart-topping hit in the United States, Australia, Canada, Norway, Italy, and Germany ninety years later.

The Tom Dooley who came to Brophy Prep my freshman year was Thomas Anthony Dooley III, who, in a 1959 Gallup Poll survey, was listed at the seventh most admired man in the world.

My Tom Dooley was a U.S. Navy officer, physician, philanthropist, devoted Catholic, immensely popular author, and avid anti-communist. He also was homosexual, though the public never knew that at the time. The CIA and the Office of Naval Intelligence knew and used that knowledge to force Dooley to resign his commission and cooperate with the CIA. The humanitarian, Catholic, philanthropist side of Tom Dooley established a string of hospitals in Laos, three of which were near the border with China. The blackmailed, anti-Communist side was regularly debriefed by the CIA about the sentiments of villagers and troop movements.

Dooley was just thirty-two years old when he was diagnosed with melanoma and came home to the United States for treatment. Fred Friendly, later president of CBS News, convinced the widely admired Dooley to go public with his treatment and his surgery was filmed for a special entitled *Biography of a Cancer*, narrated by Howard K. Smith. The special aired April 21, 1960, to great heart-rending acclaim.

Six months after that special, a frail and seriously ill Tom Dooley mesmerized me and my fellow classmates when he addressed us at Brophy. He told us how he had visited Vietnam years before, in the early 1950s, as a naval physician on board a U.S. warship and was so moved by the extreme poverty and lack of decent medical care that he vowed to return some day to do what he could to help. He told us he knew it was his mission, echoing what the Jesuits were telling us every day.

"Each one of you has a different mission," Dooley said in a soft, hoarse voice. "Some are relatively easy. Some are hard. Some are small. And some are monumental. But every mission is specifically tailored for the individual. Find your mission and live it."

Dooley told us we would be one of the last groups he would meet. He was dying and had less than six months to live. Actually, he had half that time. He died January 18, 1961, one day after his thirty-fourth birthday.

In a 1964 op-ed piece in the *New York Times*, Dr. Howard A. Rusk, considered to be the founder of rehabilitative medicine and a longtime peace advocate, captured Dooley's mission eloquently.

"Tom Dooley was a rare human being who found the single thing he wanted to do in life: to make the wretched, hungry, sick and hopeless people of Asia understand the best of America through the mercy of medicine."

The day Dooley spoke to us at Brophy changed my life. I began searching for my mission. I never quit searching.

My first real mission was Vietnam — well, not counting getting through Brophy and Arizona State University.

In 1965, male students at ASU — like male students at all land grant colleges — were required to enroll in ROTC, Reserve Officers' Training Corps. ASU had Army ROTC and Air Force ROTC. I joined the Army because the line to sign up for Air Force ROTC was too long. How was that for a smart decision as the Vietnam War was ramping up?

I enjoyed ROTC and excelled at it, rising quickly to become leader of what I called the "jock platoon," which was made up of ASU's top baseball stars. Future Hall of Famer Reggie Jackson and Rick Monday, the first player chosen in the first Major League draft, were in the "jock platoon." Reggie was a loud mouth even then. But I remember Monday as an incredibly nice man and hard worker. He would gain fame in 1976 for grabbing an American flag from two protestors trying to set fire to it in center field during a game at Dodger Stadium while he was playing for the Chicago Cubs. Monday served in the Marine Corps Reserves after leaving ASU, had a stellar nineteen-year career in the majors, and became an enormously popular broadcaster, first with the San Diego Padres, and later with the Los Angeles Dodgers.

Not much in my ROTC training served me particularly well in Vietnam. But I did learn one important lesson: that my mission was to get as many of my men home alive as possible — every day; every battle. Most Vietnam veterans were in three or four major firefights. I was in more than fifty. The mechanized infantry was like the fire brigade or the ambulance corps. When anybody got in trouble, they called on us to come save them. My mission was to do just that.

After my near-death experience at the Battle of Black Virgin Mountain, I knew my next mission was to become a Catholic priest. I wanted to serve God's people. I did everything to make it happen. And when it did, I embraced the mission with my whole heart and soul for sixteen years until those who claimed to speak for God's people pushed me away.

The surprisingly cool late Sunday afternoon in October 1986 when I drove out of Phoenix in my little red Chrysler Laser listening to the soothing theme song from *Terms of Endearment*, I prayed I would find my next mission.

I found it in my brother-in-law.

Dr. Jim Young was a struggling OB/GYN in Sierra Vista, Arizona, at the time. I moved in with him and my sister and went to work for Jim as his business manager. He was a good doctor and a horrid businessman. He had one goal: to make enough money to pay off his bills and retire in ten years. So when he threw me a lifeline, that became my next mission. Not as perilous, noble, or challenging as Vietnam or the Catholic Church, but still a mission; a focus for my new life.

Sierra Vista, in the desert one-hundred-ninety miles southeast of Phoenix, is a military town — home to Fort Huachuca, headquarters of the U.S. Army Intelligence Center and NETCOM, the U.S. Army Network Enterprise Technology Command. In other words, the place is one giant spook tank. It was where the military developed, and passed on to the CIA, its so-called "enhanced interrogation" techniques, including waterboarding.

Sierra Vista, interestingly, also was home to the first McDonald's Drive-Thru. In the 1970s, soldiers from Fort Huachuca were not allowed to appear in public in uniform — both for security reasons and an archaic sense of military decorum. David Rich, owner of a McDonald's restaurant just two miles from the base, knew the ban was hurting business so he came up with a culture-changing idea. He cut a hole in the side of his building, installed a small, sliding window, and, on January 24, 1975, began selling burgers to soldiers who could sit safely inside their cars.

Living with my sister and brother-in-law in Sierra Vista allowed me to stay off the grid. I had no house note or rental agreement; phone, gas, water, or electricity bills. Not even a library card. I refused to take the two-hundred dollars a month I was supposed to get from the church as a priestly pension. I didn't want them to know where I was. I didn't want their money and pretty soon I didn't need it.

Turning Jim Young's practice around was easy for me. During my time with the Phoenix Diocese I ran a number of boards and would bring in experts from Arizona State University to help us with everything from school curricula to budgets and human relations. I listened and learned and pretty soon I was experienced enough to serve as a consultant at a number of places, including Chapman College — now Chapman University — a private Christian school in Orange, California.

Jim had been a military doctor and only recently left to start his practice. When I got to Sierra Vista, he was practically starving. He couldn't even pay himself a salary. I turned that all around. Within six months, Jim was drawing a nice salary. Within two years, he had paid off the balloon note on his office and was the most popular OB/GYN in town. One reason was his patients appreciated the special way we treated them. Every time Jim delivered a baby, I would follow up the next day and personally deliver roses to the new mother. His patients loved Dr. Jim. I became pretty popular, too.

Those first years in Sierra Vista were stable and a stark contrast to my time in Vietnam and the Phoenix Diocese. But the respite would be short-lived.

THIRTY-SIX MONTHS AFTER Bishop O'Brien threw me out of the church, my past came back to haunt me. The personal Witness Protection Program I'd set up for myself in the southeastern Arizona desert sprang a leak. Terry Greene, a reporter for the Phoenix *New Times* newspaper tracked me down. She was doing a package of stories on predator priests, highlighting two: George Bredemann, the serial rapist who brought young boys to his "Castle" in the desert, and John Giandelone, the priest who molested my friend Harry Takata's son five years after I first reported him to Bishop Rausch for abusing another little boy.

I was reluctant to talk with Greene, but finally agreed if she withheld my name. She knew a bit of my Vietnam background and suggested a pseudonym: Perry Harper — P.H., for Purple Heart.

Greene's compelling stories ran under a group headline, "Let Us Prey," and carefully laid out both the horrid crimes of the two priests and the relentless cover-up by Bishops Rausch and O'Brien. The stories caused a minor uproar that quickly faded, but they dragged me back into an ugly world I had been trying so hard to put behind me. Private investigators and attorneys now knew a key, credible insider was somewhere out there and they quickly found me, prodding me to testify in a long string of civil lawsuits.

I put them off as much as I could, but finally agreed to be deposed November 17, 1990, in a civil case against Bredemann. That was the first of nearly a dozen depositions I gave over the next seventeen years. Depositions are no fun. They are grueling — mentally and physically. I dreaded them. But I made them my mission. I knew that without me, these victims of sexual abuse had no voice. They would be crushed by the church.

Once the depositions began, church attorneys — and every priest in the diocese — knew I was the chief whistleblower in an ongoing scandal they desperately wanted to go away. I started receiving veiled, and not-so veiled, threats. Twice, I was physically threatened by priests — once by a layman, a powerful national and civic figure. In all three cases, the threats were almost verbatim.

"Stop this stuff right now or something really bad is going to happen to you. Really, really bad."

My parents were harassed. My mother, Regina, phoned one day, sobbing. A man had parked in front of her house several days in a row. He never got out of his car, but he sat there for hours. She was scared.

I tried not to dwell on the threats, but admit I grew concerned when my own attorney warned me the risks were real. The attorney, Kenneth Freedman, had been a close friend of my younger brother, Robert Joseph Ladensack. Ken and Bob were in ROTC together at ASU. Both were officers with the 101st Airborne Division in Vietnam in 1971, though they served in different battalions. Bob was killed in an airplane crash in Thừa Thiên-Huế Province on Vietnam's north central coast November 28, 1971 — three weeks after his twenty-fourth birthday. Ken was deeply moved by Bob's death and for years afterward stopped by my parents' house regularly to see how they were doing and reminisce. In 1990, my mother told him I was testifying in a lawsuit about priestly sexual abuse and Ken asked her to get in touch with me.

"Joe is going to need an attorney," he told her. "I'd like to help. Tell him I'll do it for free. Pro bono."

When mom called, I told her I didn't think I needed an attorney. I wasn't being prosecuted. I was just telling what I knew behind closed doors. But I told her to give Ken my phone number and I would talk to him.

Ken called and was persuasive. He convinced me I needed a lawyer and insisted he be with me at every deposition.

Freedman was a fairly prominent attorney in Phoenix in the early 1990s. He had been an adult probation officer and was on the board of the Arizona Boys' Ranch, which worked with troubled youth. Truth be told, though, he probably was most noted for some of his shady clients.

Ken represented Rep. Bobby Raymond, one of seven Arizona state legislators indicted in February 1991 on charges of taking more than three-hundred-thousand-dollars in bribes from an undercover agent trying to get casino gambling legalized in Arizona. The scandal, dubbed AzScam, made national headlines and was covered extensively by the *New York Times* and network television.

Freedman's defense of Raymond wasn't particularly vigorous or effective.

"(The charges against my client amount to) political type things, if I had to describe them in a nutshell," Freedman told the *Arizona Republic.*

Raymond pleaded guilty to five felonies. He was sentenced to two years in prison, but served just six months before being paroled.

Another of Freedman's high-profile clients was Gary Patrick Callahan, a U.S. Border Patrol agent convicted of selling eighty-one pounds of cocaine to a prominent dentist in the posh Phoenix suburb of Paradise Valley. Callahan, a Marine Corps Vietnam veteran whose father fought with the Marines at Guadalcanal in World War II, had been the sole arresting officer in a four-hundred-eighteen-pound cocaine bust near the Mexican border in late May 1988. Prosecutors claimed he skimmed ninety pounds and sold most of it to the dentist.

Callahan had a lavish home, complete with an Olympic-size swimming pool, in Bisbee, Arizona. He claimed he was able to afford the mansion on a border agent's salary because he had won a California lottery.

A crack marksman who bragged he had trained with a special operations team in South Africa, Callahan was known long after Vietnam as an ardent anti-Communist. His license plate frame read: "I'd rather be killing Communists in Nicaragua."

In May 1989, Callahan was arrested on the cocaine charges and released on bond. A week before the scheduled start of his trial in July 1990, he fled to New Zealand on a phony passport and bought a yacht with two-hundred-fifty-thousand dollars his girlfriend wired him. He never had a chance to name the yacht before he was re-arrested.

Callahan was returned to Phoenix after a protracted extradition fight and stood trial in February 1993. A jury took just six hours to find him guilty, largely on the testimony of his girlfriend and her brother, who both cut plea deals. The girlfriend spent thirty months in prison. The dentist was fined five-thousand dollars and went back to his practice.

"It's awfully hard when you get two snitches," a frustrated Freedman told reporters outside the courthouse after the trial. "In essence, they're being rewarded."

Callahan was sentenced to twenty-seven-and-a-half years in federal prison in May 1993. He was released from the Bureau of Prisons facility in Seagoville, Texas, on July 9, 2014.

Sometime in late 1993, Freedman telephoned me with a dire warning.

"Joe, I don't want to scare you, but you are in real danger," he said. "Your life is in danger."

I asked Ken what he was talking about.

"You know, Joe, I have a lot of unsavory clients and they know things. I've heard on the street that somebody from the diocese wants to do you in."

"Ken," I said. "I can't believe it."

"It's true. This is serious. Be careful. Be very careful, please."

I was taken aback. Then, Ken said something even stranger.

"I've put a file in a safety deposit box at my bank and told my wife if anything happens to either one of us, she should turn it over to the county attorney."

Two months after that haunting phone call, Ken Freedman was killed in a mysterious accident. He was coming around an S-curve outside St. Joseph's Hospital—the main Catholic medical facility in downtown Phoenix—on Saturday morning, January 15, 1994, when his Corvette raced out of control and slammed into a light pole. He died in the intensive care unit of St. Joe's three days later.

Police classified Freedman's death an accident, but my brother, a Phoenix firefighter told me word around town was the crash was suspicious. Firefighters and police, of course, traditionally have close relationships and my brother told me a cop friend told him Ken's brake lines had been cut.

There never was any public evidence of foul play and the mysterious file Freedman said he put away for safe keeping never materialized. In early 2018, Freedman's widow, Mickey, told Joseph Reaves she didn't have "any documents related to Ken working with Joe Ladensack." But added: "My husband was concerned for Joe's safety" and "I never found out what caused my husband's one-car accident."

KEN FREEDMAN HAD a tendency to be over-dramatic and mysterious, so maybe that explains the ominous call about death threats and the missing file. But, as he said, he did associate with a lot of unsavory people. And not all of them were criminals, as I learned when I got another strange phone call from him before he died.

"Joe, I need you to come over to the house tonight for dinner," he said.

Need me to come over? I thought. "What's this about?" I asked.

"I can't tell ya, Joe. Just come over."

When I got there two hours later, Ken introduced me to a man dressed in a trim black suit, white shirt, and black tie.

"He's an FBI agent and he has a question," Freedman said. "I told him you'd be the best person to give him an honest answer."

Ken's guest skipped the pleasantries and asked me if I knew a certain priest.

I said yes.

"How well do you know him?"

"Pretty well," I said. "We played Little League together. I've known him since fifth grade. So, yeah, I know him really well. Why?"

"What do you know about him and women?"

I almost choked.

"I think the guy is totally asexual," I said. "He never had a girlfriend in high school. He's very passive. I mean, we used to call him Davey the WaterBug. That was his nickname in our family: Little Davey the WaterBug."

Surprisingly, the man in black thanked me.

"I'm glad you gave me that answer because he's been having an affair with my wife for six months," he said. "I didn't know whether it was started by him or my wife and you just saved his life. I'll handle this in a different way than I planned."

With that, the man stood and left.

"Ken! Ken! What are you doing?" I squealed at Freedman.

"Well, I've known this guy a long time and I knew you were the best person to answer his question."

"Ken, you need to give me a little warning," I said. "He could have mentioned any number of other priests and I'd have told him they were womanizers not knowing where he was going. I could have gotten my friend killed."

THE FIRST COUPLE depositions I gave in the early civil suits were run by what Ken Freedman called "Jack-in-the-Box" lawyers — attorneys more interested in making a quick buck than real justice for the victims. They didn't even do enough homework to know I was living in Sierra Vista, Arizona. They would call Ken and he'd tell me when and where to show up to testify. Before one hearing, Ken pulled me aside and said:

"Joe, at some point real lawyers are going to become involved in the game. If you ever hear from Dick Treon, give me a call immediately because we've got trouble."

I didn't know what he meant at the time. What he meant was the stakes were going to get a lot bigger when Treon got involved. And they did.

Treon was a product of excellent Catholic education. He earned a bachelor of arts from Loras College, a respected Catholic institution in Dubuque, Iowa, then went to the nation's oldest and most prestigious Jesuit university — Georgetown — for his law degree.

As early as June 1993, when he filed suit against John Giandelone and three other predator priests, Treon was the go-to attorney for sexual abuse victims in Phoenix. It didn't take him long to find me.

I was at my sister's house in Sierra Vista enjoying a Norman Rockwell-like Fourth of July picnic when one of my young nieces came up to me and said: "Uncle Joe, there's a man out in the driveway. He wants to talk to you."

I thought that was strange, but walked out to meet the man. A young woman was with him.

"Hello, my name is Dick Treon," he said. "I'm an attorney and this is my paralegal. We'd like to talk to you."

My stomach clenched as I remembered Freedman's warning. The fact that Treon had driven down from Phoenix with his paralegal on a holiday to seek me out seemed ominous.

Not unexpectedly, he wanted me to testify in the civil suit he had filed just five days earlier.

"I really don't want to be involved anymore," I said with what I thought was steadfast conviction.

Treon paused a second, then politely said: "Well, either you become involved or I will subpoena you as a hostile witness."

Okay, here we go again, I thought. *Well, if this guy is working for the victims, I guess I can trust him. The mission continues.*

I worked with Treon for more than a decade. At one point, he came to me and said he wanted help understanding the inner workings of the church.

"Joe, there's a lot of stuff I don't understand," he told me. "I'll pay you to come down and consult with me. As long as it takes. I just need you to tell me how the church works. I don't know how it works."

I didn't say it out loud, but I thought: *It's a medieval institution. Of course, you don't know how it works.*

For days, I drew diagrams and flow charts and outlined the chain of command in the Phoenix Diocese until I realized the key to everything Treon wanted to know — and the church wanted to keep secret — was locked in a vault.

There literally is a huge vault in the basement of the chancery. It's massive — a room-sized vault. It sounds ugly, but the Catholic Church and the Nazis have one thing in common. They document everything and they keep the documentation. If Saint Peter had his sandals fixed once, the Vatican has the receipt.

Treon's eyes lit up. They have personnel files?

"I have never seen a personnel file, but I know they have them," I said. "I've never even seen my own, but I know they have them."

Against all odds, Treon eventually convinced a local magistrate to order the Phoenix Diocese to release the personnel files. They were a treasure trove of scandal and Dick became something of national celebrity. He traveled the country giving seminars to fellow attorneys on how to pry records from their dioceses.

NINETEEN-NINETY-FOUR WAS A pivotal year in my life. Ken Freedman's death. Working with Dick Treon. And late that year, too, I wrapped up my latest mission with Dr. Jim Young, my brother-in-law.

Jim had told me in 1986 he wanted me to help him make enough money to retire in ten years. We beat the deadline by two years. Jim sold his practice and started traveling across country. I felt pretty proud of myself until I realized I had just put myself out of business. I didn't have a job. More importantly, I needed a new mission.

I heard the United Methodist Church of Sierra Vista was looking for a youth minister and thought, *I can do that in my sleep.*

When I applied for the job, I told the pastor my history with the Catholic Church. He was impressed and hired me on the spot. Little did I know that job would lead me to one of the happiest days of my life — the day I met Anita Dawson Cooper.

In February 1995, just weeks into my new job, I was leading a confirmation class for a group of seventh- and eighth-graders and told them we would take a field trip to Tucson, seventy-five miles away. We would attend a Bar Mitzvah, visit a homeless shelter, and tour the historic Mission of San Xavier del Bac, a national landmark founded by Father Eusebio Kino in 1692.

When we made the trip, Anita Cooper was the only parent to come along. Her son, Charlie, apparently told her she needed to come, when, in reality, all I asked was that parents give their permission. The misunderstanding was a blessing.

Midway through the day, we stopped for lunch at McDonald's on East Broadway Boulevard in downtown Tucson. Our pastor, David Barkley, asked us all to join hands in prayer before the meal and when grace ended, I impulsively squeezed Anita's hand. I don't know what I was thinking. It just happened.

Then, a few hours later, I found myself giving Anita a private tour of the mission, explaining to her the various functions of the church building during the Catholic Mass. She was especially interested in the *mandas*, handwritten pleas from parishioners placed around the statues of their favorite saints. Being a lifelong Methodist, Anita found it all fascinating.

The next Monday, back in Sierra Vista, the parish secretary, Manje Watson, asked how the trip had gone. I gave her a rundown of what we had seen and done and told her the kids were great.

"I also met Mrs. Cooper," I said.

"Oh, the poor widow Cooper," Manje said.

Widow, hmmmm, I thought. Anita was incredibly attractive and now I hear she is a widow. *Hmmmm.*

I learned Anita's husband, Paul Cooper, had died two years earlier at age forty-five of a rare form of cancer, leaving her with two sons — eleven-year-old Charlie and thirteen-year-old John. The

Cooper family homestead was in Arkansas, where Paul's father, Dr. Joel Aubrey Cooper, was an enormously popular Methodist minister. Dr. Cooper and others in the family were pressing Anita to move back to Arkansas so they could help raise Charlie and John, but Anita and the boys were reluctant.

I came along at the right spot and the right time.

One evening after a church meeting, Anita came up to me and asked a delightfully blunt question.

"I know why I'm single at forty-eight, but why are you?"

"It's complicated," I said.

For the next two-and-a-half hours I tried to explain I was a Catholic priest, but I'd had my faculties withdrawn by my bishop because I refused to keep silent about sexual abuse by my fellow priests.

"Faculties?" she said, her brow furrowed. "I'm a Methodist. I don't understand Catholic terminology. You've got to translate that to Methodism."

I tried, but every half hour we were interrupted by calls from John reminding his mother it was time for her to come home.

Finally, after a lot of hemming and hawing, a lot of explaining the nuances of power in the Catholic Church, and a brief telling of my time in Vietnam, Anita began to accept that I really was single. But she went home skeptical about the reasons and determined to check out my stories.

Luckily for me, she had a good friend who was able to vouch for me.

Lt. Col. Bob Bentley, the man who recruited me to be an Army Reserve chaplain in Phoenix when I was still with the diocese, had also recruited Anita's husband, Paul Cooper, to come to Fort Huachuca in Sierra Vista — a strange, fortuitous coincidence.

Anita told me later she thought of asking Bentley about me on the off-chance he could back up my military claims. When she mentioned my name, she said, the blood drained out of Bob's face.

"Joe disappeared nine years ago and the records are sealed," Bob said. "I could not find out whether he did something wrong or the

Catholic Church did something wrong. I didn't know where he was. It's a mystery."

Anita told him he could have found me easily if his wife had been using the right gynecologist. He's been here all that time working with Dr. Young.

"What happened?" he asked.

"I'll have you and your wife over for dinner," Anita told him. "I'll invite Joe and you two can go talk in another room and find out for yourself."

After that meeting, Bob assured Anita everything I'd told her was true. She was relieved, but still had a few concerns.

"I know you were exposed to Agent Orange in Vietnam," she said. "And that can come back. The priest thing may pop up again. That's another thing.

"But your personality and your values, the consistency of your character, those are solid. My two sons need a father and I need a playmate. I guess I'm willing to take a chance."

I proposed to Anita Cooper on May 13, 1995, just three months after I squeezed her hand at McDonald's. Both of us had a sleepless night wondering if we had done the right thing. More than a few of our friends and family had their doubts, as well. Pastor Barkley; Anita's sisters, Karen Widdifield, and Gwen Horton; my sister, Veronica Young, all expressed concern over the whirlwind courtship. About the only person who gave her whole-hearted support to our decision was Harriett Petzold, widow of Anita's maternal Uncle George.

A few minutes after I proposed, and Anita accepted, I had one of those "oops-did-I-really say that" moments. I told Anita: "I found a new mission. You're my next mission — you and the boys, raising the boys."

To this day, Anita still chuckles at being called a "mission." She says I was *so romantic.*

We were married August 5, 1995 — a date we choose so the wedding would be out of the way before the start of the school year. John and Charlie joined the parade of skeptics about our marriage.

"Mom, we thought we were doing okay since dad died," John said. "Why do we need him?"

I soon won them over. I was the oldest of nine children growing up and my mother was a great delegator. She basically delegated that I run the household, and I did. I learned early a lesson that I followed the rest of my life — in Vietnam, the Catholic Church, and now in my new role as step-father: Lead from the front and never ask anyone to do anything I hadn't already done myself.

With John and Charlie, I took over many of the household chores they had been assigned — doing the dishes, laundry, yard work. They were delighted.

John was an avid mountain biker and he quickly learned I was the ready chauffeur he needed at 5:30 AM on Saturdays for his outings with the Dawn to Dust Mountain Bike Club.

I won over Charlie when I convinced his mother the game of Dungeons and Dragons, which he played non-stop with his friends, was good, clean fun — not some dark, evil danger.

Shortly after I proposed to Anita, I remember sitting on a back porch swing one evening looking at Charlie and John play with the cat and dog in the backyard. I was overcome.

"I'm about to become a regular person," I told Anita. "I'm gonna have a wife and two sons and a cat and a dog. I'm gonna be a regular person."

THREE YEARS TO the day after I proposed to Anita, I got a horrible reminder of what it means to be a "regular person."

We lost John Cooper, my beloved step-son.

An Eagle Scout, John was scheduled to graduate in days from Buena High School in Sierra Vista when he and two classmates were involved in a ghastly one-car accident on Interstate 10 forty miles east of Tucson. Police said the car was traveling more than a hundred miles an hour when it flipped out of control and hit a median. None of the three eighteen-year-olds were wearing seatbelts. They all were thrown from the tumbling car. John and the senior class secretary, Stacy Ann Hemesath, died instantly of head and chest injuries. Miraculously, class president Kristen Ingrid Hoggatt survived critical brain injuries that left her in a coma for a month. She went on to serve in the Peace Corps in Uzbekistan and became an acclaimed poet and adjunct professor at the University of Arizona.

The loss of John was devastating beyond words for both Anita and me. He had taken up biking after his father's death and become so good, so quickly, that he was selected for the U.S. National Junior Cycling Team. We thought he was destined for the Olympics.

A year after his death, the U.S. Forest Service dedicated a mountain bike trail in memory of John Cooper in the Huachuca Mountains. The gesture was a small salve to our souls and we were proud John's name will be remembered as a young, energetic person enjoying life. But in June 2011, the John Cooper Trail was severely damaged by a wildfire that destroyed twenty-nine-thousand acres.

The Forest Service moved swiftly to repair the popular trail and sent in a team of experts to advise on the reconstruction in September 2011. One of men they sent in was Bernie Stalmann, a retired civil engineer with the U.S. Army Corps of Engineers. He had worked on the southwestern edge of the Arizona Trail, which runs from Mexico to Utah and stretches the entire south-north length of Arizona.

A group of young men and women from Oregon rebuilt the trail and when they finished, Anita and I invited Stalmann and several others to our house for dinner. I was seated next to Bernie and in the course of exchanging pleasantries, he told me he was a Vietnam veteran, stationed in Dầu Tiếng as an engineering officer in 1969.

I learned long ago never to volunteer too much information, especially about Vietnam, so I just nodded and encouraged Stalmann to go on. And he did, working himself into a lather about how one time during his tour this stupid lieutenant took away his flamethrowers and how he got into trouble from the brigade commander because he wasn't keeping the grass down.

Anita and I couldn't make eye contact. We would have burst out laughing. I just kept nodding and Bernie kept fuming.

I never told Stalmann I was the "stupid lieutenant" who made his life miserable forty-two years earlier.

In my office, I have a wonderful photo of Bernie Stalmann, Charlie Cooper, and five volunteers posing as they made plans to repair the John Cooper Trail. I chuckle every time I see it. John would have loved the Bernie story.

I miss him. He was my mission and he is gone.

Chapter 10

Bondsteel's Last Ride

1st Lt. Joe Ladensack

I LOST A Congressional Medal of Honor for telling the truth to two *Stars and Stripes* reporters about the Battle of Black Virgin Mountain, but I could have been court martialed if the Army ever found out what I did a few hours before the Battle of Thunder III.

My men had been fighting hard along Thunder Road for three weeks. To say they were getting pretty tired would be a woeful under-statement. I wanted to boost morale and my staff sergeant, Charles Botsford, who later would help save the day by mowing down twenty-three NVA soldiers who breached our perimeter, had a suggestion.

"You know, Lieutenant, I could probably hustle up some beer for the men if you looked the other way."

Alcohol was strictly forbidden in the field, but this wouldn't be the first time someone found a way around regulations. I hesitated, then agreed a little too quickly.

"Just be discreet, Botsford," I pleaded.

Botsford was discreet — and amazingly efficient. One day after our conversation, and just a few hours before the Battle of Thunder III, he told me he'd managed to have several cases of beer and a dozen blocks of ice delivered. They were stowed in a safe place, he assured me. I told him to wait until after dark and I would help him distribute the beer and ice to the men.

Botsford and I made the rounds early evening Thursday, September 4, 1969. We stressed to the men what they already knew, that what we were doing was strictly forbidden. Don't mess up. We gave each track two cases of beer and a block of ice.

"One beer per man each night," I told them. "Nobody gets drunk. We could get court-martialed for this. One beer."

Since five men were assigned to each track, two cases of beer would last ten days. We told the men we'd replenish the ice each day with blocks available from Vietnamese civilians along Thunder Road. The ice wasn't safe to drink, but the men could roll the beer cans across the blocks until they were cold enough to drink.

I knew I was breaking orders, but I actually felt good about it. These brave men had gone above and beyond the past three weeks. They deserved a reward. Any one of them could be dead tomorrow. A can of warm beer a day was, literally, the least we could do for them.

The Battle for Thunder III started about three hours after Botsford and I finished our rounds. First came the brief mortar feint before midnight, then, the merciless full-scale assault where our perimeter was breached and only Botsford's machine gun and the Flame tracks saved us from being overrun.

Shortly after dawn, on Friday, September 5, once the attack had been repelled, mercifully, with the loss of only one life — none in our company — I went out to inspect the perimeter.

I was aghast.

Piles of beer cans were scattered beside each of our APCs. Recon Platoon had drunk every single beer before — and maybe even during — the battle!

Shit, I screamed silently. *Time for some serious damage control.* I yelled at the men to gather up the cans and bury them as quickly as possible. They had just started when Lt. Col. Newell Vinson radioed and asked if it was safe for him to inspect the perimeter?

"I wouldn't recommend it at this time, sir," I said. "We're still cleaning up the perimeter. I'll let you know when it's all clear."

The last of the beer cans were being buried when I heard the dull thump-thump-thump of a helicopter approaching. I recognized immediately that it belonged to Maj. Gen. Albert "Ernie" Milloy, the division commander who had pinned my second Bronze Star on me three weeks earlier.

As Milloy's chopper hovered above the helipad on the northern edge of Thunder III, preparing to set down, a frenzied burst of AK-47 fire cut through the dawn sky.

"Jesus, the area's still hot!" I heard Milloy radio Lt. Col. Vinson over the company network as his helicopter banked sharply and sped away.

"Yeah, I know," Vinson responded calmly. "Lt. Ladensack told me. He said he'd let me know when the area is secured."

I did, after a little borrowed time — just enough to save my career.

CAPT. DOUGLAS BARR, commander of Bravo Company of the 34th Armor, borrowed a little too much time at Thunder III. Barr was a 1964 West Point graduate from Washington state. He was in command of the area where my Recon Platoon was stationed inside Thunder III. When the attack started in the early morning hours of September 5, Lt. Col. Vinson tried desperately, without success, to raise Barr on the radio. After numerous attempts, Vinson assumed Barr had been killed and coordinated the battle with me, since I was second in command.

The next morning, Vinson learned Barr had been in the officers' outhouse when the battle began and was so frightened he stayed there all night without access to a radio. Vinson and Gen. Milloy both gave Barr a poor OER, Officer Evaluation Report, and relieved him of command — a rare disciplinary slap for a West Pointer.

My own OER was due in a couple weeks. OERs were issued every six months. I'd arrived in Vietnam in May so my first OER was set for mid-October. The evaluations look at various personality traits then include a narrative section that lays out what an officer had done well and what he'd done wrong. Your immediate supervisor compiles the report and is known as the "Rater." His superior reviews the report and signs off on it as the "Endorser." The OER rated you on a scale of zero to one-hundred and anything ninety-seven or above sped up your path to promotion. A poor OER could lead to you being "boarded" out of the Army — that is, being discharged by an Officer Separation Board reviewing your report. When my OER came through, my Rater gave me a ninety-nine, writing the only thing wrong with my performance was my consistently disheveled appearance.

Lt. Col. Vinson was my Endorser. The minute my OER landed on his desk, he exploded and walked over to the captain — the Rater — who had written it up.

"This is the stupidest thing I've ever seen," Vinson barked. "Of course the guy looks disheveled. He's in the field all the time. Change it!"

The captain did. I got a perfect hundred on my first OER in Vietnam.

I never knew what Capt. Barr's OER rating was. But it was obviously low enough to relieve him of command and threaten his Army career. In the summer of 1970, after I was home in Phoenix and preparing to enter the seminary, Barr tracked me down and asked me to write a letter of recommendation. He said he was being threatened with involuntary separation from the Army. I wrote the letter, but never heard from Barr again. Happily, though, I learned years later that he completed a twenty-year career in the Army and retired as a lieutenant colonel. He went on to work for Boeing in Seattle as a principal engineer on their Army Weapons System Development Program.

Barr was a good man and, who knows, maybe my letter was a small help in saving his worthy military career.

SEVERAL NIGHTS AFTER the Battle for Thunder III, Lt. Col. Vinson called me in and ordered me to conduct a "Thunder Run" — a night scramble down Route 13 at top speed — from FSB Thunder III to the village of Chơn Thành, about five kilometers south. A twelve-year-old girl from Chơn Thành had walked into our base earlier in the day with what she said was information about planned NVA ambushes.

She was debriefed for several hours and now Vinson wanted her brought home safely.

I was immediately suspicious. A twelve-year-old girl with intelligence about NVA ambushes? And she just walks up to the concertina wire and volunteers to tell all? It didn't make any sense to me.

But I had my orders.

"Colonel, I'd like a couple tanks to come along with the Recon Platoon," I said.

"Forget it, Ladensack. You're making too much of this mission. It's a milk run. Just get the girl home. No tanks."

I lined up my platoon twenty minutes later and briefed them on the nature of the mission and the rules of engagement. I told them there was a good chance we were riding into an ambush and, if we were, I wanted them to do everything possible to avoid civilian casualties.

If we were ambushed on the highway, we had a Standard Operating Procedure to deal with that. We were prepared. But we had never been ambushed inside a village. I was terribly worried how we would handle a firefight with civilians everywhere.

I was still amped up and heading to my track when Staff Sgt. James Bondsteel popped up beside me. Bondsteel and I had become friends for life my second day in Vietnam when he and I charged a series of NVA bunkers and wiped them out in a battle near An Lộc. I won my first Silver Star for my actions. Bondsteel was nominated for the Congressional Medal of Honor. And because the powers-that-be couldn't risk having a Medal of Honor nominee getting killed, Bondsteel had spent the past three months living in the Tactical Operations Center, base headquarters, out of harm's way.

As the captain who wrote up my OER noted, I tended to look a bit disheveled most days. But Bondsteel was worse. At least until he went into protective custody. I barely recognized the Bondsteel who popped up beside me. His fatigues were new and crisply starched. Starched! Nobody in the field had a starched uniform. His boots were new, too, and brightly polished. His helmet was covered with a new green liner. Bondsteel looked as if he just got off the plane from the States.

"Two-six," Bondsteel said, using my call designation as leader of second platoon. "I've got cabin fever from sitting in the TOC all this time. The colonel says that since this is going to be a milk run, I can ride along. I'm coming with you."

Now, all of a sudden, I have a new set of problems beyond worrying about civilian casualties. Bondsteel was a loose cannon. If we got into an ambush, I had no idea what he would do. He loved to freelance on the battlefield and his favorite weapons were hand grenades. If he jumped off the track and got wounded, I'd have no way of getting him back. We didn't have any infantry with us. If he got killed, I would be in deep trouble — responsible for losing a Medal of Honor hero on a "milk run."

I decided the best way to control Bondsteel was to give him something to do. I made him a babysitter for the girl we were bringing back to Chơn Thành.

"Bondsteel, your job is to sit behind me, protect my back, and hang on to that little girl," I said. "Don't do anything else unless I tell you."

Bondsteel said, fine, then leaned over and whispered:

"Milk run, my ass. You know, and I know, we are going to get into one helluva fight."

Then he asked for a few extra hand grenades.

THE MONSOON RAINS were torrential as we churned down Thunder Road. Bondsteel and I were on the second track following Staff Sgt. Charles Botsford, who was using an AN/PVS-2 Starlight Scope to search through the darkness for any signs of trouble. The AN/PVS-2, mounted on Botsford's M-16, weighed seven pounds and was seventeen inches long with a three-inch circumference. It amplified starlight, hence the name: Starlight Scope. Just as we pulled in to Chơn Thành, Botsford radioed he could see two lumber trucks. One had just blocked the road, the other was pointed down the road, and between the two a few dozen men were running around with rifles.

"Stop!" I barked over the radio. "Everybody herringbone."

Herringbone formation was Standard Operating Procedure when we halted. One track would angle to cover the left side of the road. The track behind would angle right. Then left, right, left, right, so the platoon looked like a zipper down the middle of the highway. A herringbone.

Botsford's APC was the only one still pointed straight down the highway toward the lumber trucks.

I could feel Bondsteel getting restless behind me. The rain was pummeling us.

"Cool it, Bondsteel," I said, turning to him. "Make sure you've got the little girl because here's what I want you do. I want you to get her off the track and lead her down the road."

Because the tracks were herringboned, they formed a corridor that offered a semblance of safety for Bondsteel and the girl to walk down.

"You take the girl down the corridor and find out where she wants to go," I told Bondsteel.

As the two were clambering off the APC, Botsford radioed that he could see more men around the lumber trucks. "And they're moving fast," he said.

"Bondsteel," I yelled. "Just drop the girl on the side of the road. Don't ask her where she wants to go. Just drop her off and get back here."

When the girl saw Bondsteel was leaving her, she started screaming in broken English.

"No, I want to go more down road! More down! More!"

Now I am starting to get really nervous. It's clear the little girl wants to lead us into a waiting ambush.

"Bondsteel, just give her a shove and tell her to take off," I said. "We're not going to take her down the road. Give her a shove and get back up here."

As Bondsteel was climbing back on board, the Tactical Operations Center came over the radio asking for a situation report.

"I'm engaged with a potential ambush," I said hurriedly. "We've got a couple lumber trucks blocking the road ahead of us with armed men all around. Now, leave me alone. We've got to maneuver and get out of here. I can't be gabbing on the phone."

Lt. Col. Vinson came on the radio and seemed agitated I wasn't engaging the lumber trucks.

"Sir, I've made my decision," I told him. "If you want to discuss it when I get back, I'll do it, but I've completed my mission. The little girl is back at her village and I'm coming back to base as soon as I can get my platoon turned around."

I completely forgot about Bondsteel during the run back to Thunder III. All I could think about was we'd escaped an ambush. We'd dodged getting into a firefight with civilians all around us. We were racing back to the relative safety of our base and we'd be out of this unholy relentless rain in a few minutes.

When we reached the base, I ordered all the tracks back to their positions on the perimeter. Then I headed to the TOC for my session with Vinson.

"Why didn't you engage those lumber trucks?" the colonel asked.

I explained my thought process.

"I completed the mission I was given," I said. "My mission wasn't to engage the enemy inside a village where a lot of civilians could have been killed."

Vinson seemed somewhat placated and then Bondsteel spoke up. I hadn't realized until then that Bondsteel had been walking behind me like a faithful puppy since we un-assed from the track at the perimeter.

"Colonel, it was really exciting out there," he said. "I thought we were going to get into a firefight and I was all excited. But Two-Six did the right thing. He's right. We'd probably have killed a lot of civilians. In my opinion, he did the right thing."

I wasn't especially happy. I mean, I appreciated Bondsteel's words, but here I was, the lieutenant in charge of a unit and my colonel is listening to a staff sergeant rationalize my actions. Then, again, this particular staff sergeant was going to get the Congressional Medal of Honor. So I guess I could see why the colonel might appreciate his opinion.

WE NEVER SAW the little girl again. And I never understood why the colonel and his staff even talked to her. What information could a twelve-year-old girl possibly have about NVA plans? Besides, we had been taking quite a few NVA prisoners and they tended to sing like canaries. They would answer any question truthfully. They didn't care. Their attitude was: "We're going to kill all you mother fuckers, anyway, so what does it matter?"

I'd take the information from our POWs over a little girl any day.

The fact we nearly got ambushed was mildly surprising because Chơn Thành was considered a neutral village. On the far south end of the village, beyond where the lumber trucks had blocked the road, the 5th Infantry Division of the Army of the Republic of Vietnam — South Vietnam's military — had a good-sized base protected by a ten-foot berm. We were supposed to be operating with them, but I never once saw them. They just stayed behind their berms, which probably was a good thing. I had been worried they might muddle things terribly if we had gotten into a firefight that night. Not only would we be fighting off an ambush, but we'd probably have to fight off our allies in the South Vietnamese Army as well.

Backing away from that ambush was one of the better decisions I made in Vietnam.

That night was the last time I was in the field with Bondsteel. In early 1970, he was transferred to Germany, where he served until President Richard Nixon presented him the Congressional Medal of Honor on October 15, 1973. He retired from the Army as a Master Sergeant in 1985 and moved to Alaska with his wife and two daughters to become a counselor for emotionally wounded soldiers at the Wasilla Vet Center and, later, at the Veterans' Administration in Anchorage.

Bondsteel was killed April 9, 1987, on the Knik River bridge near Wasilla, Alaska, when a trailer full of logs became unhooked and slammed into his subcompact AMC Spirit. He was buried at Fort Richardson National Cemetery outside Anchorage. Bondsteel was just thirty-nine years old when he was killed.

Camp Bondsteel, a massive U.S. Army base under the command of NATO in Kosovo, was named in his honor in 1999. Three years later, the Alaska Legislature officially named the bridge where he died Bondsteel Bridge. Every year on Veterans' Day, Memorial Day, and Vietnam Veterans' Day, Wasilla resident Dave Glenn, a Vietnam veteran, stands guard over the bridge in military fatigues holding an AR-15 rifle and flying an American flag to honor Bondsteel.

I can still see Bondsteel in his brand new starched fatigues shoving that little girl down the road and sprinting through the pouring rain to get back on my track. He still had another sixteen years in the Army and another eighteen years to live. But for me, that was Bondsteel's last ride.

Chapter 11
Dragged Back In

Joe Ladensack

ANITA ANSWERED the phone and knew immediately we were being dragged back in to the Catholic Church sex abuse scandal.

I had been deposed a half dozen times during the 1990s in civil suits filed against pedophile priests, but those cases were all settled quietly without any serious media coverage. That left me feeling relatively safe. I was still in hiding in Sierra Vista, Arizona, but the dark days of my priest years seemed to be fading.

Then, on February 10, 2002, I picked up a copy of the *Arizona Republic*. A bold, banner headline on the front page screamed: "Church hid abuse, victims say."

"For more than 20 years, the Tucson Roman Catholic Diocese covered up information that priests were molesting altar boys and taking young men to their beds," the story began.

I had never worked in the Tucson Diocese, but knew immediately this story would lead back to everything I'd lived through in Phoenix. After all, the *Republic* was a Phoenix newspaper. If reporters found a scandal in Tucson, surely they would start looking into their hometown diocese.

Just one month earlier, on January 6, 2002, the *Boston Globe* Spotlight investigative team published the first of what eventually would be more than six-hundred stories on priest sexual abuse in the

Archdiocese of Boston. I was beginning to realize that what I'd known and reported in Phoenix was horribly commonplace.

By early May 2002, *Arizona Republic* reporters Bill Hart, Nena Baker, Michael Clancy, Kelly Ettenborough, and Joseph A. Reaves were writing about predator priests in the Phoenix Diocese. Reaves eventually took the lead on reporting the scandal and was nominated for a Pulitzer Prize for his work.

Within weeks, the *Republic* had uncovered enough that Maricopa County Attorney Rick Romley announced his office was opening a *criminal* investigation into the Phoenix Diocese's role in covering up decades of sexual abuse by priests. The investigation was code-named Operation Broken Oath.

I didn't know it at the time, but Romley put his top investigator, Mark Stribling, on the case. Stribling began his career with the FBI in Washington, D.C., in 1977 and worked in homicide, special investigations, and violent crimes with the Phoenix Police Department for two decades before joining the County Attorney's office.

When Anita read about the criminal investigation, she suggested I give Romley a call.

"No way," I said. "The county attorney is a political office. Who knows what kind of politics are behind this. I don't know if this is even a real investigation."

Anita shrugged.

"Well, if it is a serious investigation, they're going to find you eventually," she said.

"And if they do," I said. "I'll tell 'em everything I know."

WE FIRST HEARD from Stribling when the phone rang and a man asked Anita if he could speak to Father Ladensack. That's when we knew we were being dragged back in. If someone called and asked to speak to Joe, we knew it was friend or family. If they asked for Lieutenant Ladensack, we knew it was something to do with Vietnam. But if they asked to speak to Father Ladensack, we knew we were in trouble.

Stribling found me through a bizarre coincidence that took a quarter century to unfold. When I was associate pastor of St. Mary's Catholic Church in Chandler, Arizona, from 1976-78, one of the most active families was the Ryans. Joseph and Ellen Ryan had twelve children, two girls and ten boys. The eldest son, Joseph Jr., followed his father's career path and became an optometrist. In 1990, four years after Bishop O'Brien threw me out of the church, I saw a newspaper notice that a Dr. Joseph Ryan was opening a part-time optometry office in Sierra Vista. He would be in town two days a month. A few weeks later I stopped by the office.

"Father Joe! What are you doing here?" Joe Jr. gasped when I walked in.

We had a nice visit and I filled him in on my troubles with the pedophile priests and the bishop. He said he knew about the Harry Takata incident and was sorry to hear all the painful situations I'd been through.

Ryan went back to Chandler and told everyone in his family my story. Twelve years later, his eldest sister, Maureen Ryan, an attorney, was at a party and ran into Stribling. She knew Mark and asked how he was enjoying retirement.

"I'm working again," he said. "Rick Romley talked me into working on the pedophile priest thing."

Maureen asked how the case was going and Stribling said not very well.

"Have you interviewed Father Joe Ladensack?" she asked.

"No, who is he?"

When Maureen told Stribling my story, he remembered seeing my name linked to a number of documents he'd combed through. He had been meaning to track me down. The next day he did.

ON THURSDAY, DECEMBER 12, 2002, Mark Stribling drove two-hundred miles from downtown Phoenix to Sierra Vista to meet me for the first time. He came alone, armed with a pen, a notepad, and a tape recorder.

I liked Mark immediately. He was polite and business-like. His interviewing style reminded me of Brian Lamb, founder of the C-SPAN network who hosted the weekly, hour-long *Booknotes* program that ran for sixteen years from April 1989 to December 2004. Unlike most interviewers, Lamb never tried to make himself seem smarter than the people he was interviewing. He always started with a simple, but captivating first question, such as on his inaugural *Booknotes* program when he straightforwardly asked Neil Sheehan, author of *A Bright Shining Lie*, "Why did you write the book?"

Lamb invariably asked his guests where they went to school, the names of their children, and where their children went to school. When a guest used a big word, he stopped them and asked them to define it. Typically, during an hour-long program, Lamb spoke for five minutes or less. He let his guests do the talking.

Stribling was a lot like Lamb. He got to our house at 1 PM and came to our back door, which, really, was the side door. The house was on a corner lot with a somewhat unusual layout. Our mailing address was 2865 E. Cardinal Drive and the front door faced south onto Cardinal Drive. But the entrance almost everyone used—especially our sons and their friends—was on the east side, off a street called El Camino Real. That entrance had a double-wide rolling gate, which offered access to a circular drive with a store-bought bird fountain in the middle. Our garage and the oft-used side entrance were at the top of the circle.

When I'd agreed to meet Mark, I gave him directions to the house and told him to use the side drive. His mild manner on the phone put me at ease and I liked the idea of welcoming him through, what for us, was the customary way into our home—not the formal entrance, which in a few months would be where scores of media would camp out trying to get me to tell my story.

We had a large room in the house on Cardinal Drive that we called the "Fellowship Hall." Anita and I led Mark to a table and offered him a seat. Anita asked if she could stay for the interview and, to my surprise, Mark said no, he wanted to speak with me alone. Anita quietly, but firmly, said: "This is my home. If I can't stay here, I'll just stand outside the doorway and listen."

Mark waved his hand in a welcoming, non-confrontational manner — indicating Anita could have a seat, a gesture that put me even more at ease.

"Do you mind if I record this interview?" Mark asked.

I told him that was fine. He said he also would be taking notes and that it would take several days for the recorded interview to be transcribed. When it was, it ran seventy-seven typewritten pages and covered the ugly highlights of what I knew about sexually abusive priests in the Phoenix Diocese during my time there.

Mark started with the professional requisites: "Today's date is December 12, 2002. It's about 1 PM. My name is Mark Stribling. Present for this interview is Joe Ladensack and his wife, Anita."

He noted for the record that he had telephoned me the day before and asked to speak to me about my time as a priest. His first question was simple and straightforward — Brian Lamb-like.

"Why don't we just start off with what are you doing right now?"

I told him I was retired — that since Bishop O'Brien had suspended my faculties, I had been a business manager for my brother-in-law's medical practice, a youth minister at a Methodist Church, and then, finally, a social worker in a long-term care facility before retiring.

"All right," he said. "Now, why don't you tell me about your duties when you were in the priest... can you start with when you became a priest and..."

I cut Mark off and asked if I could give him my full background.

"I think that will be enlightening on why I'm coming forward and talking the way I am."

Mark simply said: "Great."

I went all the way back to the beginning, to my birth in Saint Claire, Michigan, in 1946, to the family's move to Phoenix in the early 1950s because all the kids had bronchial asthma. I talked about my grade

school and high school education in Catholic schools, mentioned I
went to Arizona State, enrolled in ROTC, and left with a commission
in the U.S. Army as a Second Lieutenant of Infantry.

"Spent a year in combat in Vietnam and that very much changed
how I looked at life and my goals for the remainder of my life," I told
Mark.

Most of the next fifteen minutes was spent recounting a chronol-
ogy of entering the seminary, being ordained, and rising through the
hierarchy of the church in Phoenix.

"Okay," Mark finally said. "Why don't you tell me why Bishop
O'Brien took away your faculties?"

The emotional floodgates opened. The youth ministers coming to
me about John Giandelone's rape of the altar boy who would grow up
to become a top cop, Bishop Rausch lying to me about Giandelone's
victim being the son of a Lutheran minister who wanted to keep things
quiet, Giandelone being reassigned to new parishes unpunished and
eventually molesting Harry Takata. I didn't even get into a fraction of
what I knew about other predator priests — George Bredemann and
his getaway weekends with young boys at his "Castle" in the desert, Joe
Lessard's cotton underwear romps with pre-teen boys in the rectory,
Patrick Colleary's seduction of an underage Kathleen McCabe, Lan
Sherwood and his diaries graphically detailing nearly two-thousand
sexual encounters, or the former Director of Religious Vocations with
the propensity for recruiting seminarians no one else would accept
who gave a five-hundred-dollar tip to a "cute" waiter.

Stribling seemed fixated on Giandelone and Bishop O'Brien, especially O'Brien — what the bishop knew and when he knew it.

About forty-five minutes into the interview, I recounted Giandelone's molestation of Harry Takata, the son of one of my close friends
and the second Giandelone victim I knew about first-hand. I told
Stribling how I helped the Takatas file a police report and then called
Bishop O'Brien on the Bat Phone.

"I decided I'd better call Bishop O'Brien," I said. "So, he's got a — we used to call it the Bat Phone. He had a top-secret number that all the priests had, but it was only for top-secret emergencies. It was into his house... and I figured, 'Well, this is a case where I need to call the bishop.' So, I called the bishop. And, first of all, he was quite upset that I would call him on the Bat Phone and he already said this had better be good."

Until then, Mark had basically let me talk, with few interruptions. But suddenly he stopped me.

"Okay, let me, I need to get this down."

For the next half hour, Mark interrupted me after almost every sentence, scribbling furiously in his note pad.

"Okay," he said at one point. "You're probably wondering why I'm writing this all down and it's being taped. I'm going to be asked about this real quick, so I'm writing it down."

An official transcript of that first interview shows just how excited Stribling was about the way the bishop handled that phone call.

My words, on the transcript, are noted as JL: Joe Ladensack.

MS is Mark Stribling, who was scribbling notes as fast as he could at this point.

JL: *I thought O'Brien got livid before, he was absolutely beyond himself.*

MS: *Okay, hold on just a second. Okay, so needless to say, O'Brien, Bishop O'Brien, was very upset.*

JL: *He said, Why did you go out there? Why did you call the police? You have to come to me with this immediately and to me first and to only me.*

MS: *Okay, I'm going to stop you for just a,...* as he repeated the words he was writing down... *Why did you go out there? Why did you call the police? First. You have to come to me first.*

JL: *Yeah, first.*

MS: *And not, did he say and not the police, or, or...*

JL: *Come to me first.*

MS: *Okay.*

JL: *You have to come to me first. I will handle these things.*

MS: *Okay.*

JL: *He said you owe me obedience. You took a vow of obedience and you need to — must I remind you young man? — that you need to keep your vow of obedience.*

MS: *So he says you owe me what? Obedience?*

JL: *Obedience. Yeah, when you become a priest...*

MS: *Right*

JL: *You took a vow of obedience and a vow of celibacy.*

MS: *Right... Okay, so he's yelling at you on the phone.*

JL: *Oh, he, he, he's totally out of control. I'm not sure if you've ever met the man or seen the man, but it's sort of out of character to see him that out of control. But he can get out of control.*

MS: *Okay.*

JL: *He said, Now I order you to go back to Chandler and tell that family to take back the complaint.*

At that point, I remember Stribling had a look on his face I couldn't really describe. In hindsight, I'd say it was a combination of shock and jubilation. But, at the time, it was little more than a barely noticeable tightening of the muscles in his jaw and neck and a crinkle at the corners of his eyes.

I told Mark that I reminded O'Brien I was a Vietnam veteran and invoked the Nuremberg Trials. I said I told the bishop I thought what he was ordering me to do in the name of priestly obedience was an unlawful order and I refused to do it.

Mark repeated *"refused to do it"* and wrote the words in his notebook.

I told Mark I received a phone call a few days later from the Diocese of Phoenix attorney, whose name, I said I thought, was

Mahony — Roger Mahony. I was mistaken. Roger Mahony was a cardinal and archbishop of Los Angeles from 1985 to 2011. The slip of the tongue was ironic because in 2013, Cardinal Roger Mahony would be relieved of his public religious duties for covering up child sex abuse cases in California for decades. The call I received in 1984 was actually from *William P.* Mahoney, then attorney for the Phoenix Diocese and former ambassador to Ghana under President John F. Kennedy.

Mahoney's ties to the assassinated president, of course, made him a big man in Phoenix. And his job at the diocese made him a dominant force in the church. A phone call from William P. Mahoney wasn't something to be taken lightly.

I told Stribling that Mahoney played good cop, bad cop, with me. He reminded me I had gone to school at Brophy Prep with several of his sons and told me that, "as a friend and as the diocesan attorney," he thought I should reconsider talking to the Takata family and getting them to drop their criminal complaint against Giandelone. He said Bishop O'Brien was "extremely, extremely, extremely angry" with me.

As I had done with the bishop, I reminded Mahoney that I was a Vietnam veteran and had been taught from the Nuremberg Trials that I had a moral obligation to refuse to obey an illegal order. And what O'Brien — and, now his attorney — was asking was illegal and immoral. I wasn't changing my mind.

"The bishop is really in a bind," I recounted Mahoney saying. "The bishop really is in a bind. Joe, you really have to help him."

I told Mahoney again I wouldn't get the family to withdraw the complaint and then quoted the attorney's final words for Stribling.

"He said, 'I want to give you some advice young man. You are part of the problem, not part of the solution.'"

Stribling was scribbling fanatically.

"I wish I could write faster," he said.

THAT FIRST INTERVIEW with Stribling lasted another ninety minutes. Toward the end, I told Mark I had a few things I wanted to say.

"First of all… I am the oldest of nine. My brother was killed in Vietnam, but everybody else is in Phoenix. Basically, they are all practicing Catholics. My youngest brother is an architect who does — his firm does millions of dollars' worth of business for the Diocese of Phoenix. These people are vindictive and punitive. I'm sure I don't have to mention this, but my name doesn't need to get out."

Mark didn't make any promises.

"I don't know how we are going to handle this situation," he said. "I've got to go back and talk to my people. But you've really given up some information here that we're interested in."

Mark shut off the tape recorder at 2:45 PM and collected his notes. Anita and I walked him to the door where I asked if I'd really been helpful? His eyes sparkled, but his voice was steady.

"I'm going to stop in the parking lot of that church just up the street and call my office right away," he said. "They're going to be excited to hear what you've had to say. I can tell you, you'll be hearing from me again soon. Very soon."

Anita and I were a little uneasy, but reassured. We felt we had found a friend who would accompany us as we journeyed back into the darkness once more. We were right.

Chapter 12
Snake Eyes

1st Lt. Joe Ladensack

IN LATE NOVEMBER 1969, as my tour of duty in Vietnam was winding down, Lt. Col. Newell Vinson called me to his operations center and said he was reassigning me to the rear. He said he was concerned about my safety as Recon Platoon leader. I would be taking over command of the Support Platoon, which was responsible for resupplying the battalion.

Line officers were routinely assigned administrative jobs in the latter parts of their tours, but in this case Lt. Col. Vinson had good reason to make the move. He said Lt. Dick Mailing, who was due to leave Vietnam in days, had done a poor job with the Supply Platoon. Logistics and discipline were a mess. More than a few cooks and clerks had been caught drunk or smoking dope on duty. Vinson wanted me to shake things up.

One of the many duties of an officer in the rear was to stand as "officer of the guard," which meant inspecting and supervising about thirty cooks and clerks who manned the bunker line at night. My first night as officer of the guard, I led a small convoy of jeeps, dropped two soldiers at the first bunker, and was driving away when one of them started screaming: "There's something in there!"

I immediately thought of rats because the troops were always leaving C-ration cans with half-eaten food in the bunkers. Sure enough, when I walked in the bunker I noticed three or four cans on the floor along with several paper wrappers. Then I spotted a pair of eyes a few feet off the floor in a dark corner. I figured there was a rat on a shelf, so I picked up a can and threw it in the direction of the eyes, which frighteningly started coming toward me. I made a hasty retreat.

"What was it?" asked the soldier who had first spotted the glowing eyes.

"I don't know, but it's following me out."

Just then, the soldier's face went ashen and he pointed behind me. I turned to see a giant snake — more than four feet long — sliding out the door of the bunker.

I am deathly afraid of snakes, but didn't want to look scared in front of my troops so I pulled my pistol and announced I'd kill the snake with one shot. When I aimed my weapon, the snake raised its head and we saw the horrifying hood of a monocled cobra. We had been warned about cobras during our orientations when we landed in Vietnam. Their bites were almost always fatal.

Instead of one shot, I fired six. They all missed and I sprinted to my jeep to grab an M-16, which I set on full automatic and unleashed a burst of twenty or so shots. One or two hit the snake but didn't kill it. The cobra was writhing on the ground so I jumped back in my jeep and ran over the snake several times until I was sure it was dead.

My soldiers were cheering wildly and my heart was beating so hard I thought it would burst out of my chest. I assigned a few soldiers to man the bunkers and told the rest to meet me at the NCO club.

"Beers on me for everyone," I said. "We'll rotate as soon as we can and the guys in the bunkers can join us."

We tied the dead cobra to the back of my jeep and dragged the trophy to our celebration.

When I got to the NCO club a big crowd had gathered. Someone had radioed ahead that we were bringing in a big snake and everybody wanted a look. At one point, one of our pet dogs went up to sniff the snake, which reflexively coiled around the dog. I'm not sure who jumped higher — the little dog or the soldiers who were watching.

Before we went inside the club, the battalion surgeon pried out the cobra's fangs with a scalpel. Each was an inch-and-a-half long.

Our celebration lasted till midnight and I kept my promise, rotating soldiers so the men in the bunkers could cash in their free beers. When everybody had drifted away, I made a decision—probably influenced by my own share of beers—to use the snake to frighten a racist major, who had recently taken over as the battalion executive officer. The major had forced his troops to build him a new bunker, which he refused to share.

That night, the major was drinking at the artillery officers' club. He didn't like our own officers' club. He was still out when I snuck into his quarters and coiled the dead cobra on his water bed.

Shortly after 2 AM I was awakened by a barrage of pistol fire, rifle fire, and an exploding grenade. I jumped up, grabbed my helmet, an M-16, and several ammo pouches. I was sprinting to the command center to find out what kind of attack we were under when I ran into the major, who was carrying a pistol and his M-16.

"Those fucking niggers tried to kill me," the major railed.

I asked him what he was talking about and he said he had returned from the artillery officers' club to find a cobra on his bed. He told me that even though he had a few drinks, he was able to dodge the snake when it struck at him and he had killed it using his pistol, rifle, and a grenade.

We went into his bunker. His waterbed was in shreds and a brand new stereo system he had bought with funds he made off the black market was sparking and riddled with bullet holes.

"You sure got him, sir," I said.

I told him he should sleep in my bunker for the night and I would sleep in the command center.

"Lt. Ladensack," the major said. "I want you to report to me in the morning."

The next morning, I reported to the major and he put me in charge of investigating the snake incident. I told him I had a lot of work to do supplying the battalion, with food, fuel, and ammunition, but I would get to the investigation as quickly as I could.

I was investigating myself, but as I spoke with people I learned the major had won a lot of money at the artillery officers' club and several of the losers suspected him of cheating.

A day or two later I reported to the major that I had heard stories — which, of course, probably were nothing more than bad feelings — that several artillery officers thought he had been cheating at cards. I asked the major's permission to go to the artillery officers since one of them might be a suspect in planting the cobra. The major got very red in the face and said that wouldn't be necessary. The investigation was over. He thanked me and told me I had done a good job.

I saluted the major and turned to leave.

"Lt. Ladensack," he said. "We don't ever have to speak about this incident again."

"Yes, sir."

ABOUT TEN DAYS later, I was officer of the guard again. In briefing my men, I lied and told them that I had been a zoology major at Arizona State University. I said I learned, in my studies, that cobras mate for life and told them the battalion surgeon had dissected the cobra I killed and found the snake was pregnant. That meant a much bigger male cobra was around somewhere, probably looking for revenge. I urged the men to stay alert.

For a long time, we didn't have problems with bunker guards getting drunk or smoking dope on duty.

Chapter 13
Twenty Years in the Desert

Joe Ladensack

He hath brought you forty years through the desert: your garments are not worn out, neither are the shoes of your feet consumed with age.

DEUTERONOMY 29:5

THE ISRAELITES were forced to wander forty years in the wilderness for failing to heed the word of God. I spent half that long hiding in the desert because the men of God I worked with wanted me silenced.

My Moses — the man who led me out of the desert — was a baseball-loving ace criminal investigator who once worked for the FBI. Mark Stribling came into my life in December 2002 and within six months changed it forever. I stayed in hiding another decade, but Stribling helped me reach my personal Promised Land when he and the rest of the team in Maricopa County Attorney Rick Romley's office started bringing dozens of my former colleagues to justice.

On May 30, 2002, after a series of stories by Bill Hart, Nena Baker, Kelly Ettenborough, and Joseph A. Reaves in the *Arizona Republic*, and several compelling exposés by Terry Greene of the Phoenix *New Times*, Romley announced he was launching a criminal investigation of the Roman Catholic Diocese of Phoenix.

Romley, who was raised Catholic and whose late uncle, Elias Romley, donated the bells in the tower of St. Mary's Church in downtown Phoenix and endowed the congregation hall at the city's most prestigious Jesuit high school, was relentless — vowing repeatedly that Bishop Thomas J. O'Brien and his priests would be made to "follow the law like anybody else."

The best decision Romley made during his thirteen-month investigation was putting Stribling in charge and giving him free rein to follow any lead, anywhere. Stribling not only tracked down predator priests still in the Phoenix Diocese, but traveled to Mexico, New Mexico, California, Indiana, Illinois, Wisconsin, and Florida to find others.

One of his early victories came in late October 2002 when he and fellow Detective Larry Core — an expert in computer forensics — set up an undercover e-mail account as part of their investigation of John Maurice Giandelone, the ex-priest who sexually assaulted the fifteen-year old son of my friend, Harry Takata. Giandelone was sentenced to one year in prison for that attack, but was furloughed to work in the diocesan library instead. He left the priesthood in 1992, moved to Florida, married, and had a son.

Giandelone had serially molested another boy from July 1979 through February 1980, but never was prosecuted for those crimes. That victim was Ben Kulina, who went on to become a lieutenant in the Mesa, Arizona, Police Department.

The sting operation Stribling and Core set up In October 2002 was geared to getting Giandelone to admit he molested Kulina.

First, Stribling had Kulina make four "confrontation" telephone calls to Giandelone in Fort Myers, Florida, from a secure line in the Maricopa County Attorney's Office. Recorded "confrontation" telephone calls are legal investigative tools in Arizona.

In the first call, Kulina asked Giandelone if he remembered him. Giandelone said he did and asked Kulina how he'd gotten his phone number. Ben said he found it through an internet search and hoped Giandelone could help him "work through some stuff" that happened a long time ago.

"I'm not going to talk about these things on the phone," Giandelone said. "I'm afraid."

"Why are you afraid?" Kulina asked.

"I'm afraid this whole thing might lead to me going to prison."

The second call was brief. Giandelone immediately asked Kulina if their conversation was being recorded, if Ben's lawyer was with him, and if the police were there? Kulina answered no to all three and said he was only calling to give Giandelone his home number so they could talk whenever the ex-priest wanted. Kulina gave him the phone number of an undercover line at the County Attorney's Office.

During the third call, Giandelone said he was worried Kulina was planning to sue the Phoenix Diocese.

"I don't want any trouble for my family," Giandelone said.

"That's not what I'm doing," Kulina replied. "I'm just trying to figure out stuff."

Giandelone then slipped into melancholy: "I thought you were angry with me for many, many years."

"Why would you think that?" Kulina asked.

"Because the diocese, boy did they come down on me. Your parents complained to the bishop."

Kulina pretended he knew nothing about that.

"I thought you knew," Giandelone said. "Your parents had an appointment with the bishop and then the bishop was at my door. I thought: 'Oh, geez.' You know, I've really screwed up and I never meant to hurt... do anything wrong."

Kulina asked what happened when the bishop came to see him.

"Oh, a lot," Giandelone said. "I was in deep, deep trouble. So they moved me from the frying pan into the fire, out to Chandler. They wanted me away from there so I would have absolutely no contact with you. I was lonely and it became even worse."

The fourth and final "confrontation" call was short. Kulina suggested he and Giandelone continue communicating through e-mail. Ben had become increasingly uncomfortable speaking with Giandelone and Giandelone was becoming increasingly paranoid about talking on the phone. Kulina gave Giandelone the undercover e-mail

Stribling and Core had set up: benk135@yahoo.com. Giandelone gave Kulina his email: Themathman@earthlink.com.

For the next twenty-five days, Stribling used the e-mail account to correspond directly with Giandelone.

In his first e-mail, sent Monday, October 28, 2002, Stribling, writing as if he were Kulina, apologized for not getting back in touch sooner. He said he was delayed trying to find someone with a camera so he could send a picture of himself that Giandelone had requested.

Within minutes, Giandelone wrote back. He said he had just sat down to write Kulina when his e-mail arrived. Giandelone sounded sentimental, mentioning how the two of them were "friends from old and, perhaps, we could continue to help each other grow." He closed: "Write soon, John."

The next day, Stribling wrote back, saying he, too, thought they "could continue to help each other grow." Then, in a masterful move, Stribling sent a second message at 1 AM that sounded like the emotional late-night ramblings of a lonely man. "I'm having a hard time in my life right now," he wrote. "I don't know why things are the way they are, but you helped me in the past and I hope you can help me again. I know you're not the same person you were all those years ago." Stribling, posing as Kulina, went on to apologize for his parents having gone to the bishop with their allegations against Giandelone decades ago.

"I'm sorry. I hope you can forgive me. Well, I better get some sleep. Sorry for being a pain."

Several days went by before Giandelone responded.

"Ben, you are not a pain," he wrote. "There is no need to apologize to me, rather I am sorry for anything I have done to be a pain to you. I want to help you. I just don't know what to do."

Giandelone said the delay in responding was because he had foot surgery.

Stribling wrote back on November 8 and said he hoped Giandelone's foot was better.

"I have some good memories of us, but some not so good ones, too," he wrote. "I'm confused about things that happened. I need to know things were not my fault so I can clear my mind."

Giandelone wrote back later that day.

"Ben, things are not your fault! I have done some really stupid things in my life. Can the people around me who were affected by my stupidity be blamed for my stupidity. NO. When we were together, whatever you did was my fault… good or bad. I hope I directed your actions towards the good much more than I involved you in my stupidity."

The e-mail chain continued for three more weeks with Giandelone repeatedly expressing sorrow for what he had done to Kulina and progressively incriminating himself. By early December, Stribling had enough evidence to obtain a search warrant from Lee County, Florida, and traveled with another detective, Dave Hubalik, to arrest Giandelone. Stribling had been working with Hubalik on the priest investigations for months and was less-than impressed by his partner's work. He had good reason to be skeptical — as he found out when the two of them got to Giandelone's home.

Armed with their search warrant, Stribling and Hubalik were sitting at Giandelone's kitchen table explaining that he was under arrest when Giandelone asked:

"Have you guys been e-mailing me and calling me on the phone?"

Stribling sat silent, but Hubalik jumped in: "Well, let me tell ya. He hasn't been calling you and I haven't been e-mailing."

"Oh," Giandelone said. "So *you've* been calling me and *you've* been e-mailing."

Stribling shook his head and muttered to Hubalik: "What the hell?"

Giandelone was arrested on December 3, 2002, and extradited to Arizona, where his attorney, Mike Terribile — who in the minds of prosecutors and the media was appropriately named — made a shrewd move that saved his client years in prison. In Arizona, the statute of limitations for sex crimes is seven years once law enforcement becomes aware of the crime, or should have been aware of it with normal diligence. Because Ben Kulina was a police lieutenant, Terrible contended law enforcement was aware of his molestations the day he was sworn in — more than twenty years earlier.

Instead of felony sexual assault of a minor, which would have carried a maximum sentence of twelve-and-a-half years on each count, Giandelone was allowed to plead guilty to two counts of the lesser charge of attempted sexual conduct with a minor. He was sentenced to eleven months in prison and three years' probation, during which he was not to have any contact with minors.

In Arizona, prior to 1994, inmates could be released for good behavior after serving half their sentences. Because Giandelone's crimes occurred in 1979-80, he was eligible for the early release provision.

After serving half his sentence, Giandelone was released in December 2003. He wanted to return to Florida to be with his family, but learned the terms of his probation meant he would have to stay in Arizona. Giandelone said he didn't think he could honor those terms and, in a bizarre twist, asked a judge to send him back to serve the remainder of his sentence. The judge refused, but weeks later Giandelone deliberately violated his probation by making contact with a minor. Specifically, he sent his twelve-year-old son in Florida a Valentine's Day card. That led to another outlandish court hearing during which Giandelone and his attorney asked another judge to send him to prison, while the prosecutor, sex crimes chief Cindi Nannetti, fought to keep him on probation and confined to Arizona.

"Give him prison time," Terrible told the judge. "Let's get it over with."

Superior Court Judge Jonathan Schwartz ordered Giandelone back to prison for twenty-two months. Giandelone served half of it, his probation ended, and he was released. In 2005 he moved back to Florida, where he is a registered sex offender.

THE STATUTE OF limitations and Hubalik's sloppy work both played roles in the bungled arrest of another serial sex-offending priest that Stribling tracked down.

Just one day after Giandelone was arrested in Florida, Patrick Colleary was taken into custody in Tempe, Arizona, and charged with three counts of molesting a ten-year-old altar boy, Mark Kennedy, in November 1978. Stribling had asked Hubalik to check police and sheriff's records to make sure the incident had never been reported to authorities, setting the clock running on the statute of limitations. Hubalik assured Stribling there was nothing.

Stribling knew Kennedy's family had reported the attacks to Bishop O'Brien only to be met with business as usual — threats, yelling, and intimidation. What Stribling didn't know — and what Hubalik failed to discover — was that Mark Kennedy's mother, Doris, a strong-willed woman of Irish descent, ignored the bishop's threats and filed a report with the Maricopa County Sheriff's Office. That office was run then — and continued to be run in 2003 — by arch-conservative Joe Arpaio, the self-described Toughest Sheriff in America, who was a practicing Catholic.

On January 8, 2003 — a full thirty-five days after Colleary was arrested — Arpaio produced a 1980 document that showed his office was aware of the allegations against Colleary. The statute of limitations had expired. Romley and his team had no choice but to drop the charges against Colleary.

"We un-arrested him," Stribling said ruefully and self-mockingly, knowing no one could legally be "un-arrested."

Colleary, though, had plenty more in his past for Stribling to pursue. He was on administrative leave at the time of his arrest because church officials had learned he fathered a child with a woman he raped after she came to him for counseling. In addition, Stribling found another young boy, Paul Liano, who Colleary repeatedly engaged in oral sex with during the same time frame he had been molesting Mark Kennedy. Those incidents were never reported to authorities. A grand jury indicted Colleary on two counts of sexual conduct with a minor and one count of attempted sexual conduct with a minor — felonies that could have put Colleary in prison for up to thirty-three years.

However, before the indictment was returned in June 2003, Colleary fled to his native Ireland. Two years later, Judge Phillip O'Sullivan of the Irish High Court — disgusted by Maricopa County Sheriff Joe Arpaio's treatment of prisoners, marching them through the streets of Phoenix in pink underwear — refused to allow Colleary's extradition. The ex-priest remains free in County Sligo, Ireland.

THE SAME DAY Colleary was indicted, a year and three days after Romley's office began its investigations, charges were brought against five other priests and ex-priests.

I gave Mark Stribling information on four of those six priests — Colleary, Joseph Briceno, Lawrence Lovell, and Henry Perez.

Like Colleary, Briceno managed to leave the country without being arrested. He went to Mexico and served as vicar — or deputy pastor — in a parish in Mexicali for two-and-a-half years.

Marciopa County Attorney Rick Romley wrote the Vatican asking Pope John Paul II to order both Colleary and Briceno to return to Arizona and face charges. Romley assured the pope the two priests would be treated fairly. His letter came back with a rubber stamp that claimed it was being returned unopened, but Romley said it clearly and clumsily had been slit on both sides and resealed after it was read.

U.S. Marshals finally managed to extradite Briceno from Mexico in December 2005 after Romley had left office. Originally charged with eight counts that could have put him in prison for more than thirty years, Briceno plea-bargained with Romley's successor, Andrew Thomas, to two lesser charges and was given a two-year sentence. He wound up serving just nineteen days in prison because, like Giandelone, his molestations occurred in the early 1980s and he was eligible for release after serving just half his sentence. With time served awaiting trial, Briceno went into the Arizona State Prison Complex on

December 15, 2006, and was released January 3, 2007. Locked up for the holidays, then set free.

While he was preying on young boys in the early 1980s, Briceno was close friends with two of the other priests indicted by Romley's team — Perez and Lovell. Perez died of a heart attack before he could be arrested, while Lovell, who had been defrocked as a priest in 1991, was living in New Mexico, had married, and was working as a case manager for the University of New Mexico Health Center.

Stribling drove to New Mexico to arrest Lovell, who seemed puzzled at first.

"What's this about?" he asked.

"Well, it's about, you know, some things that you did in Phoenix involving some young boys."

"Oh, it's only about the Phoenix stuff," Lovell said.

Only the Phoenix stuff! Incredible.

That sent Stribling searching for more incidents and Lovell wound up being charged with other sex crimes in Yavapai County, Arizona, where he molested a young boy at a KOA campground.

A New Mexico judge refused to honor the "no-bond warrant" after Lovell's arrest, setting him free and sending Stribling back to Arizona empty handed. But Lovell then made another absurd mistake. He had been arrested in California for molesting four altar boys, but was released after the U.S. Supreme Court struck down a California law that expanded the statute of limitations on sex crimes. Apparently assuming, wrongly, that the statute of limitations was the same in Arizona, Lovell foolishly got on a bus, rode to Phoenix, and called Stribling from the station.

"Hey, I'm at the bus station at 16th Street and Buckeye and I want to come down and get this mess all cleared up," he said.

Stribling, astonished, said he'd be right there. The bus station is actually at 24th and Buckeye, not 16th and Buckeye, but Stribling knew that. He sped over to pick up Lovell and arrested him on the spot.

The next day, Lovell's wife called Stribling from New Mexico.

"Larry said he was going to see you," she said. "Have you heard from him? When do you think he's going to come home."

Stribling couldn't help himself.

"Oh, twenty years or so."

On March 11, 2004, Lovell entered the Arizona State Prison System to begin serving a twenty-six-year sentence.

AS MIND-BOGGLING AS Lovell's colossal blunders seem in retrospect, Paul LeBrun trumped him and paid an even greater price.

Stribling flew to Indiana to arrest LeBrun on May 30, 2003, three days before his indictment was officially announced. The detective found LeBrun in a small room on the University of Notre Dame campus in South Bend and made the arrest.

"Is that your computer?" Stribling asked, spotting an open laptop.

"No, I've taken a vow of poverty and it's not mine," LeBrun said. "It belongs to the headmaster."

Stribling tracked down the headmaster and asked if he could have the computer? The headmaster said sure. Forensics experts later found a treasure trove of child pornography all over the computer.

If LeBrun had simply said the computer was his and refused Stribling permission to take it, there would have been nothing Stribling could have done without a warrant.

LeBrun was a serial molester in Arizona and Indiana throughout the 1980s and '90s. Romley's team offered a plea deal that would have sentenced him to twenty years in prison. He refused, went to trial, and was found guilty on six counts of sexually abusing boys between the ages of eleven and thirteen. On January 13, 2006 — Friday the thirteenth — Maricopa County Superior Court Judge Crane McClennen sentenced forty-nine-year-old Paul Francis LeBrun to one-hundred-eleven years in prison.

TO THIS DAY, I am amazed by the work Mark Stribling and the rest of Rick Romley's team did during their year-long investigation.

Cindi Nannetti, the sex crimes chief, was an implacable prosecutor — so implacable that Bishop Thomas J. O'Brien once referred to her derogatorily as a "pit bull."

Nannetti's fellow prosecutor, Rachel Mitchell, was equally relentless and became a respected friend of many of the abuse victims.

Together, Nannetti, Mitchell, Stribling, and Romley forced the church to turn over more than one-hundred-thousand documents, including records that revealed O'Brien was personally aware of dozens of molestations.

The church, as always, fought relentlessly to protect itself. Among the hundred-thousand documents diocesan attorneys surrendered were instructions on how to install a toilet seat and scores of other useless pages intended solely to stall, delay, and mess with investigators.

For a while, as I watched Romley's investigation gain momentum in the summer of 2002, I wondered if Bishop O'Brien and his henchmen had begun to see the error of their ways. The diocese, long represented by a string of aggressive, arrogant, bullying lawyers, unexpectedly brought in a new attorney, Michael Manning, to work with Bishop O'Brien's heavy-hitting legal team headed by of Gregory J. Leisse and James Belanger.

Manning, a devout Catholic, was then, and still is, arguably Arizona's most respected attorney. He was lead counsel in the Lincoln Savings and Loan investigation that sent Charles H. Keating Jr. to prison and led five prominent U.S. Senators — The Keating Five: John Glenn of Ohio, Alan Cranston of California, Donald Riegle of Michigan, and John McCain and Dennis DeConcini of Arizona — to be investigated by the Senate Ethics Committee.

Manning also successfully tried the case that led a federal judge to rule that then Arizona Governor Fife Symington defrauded union pension funds.

And twice he won multi-million-dollar wrongful death suits against Sheriff Joe Arpaio and the Maricopa County Sheriff's Office.

When Manning agreed to work with Bishop O'Brien, I read an article in the Phoenix *New Times* praising the move as a significant step toward transparency. "[Manning] nearly always finds the highest moral grounds in monumental battles," the newspaper wrote glowingly and accurately.

Manning, who told colleagues he only agreed to work for O'Brien after he was promised full cooperation and transparency, convinced the diocese to comply with a series of grand jury subpoenas. He also assembled a team of seven attorneys, led by former FBI chief James Ahearn, to review more than thirty years of church personnel files. The team eventually turned over more than sixteen-thousand pages of documents from their search and Manning convinced O'Brien to admit, in a letter he made public, that more than fifty priests, former priests, and church employees had been accused of criminal sexual misconduct with minors in the Phoenix Diocese in the past three decades.

Those successes, significant as they were, masked the deep opposition Manning continued to face from Leisse, whose favored tactic was to stonewall. By late 2002, after just six months on the job, Manning had enough. He quit without publicly saying why.

"Effective last Sunday night, I'm no longer counsel for the bishop or the diocese," Manning announced in a statement I read in the Friday, December 13, 2002, editions of the *Arizona Republic*. "I can't ethically say any more. That's up to the client, under our rules of practice."

"Last Sunday night" would have been December 8, 2002 — just five days after Stribling arrested John Giandelone in Florida and four days after Patrick Colleary was arrested in Tempe, Arizona.

Phoenix Diocese spokeswoman Kim Sue Lia Perkes told reporters Manning's resignation was a mutual decision and had been discussed before the Giandelone and Colleary arrests.

Given Manning's impressive history of doing the right thing, I couldn't help but think the timing was curious. Still, all I could do was speculate and hope. What I did know, given my experience, was the church was back in full siege mode.

Then, miraculously—or perhaps not so miraculously—three days after Manning quit, Mark Stribling found me in Sierra Vista.

I learned later that not long after Manning resigned, he asked for a meeting with Romley to pursue a possible settlement. Manning enlisted another prominent Catholic attorney, Ernest Calderon, president of the Arizona Bar Association, to join him in proposing an agreement—not as counsel, or former counsel to the bishop or diocese, but rather as "concerned Catholic lawyers."

Romley was initially reluctant to meet Manning and Calderon since neither represented the bishop or the diocese. Manning, though, convinced the county attorney that he and Calderon had broad support from highly placed officials in the diocese who were interested in putting the era of scandal behind them and rebuilding the church's relationship with its followers and the public.

Fifteen years later, in 2017, Manning told Joseph A. Reaves that he, Calderon, and Romley agreed to a deal that would have been "wonderful for both sides and would have served every purpose either side could hope for"—a deal that would have been far better than the fate that eventually awaited the bishop.

They took the proposed deal to Bishop O'Brien, who seemed inclined to accept it, but refused at Leisse's urging and under orders from Pope John Paul II's representative in New York—Papal Nuncio Gabriel Montalvo Higuera.

Under the deal, O'Brien would have requested the pope to appoint a co-adjutor bishop for the Phoenix Diocese in return for an end to any threat of criminal indictment. Co-adjutors are bishops-in-waiting with guaranteed rights of succession. They share power with the incumbent bishop.

"Failing to get that wonderful deal approved is the single biggest disappointment of my forty years as a lawyer," Manning told Reaves.

Months after Leisse helped scuttle the deal, he filed suit in federal court accusing Manning, Calderon, Romley, and the Phoenix *New Times* newspaper of conducting a "campaign of defamation, threats, intimidation, ridicule and disinformation" against him and O'Brien. U.S. District Court Judge Mary H. Murguia threw out the case in less than six months, an especially quick dismissal in the litigation world.

I never knew about Manning's behind the scenes efforts to broker a deal at the time. But looking back now, I wish he and Calderon would have succeeded. My years in the desert would have ended a little sooner.

Chapter 14
Moon Man Christmas

1st Lt. Joe Ladensack

THE DAY NEIL ARMSTRONG stepped onto the moon, I was busy — so busy I missed the whole thing.

July 20, 1969, was my first day commanding Echo Company, the makeshift unit pulled together shortly after we were massacred at the Battle of Black Virgin Mountain. The next morning, I took my three platoons for ten days of desperately needed training in the field, where we were cut off from all non-military communications. We didn't learn of the moon landing until August 3rd and that afternoon we were rushed to Route 13 to counter an NVA attack. We didn't have a lot of time to dwell on Armstrong's moon walk, as amazing and historic the moment had been. Little did I know, though, that in just a few weeks I'd be shaking Neil Armstrong's hand and he'd help me figure out how to pay for my religious education.

Five months to the day after Apollo 11 landed on the moon, I was summoned to the Tactical Operation Center by Lt. Col. Lee D. Brown, who had just replaced Lt. Col. Newell Vinson as battalion commander. Brown told me I was to report to the airfield at Dầu Tiếng the next morning at 0700 for a special mission. He said he couldn't tell me what the mission was or how long it would last, but it was important.

At the time, I was working hard to organize a battalion Christmas party I was excited about and asked if someone else could take the mission.

"No, you have been selected by name," Lt. Col. Brown said. "Make sure you're at the airfield at 0700 hours. That's all."

When I showed up the next morning, two other lieutenants were booked on the same flight and both confided they, too, had been chosen for a "secret mission." We boarded the aircraft and landed in Lai Khê twenty-five minutes later. A major greeted us, loaded us into a truck, and told us we'd be briefed after lunch in a bunker he pointed out.

Inside the bunker after lunch the three of us were joined by seventeen other lieutenants. A colonel strode to the front of the room and reminded us, for what seemed like the hundredth time in two days, that what we were about to be told was top secret. We were to tell no one about the briefing.

"Bob Hope is coming to Lai Khê with his entire tour to put on a Christmas show," the colonel said. "Security is our top priority. Each of you will be given a special assignment."

Hope had been entertaining U.S. troops since 1941. He traveled to combat zones during World War II and the Korean War and made nine consecutive Christmas tours to Vietnam from 1964 to 1972. Security was so tight during the Vietnam trips that Hope himself sometimes didn't know until the night before where he would be performing.

The 1969 tour was the most ambitious of Hope's career, a grueling sixteen-day trip that began with a stop at the White House for a state dinner with President Richard Nixon before moving on to Germany, Italy, Turkey, Thailand, Vietnam, Taiwan, and Guam. In Vietnam, Hope put on five shows, the first of which was at Lai Khê on Monday, December 22, 1969.

Lai Khê, at the time, was known as "rocket city" because it was attacked almost every night and the colonel who briefed us said there was credible intelligence the North Vietnamese Army would attempt to shell one of Hope's shows. That explained the hush-hush warnings, but our assignments had little to do with security. We were to be escorts for Hope and his entourage.

The way those assignments were doled out was almost as entertaining as Hope's show. The colonel had a roster of our names and called out one at a time. After each name, he drew a slip of paper from his hat to determine who the escort would be paired with.

First out of the hat was "Bob Hope's teenage son."

We exploded in laughter and someone shouted: "You're going to be a baby sitter"

The next lieutenant's name was read and his assignment pulled from the hat.

"Bob Hope's luggage."

The laughter grew even louder.

A friend of mine from Fort Benning was called and his piece of paper read: "The Golddiggers."

"The Golddiggers?" he asked. "What are the Golddiggers."

I told him I'd take them off his hands, but the lieutenant standing next to him ruined my potential coup by telling my buddy who the Golddiggers were.

"They're a dozen gorgeous singers and dancers from the Dean Martin television show," he said.

My buddy decided to keep his slip of paper.

When my name was read, I hit the jackpot: "Suzanne Charny."

Oh, boy!

I was the only person in the room who knew who she was. She was a gorgeous, sexy dancer — an exotic dancer. She'd had a wonderfully erotic scene in a short black-sequined dress in the Ray Fosse movie *Sweet Charity*, which had been released in April, just before I arrived in Vietnam. I wasn't going to trade my piece of paper for anything.

When all the names had been read, the colonel briefed us on the logistics of escorting our guests and told us to report to the airstrip the next day at ten-hundred hours. Yet again, he warned us not to tell anyone anything about what we were doing.

The next day, when we assembled alongside the airstrip, I found my jeep was first behind Maj. Gen. Albert "Ernie" Milloy, the division commander who had pinned my second Bronze Star on me in the field in August. When I saw that, I assumed Milloy was responsible for me being "selected by name" for the escort assignment — probably with a not-so-subtle nudge from his aide, Capt. Dudley "Pete" Combs, my former company commander.

We sat in our jeeps in the baking sun for an hour until we saw four C-130 aircraft coming in for landings. The first plane landed hard and blew several tires before stopping at the very end of the runway. Hope was aboard the aircraft and joked about his scary landing during the opening monologue of his show two hours later.

"The Lai Khê airstrip is the only one where the last fifty feet is up the side of a rubber tree," he said with his trademark Vaudevillian deadpan.

As soon as all four C-130s had landed, our column of jeeps sped across the runway to greet our guests. Bob Hope was the first person out of the lead aircraft. He greeted Gen. Milloy, then walked straight over to me and shook my hand.

"Where are you from, lieutenant?" he asked.

I told him Phoenix, Arizona.

"Ah, you have a great golf course there."

"Yes, sir, the Phoenix Country Club was part of my paper route when I was a boy," I told him.

"I bet you found a lot of my golf balls then."

We both laughed and Hope asked: "Tell me, lieutenant. How close are the enemy?"

"Do you see that gate?" I said pointing a few hundred yards beyond the airstrip. "They're right on the other side."

Hope nodded, said goodbye, and walked back to Gen. Milloy's jeep. I felt a personal connection during his monologue later when he used my information in one of his gags.

"Lai Khê is so close to the action," he quipped, "that we had to give half the tickets to the VC (Viet Cong)."

After my brief, memorable chat with Bob Hope, the column of jeeps moved out. I had an enlisted soldier as driver in my jeep. I sat next to him with Suzanne Charny behind him and Theresa Graves, a beautiful African-American actress who later would become a regular on *Rowan & Martin's Laugh-In* show, behind me. Both women were dressed for the show, Graves wearing what then was her trademark "hippie" style pant suit with bare midriff and a coiled headband around her long pony-tailed hair, and Charny in an incredibly revealing short black dress with a plunging neckline.

This may be hard to believe, but I paid little attention to either woman. We had been told not to interact with the performers — to simply escort them from the airstrip to the bunkers behind the outdoor stage as quickly as possible. That was my mission and I carried it out, but I must admit years later that I wish I'd paid a little more attention to my passengers that day.

The show began at 1 PM with Les Brown and His Band of Renown beating out their rousing hit, *Sentimental Journey*, which had been a favorite of U.S. soldiers since its debut on the top of the charts just as World War II was ending. Gen. Milloy came on stage and introduced Hope, who reeled off a series of one-liners, including the ones about the short airstrip and giving half the tickets to the Viet Cong.

"Well, here we are back in Vietnam," he said, pausing for effect and leaning on the golf club he always carried as a prop on his tours. "Those hijackers are never around when you need them."

The crowd of three-thousand, most of whom had been sweating in the hot sun for four hours, roared.

"We would have been here sooner, but that Ho Chi Minh trail is murder during rush hour."

He went on for five minutes and each quip drew more laughter and applause than the one before — especially when he made them personal.

"Now I know why they call this outfit the Big Red One," he said. "That's what my backside looked like when the mosquitos got through with it."

Probably the crowd's favorite joke was when Hope recognized Lai Khê was part of the Michelin Rubber Plantation.

"These men have a tremendous mission stationed here in the middle of this huge rubber plantation — guarding next year's supply of bras and girdles."

I had a front-row seat to the show. All the escort officers were seated up front. It was great. One of the highlights was when my jeep-mate, Theresa Graves, finished her medley and flashed the peace sign to the audience and was greeted with several thousand in return.

Toward the end of the show, Gen. Milloy recognized a squad of soldiers who had ambushed an NVA rocket team near Lai Khê the night before. They, too, were seated near the stage and Hope waded into the group to shake each man's hand and thank them.

Hope gathered the entire cast on stage at the end of the show and made a mistake that would haunt him the rest of his life. Wanting to wrap things up with an upbeat message, he talked about his trip to the White House at the start of the tour and said President Nixon told him he had a plan to end to war.

Several soldiers booed at the mention of President Nixon. A couple hundred more joined in — still only a smattering of the huge crowd, but enough to visibly upset Hope.

I felt then, and still feel today, that the boos were directed at Nixon. The president was incredibly unpopular with the troops, who had heard enough of his "light-at-the-end-of-the-tunnel" promises and his stalled Paris Peace Talks. We believed Nixon could care less about us. But Hope took the boos personally and was hurt by them.

More than twenty years later, I saw Bob Hope on the *Today* show promoting an album his wife, Delores Reade Hope, had just recorded at age eighty-four after abandoning her singing career for five decades to be by Hope's side. Naturally, Hope's lifelong history of entertaining U.S. troops overseas came up and he was asked about the Lai Khê show. Hope frowned, said it was the first time he was booed at one of his traveling shows, and admitted he had never gotten over it. He said he learned his lesson and never again included anything close to political commentary in his shows.

The Lai Khê show ended shortly after the brief booing episode when Hope asked Connie Stevens to sing "Silent Night," the traditional closing number, which always brought the audience of homesick warriors to tears.

After the show, I got to shake Neil Armstrong's hand and listened as he told a group of soldiers about the GI bill and stressed how important it was for them to get a college education when they returned home. I took the message to heart even though I already had my undergraduate degree. When I returned home from Vietnam, I learned that money from the GI bill could be used at any accredited college in the United States. That included St. John's College and Seminary, so I followed Neil Armstrong's advice and got the government to pay for six years of religious education.

At one point during my studies, the treasurer of St. John's asked me to sign over my GI benefits to the seminary. I refused and used the money to pay for books and tuition with enough left over to buy myself a new 1976 Dodge Monaco just before I was ordained.

The Bob Hope show was a happy highlight of my tour in Vietnam, but I never felt a more profound sense of sadness than when I boarded the aircraft at Lai Khê that night. Only a few hours earlier, I'd been part of one of the greatest shows on earth — a joyous, laugh-filled gathering of several thousand brothers. Then, before I even had time to fully appreciate it all, I was headed back to war — on a mission to kill other brave men who we were told were our enemies.

I wrote my parents about how great the show had been and told them about Suzanne Charny. I knew they wouldn't know who she was and when the Bob Hope special aired in January, as it did every year, they would be surprised. I heard later that the whole family, including my girlfriend, Lorraine Dwyer, watched the show together. My brother Bob, who would die in Vietnam in less than a year, told me that when Suzanne Charny appeared on the screen in her short sexy outfit, "You could have heard a pin drop" — for a few seconds, anyway, until one of my younger brothers, Paul John, who was five at the time, exclaimed: "She's a stripper!"

Bob said it was a long while before anybody in my fervently Catholic family said anything.

I GOT OVER my depression after the Bob Hope show by throwing myself full speed into preparations for the big battalion Christmas party I had been planning for weeks before I was called away. Since he had just taken over as battalion commander, Lt. Col. Brown wanted the party to be special and I had the connections to make it happen. I'd always been pretty liberal giving out passes to my men, who put their time in Saigon to good use. They were Class-A scroungers. When I asked around about how we could make Christmas memorable, I was floored by the treasure trove they came up with. Calling in favors from friends in Saigon they offered up: a container filled with one-thousand new uniforms... several crates of new socks, tee-shirts, candy, and various toiletry items from a church group in Kansas... a portable hot shower unit with ten heads... a half-dozen boxes filled with small artificial Christmas trees... and a Korean USO troop with girls who could sing almost all the current pop songs in English.

My own contribution rounded things out nicely. I had four cases of Bacardi Rum my Recon Platoon liberated from the burned hulk of a PX truck that had been ambushed on Route 13. Every officer and senior NCO in the battalion would get a bottle.

Enemy activity in our area at the time was near zero, so I decided to stage the party in the middle of a large natural clearing in the rubber plantation. We secured the perimeter and spent two days hauling in supplies.

On Christmas Day, the line companies pulled into our clearing one by one. As they did, we had them refuel and re-arm their APCs and stock enough C-rations and water for three to five days. Then we surprised the men by showing them to the hot showers and passing out new uniforms, socks, tee-shirts, candy, and the toiletry items. Our mess crew served up a hot meal before everyone filed in for the USO show.

Our division commander had assigned helicopters to fly in special Christmas dinners to each battalion, but since we had arranged our own hot meals at the rubber plantation, we didn't need the extra chow. When the choppers landed at our base at Dầu Tiếng, the pilots got an unexpected break and enjoyed their own hot meal without having to deal with us. Of course, they had to come up with excuses why they stayed on the ground an hour or so longer than scheduled, but they proved pretty creative: unexpected maintenance issues, refueling snafus, offloading problems. As each crew prepared to take off, we arranged one more surprise: a specially wrapped bottle of "Recon Liberated Bacardi Rum."

Late on Christmas afternoon, Lt. Col. Brown radioed me that a company of leg infantry from 28th Infantry Regiment, the Black Lions, had been temporarily assigned to us. Their battalion wasn't able to provide Christmas dinner for them. Could I do something?

No problem. We had plenty of extra uniforms, socks and candy. There was more than enough left over food to feed them. They got hot showers and seats at the USO show. One of the soldiers told me later he thought he had died and gone to heaven.

The day was a great success and Lt. Col. Brown was on hand to see it all, which was a bit of a surprise since, at the time, it was unusual for the commander of the 2/2 to be in the field with us.

Shortly after the USO show, Brown called to tell me the party we'd put on exceeded his greatest expectations.

"And thank you for the special gift," he said of his own bottle of Bacardi. "Make sure the Support Platoon is rewarded for their hard work."

The colonel didn't know it, but more than half the men already were being rewarded. I'd given them passes to spend the night in Saigon.

Before he signed off, Lt. Col. Brown told me to look to the east. I did and saw tracers and illumination rounds lighting the night sky and heard the faint singing of "Silent Night." For the second time in four days, the song brought tears to my eyes. And for the second time in four days, I was overcome with sadness.

Happily, the sadness was short-lived because as the last refrains of "Silent Night" began to fade, the tracers and illumination rounds to the east were joined by hundreds of bottle rockets, fire crackers, and flares seemingly fired from everywhere. Every man in the company seemed to have gotten hold of fireworks. And they were unleashing them in a crazy, joyous, childlike celebration.

Lt. Col. Brown, who had been so sentimental and wistful at the first display of tracers and illumination rounds, was enraged at the impromptu fireworks display in his own camp. He dressed us down the next morning and swore that, "By God, we won't have a repeat on New Year's Eve."

He said he was assigning military police to enforce his crackdown on New Year's Eve pyrotechnics.

A week later, on New Year's Eve, I was celebrating with my old friend 1st Lt. Toney Mathews, who'd been my forward observer and, with me, was the last to leave the field at the Battle of Black Virgin Mountain. We were partial to Cuba Libres — rum and coke — in those days and we'd had a few sitting around a tiny Christmas tree a buddy had sent Toney from Hawaii. We decided to have a little fun.

I grabbed a radio and Toney and I loaded an M-2 60-mm mortar onto the back of my jeep, its bi-pod legs weighed down by sandbags.

At midnight, we piled into the jeep. Radio traffic told us where the MPs were patrolling. We drove to the other side of camp and fired off two or three M-301A1 illumination rounds that soared into the night sky and made day out of darkness.

When the MPs scrambled to find us, we sped in the opposite direction and fired two or three more.

Within minutes, the entire camp exploded in another joyous burst of fireworks and bottle rockets. The men realized the MPs were power-less to stop us and were more than ready to join in the fun.

Toney and I returned to his bunker to celebrate with one last Cuba Libre and Lt. Col. Brown never found out who set off the mayhem.

Years later, in August 1997, at a reunion of Alpha Company held in Harrison, Arkansas, one man after another came up to me and showed me pictures of their APCs decorated with small Christmas trees, bright-colored glass balls, garland, and tinsel. Almost every one of them said Christmas and New Year's 1969 had been the best of their lives.

I was incredibly proud to have been a part of it.

Chapter 15
A Sacred Salute
Joe Ladensack

I WAS MANNA from heaven for Mark Stribling.

When he started rounding up the bad priests of the Phoenix Diocese in 2002, he made the world a better place. And I was eager to help him. The minute he left my house the day we met in Sierra Vista, Arizona, he telephoned lead prosecutor Cindi Nannetti, and told her he had found a gold mine.

"You're not going to believe this guy," he said and began telling her about me. "This is good! This is real good!"

Nannetti had worked with Stribling for years and later told me she had never heard him so elated. He was normally low key. She was the emotional one. But, on the phone, after hearing my stories, she said Mark could barely contain his excitement. His voice was high-pitched and squeaky.

Stribling went in to the Maricopa County Attorney's Office the next day and briefed Rick Romley and his two top assistants, Paul Ahler and Bill Culbertson, about me. He talked at length about my war record, my years with the church, and my credibility as a witness.

"He's probably the most credible witness I've ever interviewed and you guys know I've interviewed thousands of witnesses," Stribling told his bosses.

Culbertson wasn't convinced and openly questioned my military history — my long list of medals and honors.

"Nobody does that," Culbertson said.

"He did, I saw all the medals," Stribling shot back.

"You make this guy sound like he's ten feet tall," Culbertson said.

"No, he's kind of a smaller guy, actually," Stribling chuckled.

"Well, we've got to vet this guy," Culbertson said. "If we're going to bring him to the grand jury and use all his information, I want his war records. I want his DD-214."

Defense Department Form 214, commonly called DD-214, is a certificate of release or discharge from active military duty. It includes, among other things, a veteran's date and place of entry into active duty, home address, last duty assignment and rank, military job specialty, separation information, and decorations, medals, badges, citations, and campaign awards.

Stribling, with my permission, obtained a copy of my DD-214 from the National Personnel Records Center in St. Louis and laid it out in front of Culbertson. The packet contained a three-page cover letter from an archives technician that listed my two Silver Stars, six Bronze Stars, Purple Heart, Republic of Vietnam Cross of Gallantry, and a long series of lesser honors, including the Army Commendation Medal, National Defense Service Medal, Vietnam Service Medal, Army Service Ribbon, Combat Infantryman Badge, Republic of Vietnam Campaign Ribbon, and Marksman Badge with Rifle Bar. Accompanying the cover letter were twenty-six pages of citations for the awards along with my separation papers.

Culbertson's doubts were allayed and at 9 AM, Friday, January 3, 2003, I appeared before a grand jury investigating the cesspool of immorality in the Roman Catholic Diocese of Phoenix. It had been just twenty-two days since Stribling knocked on my door in Sierra Vista.

The grand jury I appeared before was the second empaneled to investigate the Phoenix Diocese. The first, seated in July 2002, disbanded November 6 because several jurors dropped out. A new grand jury was convened almost immediately, but had to start over from scratch.

In January 2003, the Phoenix Diocese was one of ten Catholic dioceses and archdioceses across the country facing criminal scrutiny.
At the time, thanks to the prodding of crusading attorney Michael
Manning, the diocese had turned over nearly one-hundred-thousand
documents to the grand jury. But, after Manning resigned in December 2002, the church returned to its long-standing stonewall tactics
and was refusing to surrender an additional thirty-five hundred documents Romley's office had subpoenaed. Greg Leisse, the diocesan
attorney, arrogantly claimed that Canon Law—church law—"trumps"
state law.

The highly publicized and fiercely pitched fight over those documents — and the church's renewed intransigence — served as the back-
drop to my grand jury appearance.

A day before I testified, Cindi Nannetti and several other members
of Romley's team put me through the paces, grilling me for five hours.
It was the worst interrogation I had in all my years of testifying against
the church — worse than any of the grueling depositions in the civil
cases of the 1990s.

Nannetti led the questioning, telling me she would be asking most
of the same things before the grand jury the next day. Cindi was a
strong, confident, intelligent woman and, despite her toughness, put
me at-ease — at least, as at-ease as possible given the fact I was about
to swear under oath that the leaders of the church I loved had engaged
in unlawful, immoral acts for decades.

I know this sounds ridiculous, but at the time, I didn't even know
what a grand jury was or what it did. In my mind, all I knew about
grand juries was that they were used to bust the mafia. I didn't even
know who served on a grand jury. I thought, maybe, it was a whole
bunch of judges.

While I may have been in the dark about grand juries, my neigh-
bors knew all-too-well what I would be facing when they learned I was
going to testify. Several of them — all Catholics, who knew the power
of the church — begged Anita and me to move in with them for our

own safety. We passed on those offers, but became concerned enough to have a locksmith come out and check the security of our place. He spent an hour and reassured us we were safe: "This place is a fortress," he said. "You're good."

The morning I appeared before the grand jury, Anita and I were escorted to a small office to wait until I was called. In the office, a young police officer with the nametag "Canidate" was busy writing a report. I asked him if he was related to Trung Canidate, a former University of Arizona running back, who was a first-round draft pick of the St. Louis Rams three years earlier.

"Yes, sir," the officer said. "I'm his big brother."

I told Officer Canidate he must have been a good big brother because I'd seen Trung interviewed several times and he was impressive.

"Yes, sir. He's a good man."

MARK STRIBLING CAME into the little office and escorted me to the grand jury room. Anita thought she would be able to accompany me, but Stribling asked her to wait on a bench just outside the door.

The grand jury room was anything but grand. The building it was in was a crowded concrete jumble. The room itself was a mess. I remember thinking: *This is a* **grand** *jury and this is as good as you can do for a room. This is really crummy.*

Jurors were seated in metal folding chairs to my left when I entered. Three sat with legs dangling over the edge of a folding table along the wall. A couple stood the entire time. Most of the jurors were dressed in tee-shirts, sweatshirts, and blue jeans and all but one or two of the men looked as if they hadn't shaved for two or three days. Frankly, they were a motley crew. I could picture them all walking out of a Home Depot early on a Saturday morning.

On the right side of the room was a small desk where Cindi Nannetti was seated. Stribling walked over and sat to her right. Behind them were two or three of Romley's lieutenants, including Bill Culbertson, my personal "Doubting Thomas."

I was directed to a folding chair facing the jurors and slightly in front of, and to the left of the attorneys. Nannetti began asking questions, most of which we covered the day before, but several new ones, as well.

At the time, I was the first, and only, priest to voluntarily testify before a grand jury in a criminal investigation against the Catholic Church. Other priests, including bishops and archbishops, eventually testified in several other jurisdictions, but almost all were "hostile witnesses" who were subpoenaed and forced to testify. I was the only "snitch" — the Serpico of the church.

Nannetti's questions focused on Bishop Thomas J. O'Brien and what I knew about his actions covering up sexual abuse by my fellow priests. She led me through the "Bat Phone" incident where O'Brien ordered me to go back to the Takata family and get them to recant everything they had told the police about John Giandelone's molestation of their son. I repeated the Nuremberg Trials line about refusing to obey an illegal order. We spent nearly an hour covering that incident alone.

After a short restroom break midway through the morning, we came back and Nannetti questioned me about other abuse cases I knew firsthand. Stribling had done a comprehensive job going back through all the depositions from the civil suits in the 1990s where Bishop O'Brien denied he was aware of any allegations. His research, Nannetti's questions, and my testimony methodically laid out how the bishop repeatedly lied under oath.

The jurors were allowed to ask their own questions and toward the end of my testimony one wanted to know why I had become a priest after my tour of duty in Vietnam? I told him about my near-death, out-of-body experience at the ghastly Battle of Black Virgin Mountain. I told him of my deep faith and unswerving desire to find my mission in life. Then I decided to lighten things up a bit by dropping one my favorite lines. "I joined the priesthood looking for a Band of Brothers," I said, pausing for effect. "Instead, I found the Village People."

That broke the place up.

Sitting on a bench outside the jury room, Anita heard the outburst of laughter and knew, for the first time, that everything was going well.

I managed to make a few other jokes before Nannetti was finished with me and asked the jurors if they had any last questions.

Three men in the back of the room stood up in unison. They all were unshaven and looked like blue-collar workers. They could have been a plumber, carpenter, and electrician straight out of central casting.

One man spoke.

"All three of us are Vietnam vets and there's an awful lot about Vietnam vets that people aren't proud of," he said. "We just want to say we are proud of your service. We are proud of what you are doing here today. And we are proud that we can call you a brother and a Vietnam vet."

Then all three saluted me.

I don't know how I didn't break into tears. That meant the world to me. All the horrors of Vietnam; all the agony and suffering of my years as a priest; all the worry, fear, second-guessing; the death threats; the gut-wrenching depositions; the years in isolation — they were absolved in one spontaneous, sacramental gesture of respect from three brothers I only just met.

I LEFT THE grand jury room and hugged Anita. I was convinced my testimony would go a long way to curbing the nightmare of sexual abuse by priests in Arizona — and, hopefully, across the country. I was right, it did. But it took a lot longer than I thought.

For six weeks after my testimony, Romley's office and the diocese continued to battle in the courts over the release of priest personnel records. On New Year's Eve, four days before I went before the grand jury, Maricopa County Superior Court Judge Eddward (cq) P. Ballinger Jr., handed the diocese a major setback. He ordered the church to surrender two-thousand-two-hundred-eighty-six of the thirty-five-hundred personnel records that diocesan attorneys claimed were protected by attorney-client privilege.

More than a month later, a three-judge panel of the Arizona Court of Appeals upheld Ballinger's order.

"We conclude that the trial court applied the correct standard to determine whether the documents in question were protected by attorney-client privilege," wrote judges Susan A. Ehrich, G. Murray Snow, and Patrick Irvine in a unanimous decision. "We deny (the diocese) relief."

The diocese could have carried its appeal to the Arizona Supreme Court, but decided, surprisingly, on February 10, 2003, to give up and hand over records.

"We're not going to appeal," said diocesan attorney James Belanger. "We don't agree with the ruling, but we've had our hearing and we will move ahead."

Moving ahead proved costly for the diocese, in general, and, Bishop O'Brien, in particular. Among the documents turned over to Romley's investigators was a three-page typewritten memo with another page of hand-scrawled notes attached. The memo and notes had been written years earlier by O'Brien's personal attorney, Jordan Green, shortly after the Phoenix *New Times* newspaper published an article entitled *Let Us Prey* on October 25, 1989. In the article, reporter Terry Greene cited several anonymous sources to expose — more than a decade ahead of any other media — incidents of sexual abuse by Phoenix priests, including John Giandelone's molestation of Harry Takata Jr.

I was one of those anonymous sources.

> *Former priest Perry Harper, who once held a high post in the diocese, says he left the priesthood because he was angered by what he saw as Bishop O'Brien's toleration of corruption, including homosexual acting-out by some priests. But Harper (not his real name) acknowledges that he was fired by O'Brien and is still annoyed at him. Harper is now a white-collar worker in a small town and consented to an interview only if his real name was not used.*

Harper says he was "suspended" by O'Brien after an argument. "I told the bishop a couple of years ago that I was fed up with him and all the garbage that he was keeping quiet," says Harper. He claims that he told the bishop that he would also start telling the police about criminal behavior by priests. "I told him I could no longer carry out my vow of obedience to him," Harper says. "The bishop told me I'd lost my faith. Essentially he fired me. I had already decided to quit."

I loved the name Perry Harper. It was a clever play on my Purple Heart and melded two of my life's great missions — Vietnam and the church.

Obviously, Greene's article caused huge concerns for O'Brien. His attorney, Jordan Green, in an attempt to pull together the facts in case he needed to mount a criminal or civil defense, compiled the three-page internal memo, then supplemented it with hand-written notes. Instead of defending O'Brien, those documents confirmed in black-and-white that O'Brien and former diocesan attorney William P. Mahoney had conspired to obstruct justice.

"Mahoney said the bishop had requested that he call Ladensack," Green wrote on page three of his memo. "Mahoney asked Ladensack to visit with the Takatas and persuade them to drop the criminal charges. Ladensack said no. Mahoney said the bishop can order you to go to the family and try to persuade them to drop charges."

On March 15, 2003, just weeks after the documents were released, Stribling came to visit me again in Sierra Vista and showed me Green's memo and notes. He recorded our conversation because had a concern about one confusing word in the memo.

After the line about Mahoney asking me to persuade the Takatas to drop charges was another sentence that contained the troubling word.

"Ladensack responded by saying, 'The bishop has **not** told me to do it and I won't do it.'"

Stribling read the sentence to me and said: "I'm wondering if this *not* is correct. You can read that for yourself and see."

"Yeah," I said. "I think that the *not* is not consistent with what I was thinking or saying. The bishop has told me to do it, and I won't do it... I can't make any sense of: 'The bishop has *not* told me.'"

Stribling continued to grill me for several minutes before finally accepting my account of the incident.

"Okay, I just wanted to clarify that."

Stribling stayed long enough that we had to break for lunch and we covered many of the topics we'd gone over in our first meeting and my grand jury testimony. Then, just before leaving, Stribling asked the one question every good detective or prosecutor needs to ask before bringing criminal charges.

"Do you have any motivation at all to make up this story about the 'Bat Phone' or any of this other stuff? To get back at anybody or anything like that?"

"No, no, no," I said. "If you'd ask me a lot of different ways, 'Would I be happy if the bishop simply resigned?' I'd say, 'Yeah. I'd feel that justice would be met.' But would I also feel fine if the case was dropped? 'Yep, we did the best that we possibly could — given our society and our legal system and all the politics and all that stuff.' I'd feel fine. I do not need to be vindictive, see anybody punished."

Years later, I read a transcript of that conversation with Stribling and still felt the same. I've never been a vindictive person. And I think we did the best we could — people like me, Stribling, and Joseph Reaves, especially. But Terry Greene and scores of others, as well. I do, however, wish there had been a little more justice for the scores of young men and women who were hurt and abused. And maybe that justice could have come with a little more punishment for the priests who preyed on them and those who covered up their crimes.

FOUR DAYS AFTER Stribling visited me in Sierra Vista and showed me Jordan Green's memo, Deputy County Attorney Cindi Nannetti drew

up a draft indictment accusing Bishop Thomas J. O'Brien of three felony counts — one of obstructing justice and two perjury charges.

But before presenting the draft indictment to the grand jury,
prosecutors wanted the jurors to hear from O'Brien himself. Stribling and Nannetti spent weeks trying to convince the bishop to
testify, then forced his hand. Stribling went to Jordan Green's office
in downtown Phoenix on Thursday, April 25, 2003, and served a
subpoena commanding O'Brien to appear before the grand jury
Tuesday, May 6, at 9 AM.

I didn't know — no one in the public or media knew — that the
pressure from Nannetti and Stribling for O'Brien to appear in person before a grand jury and answer questions under oath had finally
forced the bishop and his attorneys to cave.

Three days before the May 6 deadline, O'Brien signed a carefully
crafted document confessing at least part of his sins and agreeing to
a long list of conditions that both curtailed his powers and forced
changes in church policy on sexual abuse.

County Attorney Rick Romley and his staff kept the signed deal
secret for a month while they worked to serve indictments on six
of O'Brien's predator priests. Romley wanted to announce O'Brien's
humiliating admission and the arrests of the six priests at the same
time, but was handcuffed by legal restrictions.

Prosecutors are required to serve indictments on individuals before
publicly announcing criminal charges, but three of the six priests
couldn't be located for weeks. Finally, Ballinger, the strong-willed
judge who earlier ordered the diocese to hand over those personnel
records, issued a ruling allowing the indictments of the missing priests
to be unsealed.

The morning of June 2, 2003 — thirty days after the agreement was
signed in secret — Joseph A. Reaves had a front-page story in the *Arizona Republic* under a screaming, bold, two-deck headline that read:

BISHOP O'BRIEN ADMITS COVER-UP
IN HANDLING SEXUAL ABUSE CASES

Beneath the banner headline were three sub-heads:

Surrenders some authority after making offer to resign

Avoids possible indictment in Romley's criminal probe

Admission thought to be most candid by any bishop

The lead of the story read:

Bishop Thomas J. O'Brien has acknowledged that he covered up allegations of sexual abuse by priests for decades and will relinquish some of his power as head of the Phoenix Diocese to avoid possible criminal indictment, The Arizona Republic has learned.

Shocking stuff. But I was oblivious to it for hours. I had been in the habit of going to a neighborhood convenience store to get the *Republic* and the local paper fairly regularly to see if either had any news on the church scandal. That morning, though, I hadn't gone out and was sitting in my living room around 10 AM when Mark Stribling called.

"Turn on the TV," he said.

I did, and saw Romley standing before the cameras confirming what Reaves had reported, hailing the agreement as historic, and announcing the indictments of the six priests.

Under the agreement, Romley explained, O'Brien would avoid prosecution in return for admitting his role in covering up sexual abuse by priests under his control and granting a number of concessions.

O'Brien would appoint a Moderator of the Curia — the canonical equivalent of a chief of staff — to take over the bishop's authority to deal with issues involving sexual misconduct.

The diocese also was required to implement a training program to educate Diocesan personnel on sexual misconduct issues, to employ a Youth Protective Advocate, to create a Victim Assistance Panel and to pay out seven-hundred-thousand dollars — three hundred-thousand to be used for counseling victims of child sexual abuse… three-hundred-thousand dollars to the Maricopa County Attorney's Victim Compensation Fund… and one-hundred-thousand to reimburse Romley's office for investigative expenses.

Romley later admitted he wanted the bishop to resign, but Papal Nuncio Gabriel Montalvo Higuera refused to allow it, fearing it would signal the church buckling to civil authorities.

The nuncio, however, couldn't stop Romley from extracting an embarrassing eighty-two word written statement from O'Brien admitting guilt in the decades-long cover-up of sexual abuse by priests and church employees.

> *I acknowledge that I allowed Roman Catholic priests under my supervision to work with minors after becoming aware of allegations of sexual misconduct. I further acknowledge that priests who had allegations of sexual misconduct against them were transferred to ministries without full disclosure to their supervisor or to the community in which they were assigned. I apologize and express regret for any misconduct, hardship, or harm caused to the victims of sexual misconduct by Roman Catholic priests assigned to the diocese.*

O'Brien signed the agreement, with his statement attached, twice in the presence of his attorneys, acknowledging his actions both as an individual and as head of the Phoenix Diocese.

The deal saved Thomas J. O'Brien from becoming the first Roman Catholic bishop indicted on criminal charges in the worldwide sexual abuse scandal.

Without question, the deal was historic. Still, I was frustrated it wasn't, frankly, more damnatory.

And I wasn't alone.

"I'm real disappointed he's being let off the hook criminally," said Kathleen McCabe Lechler, who was abused by Patrick Colleary when she was a seventeen-year-old high school student in 1974. "The buck stops here. He needs to pay the price."

Shari Roy, another of Colleary's victims who gave birth to a child in 1978 after she was raped by the priest, echoed the disappointment.

"He truly should be held accountable and sent to jail," Roy told the *Arizona Republic*. "O'Brien is as evil as the predators."

Sue Watson, whose son was molested by George Bredemann, was outraged.

"That there are no charges against the bishop is just unbelievable to me when you think of the crimes that have been committed," she ranted to *Arizona Republic* reporter Connie Cone Sexton the day the plea agreement was announced. "It's just a slap in these kids' faces."

Romley, not surprisingly, had a different take.

He was convinced the immunity agreement, and the concessions he negotiated with the diocese, would do more to help the church and community move past the sex abuses scandal than indicting the bishop. Besides, Romley knew going to court was always risky. Something as simple as the confusion over the word "not" in Jordan Green's memo about his conversation with me after the Takata incident could be used to cast doubts on my credibility and scuttle the prosecution.

Cindi Nannetti and Rachel Mitchell spent days talking to the families of victims who were disappointed. They pointed out the reality that even if the bishop had gone to trial and been convicted, no judge would have given him jail time. Besides, O'Brien could claim he was railroaded and continue to deny he did anything wrong.

Under Romley's agreement, at least the bishop clearly admitted his guilt.

Or so it seemed.

Within hours of Romley's announcment, Bishop O'Brien called a news conference of his own and denied any criminal wrongdoing.

"It was never my intention to obstruct or interfere in any way," he said. "I certainly never intentionally placed a child in harm's way. To suggest a cover-up is just plain false. I did not oversee decades of wrongdoing."

The bishop followed that about-face with another claim of innocence in an open letter read from the pulpits of the diocese on Sunday, June 8, 2003.

Dismissing his eighty-two word statement as a "so-called confession of guilt," the bishop wrote: "In my mind, I was not confessing criminal activity. I was acknowledging that we made mistakes."

Romley was irate.

He called O'Brien's legal team and threatened to withdraw the immunity agreement and prosecute the bishop for obstruction of justice and perjury if he didn't stand by his written admission of guilt.

Within days, the bishop and his attorneys caved again. O'Brien's tone changed.

He quit denying his guilt and began working diligently at taking a low profile.

Little did he know, his worst days were yet to come — and come quickly.

Chapter 16
Coming Home

1st Lt. Joe Ladensack

MY FIRST FIFTY DAYS in Vietnam, I earned two Silver Stars, a Bronze Star, and was told I was being nominated for the Congressional Medal of Honor. I still had nine months left on my tour. Two-hundred-seventy-two more days.

Somehow I made it through, winning five more Bronze Stars and the respect of some mighty good men. On January 12, 1970, those men, and the rest of the 1st Infantry Division, were told they would be going home in April as part of President Richard Nixon's promised withdrawal from Vietnam.

Maj. Gen. Albert "Ernie" Milloy, the division commander who had pinned my second Bronze Star on me in the field in August, announced the withdrawal with typical military bravado.

"We have worked ourselves out of a job," he told his jubilant troops, then prodded them to remain vigilant.

"Until we leave, we need to make every day count."

It didn't take long for the men to recast the general's words into a phrase they found infinitely more inspiring: "Count every day."

A few days after Milloy's announcement, Battalion Commander Lt. Col. Lee D. Brown called me to the Operations Center and told me we would be moving twice in the next three months — once south down Thunder Road from Dầu Tiếng to Lai Khê and then several weeks later farther south to a warehouse staging area at Dĩ An, on the outskirts of Saigon. We would be turning in all our equipment, from pencils to APCs, before disbanding and I would be in charge of getting it done.

I called in the battalion first sergeants and briefed them on my plan. We would start by turning in unnecessary equipment when we set up in Lai Khê, then eventually unload our APCs and other big stuff at Dĩ An. That would allow everyone to prioritize what they wanted to surrender and ensure that most of the work was done before we got to Dĩ An and be forced to scramble to get everything done at the last minute.

Things went smoothly until we got an unexpected and sickening change of plans. We'd originally been told all seventeen-thousand men of the Big Red One would be going home. Instead, in early April, we learned only one-hundred-forty of us would actually return to Fort Riley, Kansas. While the Big Red One was technically withdrawing from Vietnam, the only members of the division who were going back Stateside were those who had completed a year in country. Everyone else would be reassigned to other divisions.

I felt physically ill when I realized thousands of brave young men had a seductive safety net dangled in front of them only to have it abruptly withdrawn. Obviously, there was nothing I could do about it, but I could, at least, try to dull the disappointment. I began stocking up on steaks and beer and rounding up USO acts to perform at a series of parties during the three to five days off the men would have before being reassigned to their new units.

Those days were extremely emotional for me. As we turned in our APCs, many of the enlisted men I served with stopped by to say good-bye. We shared memories that we knew would shape the rest of our lives. Sadly, many of those lives would be cut short in the coming months. Most of those left behind were assigned to new units that invaded Cambodia from May 1 to June 30, 1970. I recognized far too many of the names on the death rolls from that campaign, which triggered wide-scale protests back home in the United States.

That betrayal was weighing heavily on me when I was called to company headquarters to meet a young lieutenant I didn't know. He was the assistant to the battalion's S-1, the executive officer in charge of awards and ranks. His desk, a plank of rough plywood sitting on two saw horses, was piled high with personnel records flapping in the breeze of a portable fan.

"You got a Silver Star for Núi Bà Đen, didn't you?" the young officer said when I introduced myself.

"Yeah."

"Well, division has just authorized us to give somebody the Distinguished Service Cross," he said. "Everyone we've talked to says nobody deserves it more than you."

I was stunned. Stunned and angry.

"No way," I said. "I don't want it."

"What?!," the lieutenant screeched. "What do you mean?"

"You heard me," I said. "I don't want it. I don't want to just take a handout as if I'm some homeless person. Oh, a DSC. Isn't that nice."

What a sick way to handle the nation's second-highest honor for valor in combat. I was so mad. I thought about everything that had gone wrong lately. The generals had said the division was going home, so get all your men ready to ship out. Then, just days before we were supposed to leave, they come to me and say, "Oh, here's a list of the guys who don't have enough time in Vietnam. Get them into trucks so they can go get killed somewhere else."

And now, on top of all that, here they were trying to hand out the Distinguished Service Cross like it was candy at Halloween. Here, take one.

I was furious and my mood didn't improve two days later, on my last night in Vietnam, when the battalion held a farewell dinner for officers. It was a depressing evening. I looked around and realized the only officer I'd served with for any length of time was Lt. Col. Brown. The rest were all relatively new. They knew nothing of the brutal bunker-to-bunker fighting I'd survived my first two days in Vietnam in

May. None could begin to imagine the unthinkable fiasco of the Battle of Black Virgin Mountain. And while they'd all heard of Thunder Road, not one of them knew the gut-gripping fear of seeing NVA sappers cutting through razor wire in the pitch dark night about to overrun a fire support base.

They would learn. Most would survive their own nightmares, as horrible as — or, maybe, even worse than — mine. But on that last night, the new officers were still untested. Untested, but full of bravado. The drunken toasts they made rang hollow and immature. It was sad. I felt depressed and very much alone on my last night in Vietnam.

THE NEXT DAY I joined six other men who made up the honor guard to bring the 1st Division's colors home. Lt. Col. Brown had notified me in writing two months earlier that I'd been chosen "to escort the unit's colors back to Fort Riley."

"We have considered the merit of all our men," he wrote. "It was not an easy task to decide who should represent the 2d Battalion (Mech), 2d Infantry of the Big Red One; so many have exhibited meritorious qualities, thereby earning the Big Red One the tradition it so proudly bears."

Lt. Col. Brown said he and my company commander had personally chosen me for "an honor to be cherished" because of my "impressive accomplishments" and wished me a "safe, rewarding, and triumphant" trip home.

That trip home started with a flight to Alaska where the honor guard rehearsed the ceremonial duties we would perform at Fort Riley. We pretended to walk off the plane. We marched in formation and handed off flags until we had everything down to perfection.

We landed in Kansas a few days before the April 15 ceremony and I was enjoying a peaceful nap one afternoon when I was jolted out my bunk by five soldiers who had served with me in Alpha Company. We had a raucous reunion and I treated them all to a steak dinner — a simple thing, but a ritual that, for me, symbolized a long-awaited homecoming and the start of my purge of Vietnam.

The day of the ceremony we handed our flags to soldiers of the 24th Infantry Division, which was being deactivated and absorbed into the Big Red One. The only flag we didn't hand over was mine, the 2/2 — 2nd Battalion (Mechanized), 2nd Infantry Regiment of the 1st Infantry Division. We were being replaced by a tank battalion. Since there was no one to receive the 2/2 flag we took it behind the bleachers and placed it in the back of a truck that hauled the proud colors away for storage.

Two days later, I flew home to Phoenix. My mother, Regina, and seven of my siblings were waiting at the airport, but I hardly got the rousing welcome I'd imagined. I walked up to my mother and said: "I'm home."

Incredibly, she raised up on her toes and peered intently over my shoulder.

"I'm looking for my son. He hasn't come off the plane yet."

I know war changes everyone, but my own mother not recognizing me? I couldn't believe how much that hurt.

Then my little brother, Paul — the same little brother who recognized Suzanne Charny in the video of the Bob Hope Christmas Show — came to my rescue.

"Mom, it's Joe!"

"Yep," I said. "It's me, Joe. I'm home."

My poor mother never intended to hurt me. But she did. The anonymous reception I received from my own family personified the experience of far too many proud Vietnam veterans who came home to an angry, divided nation that rarely recognized the sacrifices and horrors that changed them forever.

I was on thirty days' leave when I landed in Phoenix. But two weeks in I packed up my car and headed to my next duty station at Fort Lewis, Washington. After everything I'd gone through in Vietnam, I couldn't stand being treated like a high school kid any more. My family never understood that. I had to get away.

Chapter 17
Hand of God

Joe Ladensack

THE PRIDE I FELT when those three Vietnam veterans stood and saluted me in the grand jury room was drowned by the rage that swelled when I heard Bishop O'Brien trying to renege on his admission of guilt. But no emotion can describe what I felt — what most people felt — just twelve days after the immunity deal when the bishop killed a man.

Driving home alone on a Saturday night from a confirmation ceremony in the small town of Buckeye, Arizona, forty miles west of Phoenix, the bishop struck a drunken pedestrian who was jaywalking across a poorly lit street. O'Brien didn't stop. He drove off in the night and left a dying man on the ground, not knowing another driver who witnessed the crash followed him and wrote down his license plate.

O'Brien failed to report the incident. He went home Saturday night and spent most of Sunday at a Father's Day pool party at his sister's house, where he stayed overnight. Parked at her house was his new 2003 champagne-colored Buick Park Avenue, its windshield shattered and right front fender dented.

Police traced the license plate they'd been given to a vehicle registered to the Phoenix Diocese and tried to contact O'Brien on Sunday. Unable to reach him, they phoned Monsignor Dale Fushek, the bishop's second-in-command. They told Fushek a witness to a fatal hit-and-run accident had copied down the license plate of a light-colored Buick fleeing the scene.

Fushek told detectives the diocese had several cars, including O'Brien's, that matched the description, but he didn't know the license plate and couldn't check it out until Monday morning.

As soon as he hung up, Fushek called O'Brien, who was eating dinner at his sister's house. Fushek let him know the police were asking questions about a hit-and-run accident that apparently involved a car registered to the diocese and told him where the accident occurred. He asked the bishop if he had been in that neighborhood Saturday.

"I might have been," the bishop replied.

Might have been?

Fushek was flabbergasted. O'Brien, though, was unfazed. He still didn't call the police.

First thing Monday morning, O'Brien told his secretary, Julie Deck, that his windshield was damaged and asked her to arrange to have it repaired. But before she could make an appointment, police showed up at O'Brien's home in north-central Phoenix. They knocked on his door and telephoned him from outside, but got no response. They were still outside a half hour later deciding what to do when the bishop's housekeeper, Doris Knowles, arrived for work. She told the officers she couldn't let them in, but would ask the bishop if he would see them.

"Why are they here?" Knowles later testified the bishop asked her. "Did they tell you?"

O'Brien eventually let the officers in and, when they asked, showed them his damaged Buick parked in the garage. He admitted he had been driving the car Saturday night and hit something, but thought it was a dog or cat — or, maybe, someone had thrown a rock at his windshield. When officers asked why he failed to report the accident even after he learned authorities were looking for him, O'Brien said he didn't know how to contact the police.

Late Monday, June 16, 2003, police arrested Bishop Thomas J. O'Brien, who, at the time, was the highest-ranking cleric of the Roman Catholic Church in the United States to be charged with a felony.

News photos of O'Brien being led away showed him looking stunned, dressed in his Roman collar, a black short-sleeve shirt, and black dress slacks.

Just as he had done before Rick Romley's news conference two weeks earlier, Mark Stribling called to give me a heads-up.

"Joe, you need to sit down," Stribling said over the phone. "You won't believe what's happened."

Stribling was right. The news *was* hard to believe. But when I thought about it, the way O'Brien handled the hit-and-run was a perfect example of how he handled everything.

First he denied it. Never happened.

Then, it was somebody saying something bad happened, but he didn't know what they were talking about.

Then, cover it up: I hit a dog. Oh, my windshield just broke. Call my secretary and we'll get my windshield fixed.

Then, when the police show up, don't answer the door. Maybe they'll just go away.

Finally, "What's this all about? Why are you here?"

Just typical.

The night O'Brien was arrested he was taken to the Madison Street Jail, which was so shabby and dilapidated that it would be closed for a decade because it failed to meet corrections standards. The trauma of being arrested and hauled into the kind of squalor he could only imagine in his worst nightmare, was too much for the disgraced bishop. His blood pressure spiked. He fainted and was rushed to nearby St. Joseph's Hospital.

For years, I joked every time someone would mention the bishop fainting when he was brought to jail.

"You know why he fainted?" I'd ask. "It's simple. He goes in there to get booked and, all of a sudden, he hears the prisoners singing 'Here Comes the Bride.'"

It is a terrible shame that someone had to die, but I couldn't help thinking what goes around, comes around. It was almost as if the Hand of God was responsible. The bishop dodged criminal charges for covering up widespread sexual abuse and lying about it for decades. Then, almost before the ink dried on the news stories about his immunity deal, he is arrested for running over a man, killing him, and fleeing the scene.

There had been widespread calls for O'Brien to resign in the days after his written statement confessing guilt in the sexual abuse scandal, but he and his legal team dug in. Even now, after his arrest, they were still determined to hold on.

"He's still bishop and he's still in charge," O'Brien's spokeswoman, Kim Sue Lia Perkes, said hours after O'Brien was released on forty-five thousand dollars bond.

But even as she was making that proclamation, O'Brien was being told by his superiors in the church that he had to go. Just before noon on Tuesday, June 17, the pope's chief representative in the United States — Papal Nuncio Gabriel Montalvo Higuera — telephoned Archbishop Michael J. Sheehan of Santa Fe, New Mexico, and told him his duties were being expanded to include temporary control of the Phoenix Diocese. The Vatican would be demanding O'Brien's resignation.

O'Brien, his shoulders slumped and eyes moist, refused, at first, to accept his fate. Members of his inner circle gathered around him to tell him he had no choice. Monsignor Fushek, O'Brien's close friend, tried to console him.

"You will still be a bishop," he told O'Brien. "You will always be a bishop. You just won't be the bishop of the Phoenix Diocese."

Fushek spent three hours comforting and cajoling before O'Brien relented and wept.

I had gone to school with Fushek and knew him fairly well. But apparently not well enough. Mark Stribling was always asking if I could tell him anything about Fushek.

"All I know is his affect is really weird and that he was a back climber," I told Mark. "He works a lot with youth and he's a back climber in the church. He has a national board with all kinds of bigwigs on it."

Fushek, at the time, was the extremely popular pastor of St. Timothy Parish in the Phoenix suburb of Mesa. He founded Life Teen, an international ministry for young people, and oversaw many of the biggest events in the Phoenix Diocese, including the visits of Pope John Paul II and Mother Teresa.

In November 2005, two-and-a-half years after O'Brien resigned and after years of rumors about his own character, Fushek was charged with ten counts of misdemeanor sexual activities with seven boys and young men. Stribling made the arrest, going to the posh Biltmore Hotel in central Phoenix where Fushek had a suite for long periods.

Mark later told me arresting Fushek was "one of the most pleasurable things" he had done in his career.

"He was living pretty high on the hog," Stribling remembered. "We went to the Biltmore and waited for him. He drove up in a BMW and when he got out, I went up to him and said: 'Excuse me, sir.' I told him who I was and arrested him. I cuffed him and as I shoved his head into the back of a police car, I said to myself: 'Yes!'"

Fushek fought the charges for five years and eventually pleaded guilty to one misdemeanor count of assault involving the "flicking" of a young man's genitals. By then, he had been defrocked by Pope Benedict — not for sexual misconduct, but for leading non-Catholic religious services.

Father Dale somehow remained incredibly popular and went on to found his own non-denominational church, the Praise and Worship Center, in Chandler, Arizona.

BISHOP O'BRIEN'S TRIAL on felony charges of leaving the scene of an accident began January 20, 2004, and lasted one month. I followed it carefully every day through the *Arizona Republic* and, frankly, thought the defense presented a lame case. Of course, they had little to work with. O'Brien's windshield was caved in so badly that no rational person could possibly believe the damage had been caused by anything but a 240-pound man crashing through it. How do you defend a man who says he failed to report an accident because he didn't know how to call police? What could possibly explain the rush to get his windshield repaired?

I learned later that Romley's office had received information the bishop may have been drunk the night of the fatal accident. His team was never able to corroborate the allegations, although a few days later, shortly after O'Brien was indicted, investigators received another call from an employee of a See's Candy store in downtown Phoenix claiming the bishop had just left and was "very drunk." Phoenix Police followed up several hours later, but O'Brien denied he had been drinking.

On Tuesday, February 17, 2004, resigned Bishop Thomas J. O'Brien was found guilty on felony charges of leaving the scene of a fatal accident. I have to admit, I was gratified. But thirty-eight days later I was sick to my stomach when Judge Stephen A. Gerst let O'Brien walk free.

Gerst could have sentenced O'Brien to forty-five months in prison. Prosecutors asked for a minimum of six months. Instead, Gerst gave the bishop one-thousand hours of community service, four years' probation, and suspended his driver's license for five years.

The judge tried to justify his leniency with a rambling PowerPoint presentation detailing ninety-nine other hit-and-run cases and the relatively light sentences those defendants received. Anita and I listened in astonishment to a live radio broadcast of Judge Gerst's arguments as we made the three-hour drive from Sierra Vista to Phoenix to visit my parents, both of whom had recently been diagnosed with cancer.

County Attorney Rick Romley was in the courtroom for the sentencing. He had spent much of the day in official motorcades and attending speeches by President George W. Bush, who was in Phoenix that day. Romley was as stunned as we were.

An hour after the sentencing hearing, the county attorney made what for him was the unprecedented move of criticizing a sitting judge.

"The message (Judge Gerst) sent today is that if you are a person of some note, then you are to be treated differently," Romley told a crowd of reporters.

O'Brien left court smiling and shaking hands with friends and family. Romley left shaking his head. My hands shook in anger as Anita drove.

I remembered how disappointed I was when the bishop wasn't indicted for obstruction of justice in the sex abuse scandal. Now I realized it didn't matter. The bishop could probably get away with murder. He certainly could get away with manslaughter. The fix was in.

O'Brien did eventually lose one court battle. His community service sentence required him to visit terminally ill patients at local hospitals and hospices. Because his license was suspended, the bishop had a chauffeur. Even so, O'Brien went back to Judge Gerst and asked that his travel time to and from his visits be counted as part of his community service hours.

Gerst initially indicated he was willing to grant the bishop's request, but Romley filed a motion arguing that if the travel time were deducted it would appear a guilty felon was controlling his own sentence. Gerst reluctantly refused O'Brien's request.

At least that was something.

O'Brien served his one-thousand hours and I never had to see him again. Thirty-one years after he threw me out of the church and fourteen years after he killed a man, I was dying and he was still living peacefully in the same five-bedroom, six-bath, forty-one-hundred-square-foot house the diocese gave him when he became bishop in 1981.

Guess we've both been hard to kill.

Chapter 18

I Left Everything On the Field

Joe Ladensack

IN LATE FEBRUARY 2013, my oncologist gave me the choice of having another round of chemotherapy or having six weeks to live.

The first round of chemo in 2007 had put me in remission, but it was a horrible, nearly fatal experience. I figured a second round would certainly kill me. When I refused treatment, my doctor suggested I enroll in hospice and get my affairs in order.

Since my adult life had been ruled by a sense of mission, I had to come up with a plan fast. In the next six weeks I needed to sell our house in Sierra Vista, buy a new house in Tucson, and sort, pack, and move forty years of possessions. We did it, with the help of the many friends Anita and I had made in our twenty seven-years "hiding" in Southern Arizona.

Once we unpacked and made our home in Tucson somewhat livable, Anita reminded me I needed to enroll in hospice. I made an appointment with a new physician just down the street. He took one look at my medical records and arranged for a hospice team to come to our home the next day. He told me I should go home and enjoy my "Indian Summer."

Mission accomplished, I started to compile a bucket list.

First, was to help Bill Sly complete his book on the Battle of Núi Bà Đen — Black Virgin Mountain — in July of 1969.

Second, was to call attorney Richard Treon and thank him for his incredible support during the long years we dealt with the emotional legal battles against the Diocese of Phoenix.

Third, was to contact Joseph Reaves and have the conversation I regretted being unable to have with him in 2002-2003.

Bill Sly's book, *No Place to Hide: A Company at Núi Bà Đen*, was self-published in 2016, the culmination of twenty-two years of work by Bill and more than a decade of help from Anita and me. In the days after the book's publication, I spoke with the families of survivors of the battle and shared with them the sacrifices their loved one's had made on that miserable, god-forsaken mountain four decades ago. I told them about the final moments of their husbands', fathers', and brothers' brave lives and how proud I was to lead them.

Next came Richard Treon. My long conversation with him was touching and helped bring closure to the relationship of two old soldiers who had fought the good fight for the many victims of abuse at the hands of the priests and bishops of the Diocese of Phoenix.

When I contacted Joseph Reaves, he graciously accepted Anita's and my invitation to visit us in our new home in Tucson. I would finally meet the man I'd never known, but who'd fought alongside me in the tortuous battle to try to bring justice to the scarred victims of abuse.

Luckily, my life lingered past the doctors' expiration date. I was thrown out of hospice after eighteen months. They told me I wasn't dying fast enough. That was four years ago.

The extra time allowed me to do more than merely finish my bucket list. I was blessed with year two more missions that I feel, now, brought my life full circle.

The first was this book. The two-year project was an exciting creative outlet — for me, for Anita, and, I believe, for Joseph A. Reaves. Rekindling forty-eight years of fighting for my country and my faith, brought about more much-needed healing than I could have imagined.

I am proud, too, that our son, Charlie — and perhaps, one day, his children — will always have these pages to better understand my life, my struggles, my victories, my agonies — and, most of all, my many, many blessings.

The second luxury of having outlived my "Indian Summer," was being allowed to comfort one last shattered soul.

In August 2017, I learned a lawsuit had been filed against Bishop Thomas J. O'Brien, accusing him of the very sin he had spent decades hiding for others. A former altar boy, whose life had been in shambles for four decades, claimed—with graphic detail—that O'Brien serially molested him from 1977 to 1982.

Finally, thirteen years after confessing to decades of crimes against children in return for immunity, then compounding his arrant heartlessness by plowing over a pedestrian and leaving him to die on a darkened street, Bishop Thomas J. O'Brien was forced to face his worst nightmares.

The lawsuit, filed in Maricopa County Superior Court, claimed the young boy repressed memories of the assaults and only recovered them in September 2014, at age forty-four, as he was preparing to have his own son baptized in the Catholic Church. During rehearsals for the ceremony, the sight of a brilliant white towel the priest was using to dry his hands of holy water triggered memories of molestations long buried.

"Basically, I blew up," the weeping man remembered in August 2017 when I met him in a confession-like session with his lawyers present. "Something about the towel triggered memories of O'Brien cumming on me."

Court documents detailed the moment.

"In (one) instance, O'Brien summoned (me) from class and induced (me) to orally copulate (him) until he ejaculated on (my) face. O'Brien subsequently cleaned (me) with a white cloth while repeating to himself: 'I am not a sinner.'"

According to the lawsuit, the bishop then told the young boy — identified only as Joseph W. — to do penance by praying the rosary in a pew of a large, empty church.

Attorneys for the Diocese of Phoenix issued a statement on O'Brien's behalf saying the former bishop "categorically denies the allegations." They also made a point of noting "O'Brien was never assigned to any of the parishes or schools identified in the lawsuit."

That was a blatantly bogus defense. True, O'Brien never was assigned to the two parishes or elementary schools named in the complaint. But, at the time of the first alleged assaults, O'Brien was Vicar General of the Diocese. He had free rein of every parish. He could be anywhere he wanted any time. And by the time the then-twelve-year-old boy claims the molestations stopped, O'Brien had even greater leeway as bishop, the unquestioned leader of the diocese.

The attorneys who filed the suit, Timothy C. Hale of Santa Barbara, California, and Carlo N. Mercaldo of Tucson, Arizona, showed me a half-dozen photos of their then-young client with O'Brien at confirmation services and other religious gatherings from the late 1970s and early 1980s. Among the snapshots was one of the boy standing near O'Brien in an alcove where he told the lawyers O'Brien first kissed him on the mouth.

I didn't know about the lawsuit for nearly a year. Almost no one knew. The suit was public, of course, as soon as it was filed on September 14, 2016, but the media didn't get hold of it until oral arguments were heard in Judge David K. Udall's courtroom in August 2017.

Like most everyone, I was appalled to read the chilling allegations. I can't say I was shocked. Nothing about the Catholic Church and sexual abuse will ever shock me again. But I was horrified. And I knew immediately I had a new mission. I needed to do what I could to help the attorneys who were pursuing justice and the man who had the courage to seek that justice.

Repressed memory cases have always been a hard sell. Combine that with the use of a fictitious name and I knew Joseph W. was in for a tough battle.

Arizona is one of twenty-eight states, as of January 2017, that accommodate repressed memory cases by extending the statute of limitations. For most sex crimes in Arizona, the statute of limitations is seven years, which would mean that Joseph W.'s deadline for filing suit would have been in 1989 — a lifetime ago. But under Arizona's so-called "delayed discovery rules," the statute of limitations only starts tolling the day a victim "recovers" his or her memory and runs for two years.

Joseph W. claimed the white cloth incident that "triggered" the return of his memories took place September 28, 2014. His lawsuit was filed in 2016, two weeks before the statute of limitations would have blocked him from pursuing a case and spared O'Brien the misery of yet another dark shadow over his ministry.

Psychologists, psychiatrists, and other mental health professionals disagree ardently over the reliability of repressed and recovered memories. *Psychology Today* magazine has written extensively about what it calls the "Memory Wars" pitting an army of mental health experts who insist recovered memories are valid, particularly in sex abuse cases, against an equally sizeable force who argue such recollections are often manufactured by the mind and are wholly untrustworthy. Both sides have a plethora of scientific studies to back their positions.

I agree with Lindsey Pratt, a psychotherapist in New York city who specializes in sexual trauma and abuse.

"In simple terms, our brains only allow us to experience what we are able to withstand," Pratt writes. "This is one of the reasons why repression of traumatic childhood memories is so common, as children are not as well equipped to cope or make sense of fear, panic, anger, shame, or sadness as adults may be."

Who could ever make sense of the fear, panic, anger, shame, and sadness of being sexually molested at age seven by man who tells you he is God's representative on earth?

One week after news of Joseph W.'s allegations became public, I was in his lawyers' offices. Joseph Reaves arranged the meeting. Tim Hale flew in from California and we gathered in a long conference room lined with awards and citations at the Mercaldo Law Firm, just a couple miles from my home in Tucson. In addition to the four us, we were joined by John Murphy, a paralegal specializing in research on the case.

The session lasted two hours and I shared quite a bit of information about O'Brien and dozens of "bad priests" I'd known through the years, including the names of at least eight sexual predators previously unknown to the attorneys. Hale, Mercaldo, and Murphy had compiled a list of sixty priests from the Phoenix Diocese known to be sex offenders. They were asking the court to declare the diocese a public nuisance and the more names they had the better.

Near the end of the session, I asked if I could meet the man who filed the suit. Hale and Mercaldo said they'd ask their client and let me know if he was willing.

Two weeks later, we were all back in the same conference room with Joseph W., who freely volunteered his real name and poured his heart out, weeping often, head buried in his palms, for nearly three hours. He told me I could ask anything. Nothing was off limits.

Joe brought with him a six-page diary he had written as a child. Bound in purple construction paper, the cover was rimmed with drawings of multi-colored flowers forming a frame around curly-cue letters that spelled out: "My Life 1-6 Grade" by (his full name in tidy print letters)

The first five pages told the history of his grandparents, parents, and eight siblings along with a list of his teachers in each grade one through six. The final page was titled: "Comming Life" — the misspelling uncorrected by a teacher who circled every other mistake in the mini-diary.

"My dream of the future is to have four kids, two boys and two girls," he wrote about the time he claims the abuse stopped. "My occupation will hopefully be computer electronics.

"My life will be easy, I think. It will be easy because I'm gonna (gonna circled) be doing something I think is neat and fun.

"The things I plan for my kids are I'm gonna (circled) send them to a good school. I'll give them some things that they want. I don't want to spoil them.

"One of the things I hope to learn is how to fly a plane.

"The end."

I learned during those three emotional hours that some of Joseph W.'s dreams came true. Others were crushed.

He and his wife, Susan, have three kids, not four — two boys and a girl. Joe became a successful executive in a tech-related company, managing accounts that include the University of Arizona and the city of Tucson. His children are going to good schools and doing well.

But Joe's life has been anything but the easy one he predicted for himself in sixth grade.

The worst of it began the first time he says O'Brien kissed him on the mouth — before any oral copulation began — when Joe decided to confide in his father, a rabidly devout Catholic with nine children.

"My dad beat me with a hair brush and told me I was never to mention it again," Joe told me, weeping and burying his head in his open palms for the first of scores of times during our meeting.

"My wife always thought it was strange when we were dating that I didn't have any childhood memories. Now I wish the memories had never come back. I wish that more than anything."

After graduating from high school, Joe applied to Embry-Riddle Aeronautical University in Prescott, Arizona, hoping to fulfill his dream of learning to fly an airplane. His father withdrew the application and told Joe he needed a more practical degree so he enrolled at the University of Redlands, a private, independent liberal arts institution an hour due east of Los Angeles.

At Redlands, Joe never had a roommate. He didn't really know why at the time, but he slept in a closet all four years of school. He felt safe in the small, dark room.

The more I heard Joe tell his story, the more credible I found him to be. One small, but important sign of his earnestness came when he showed up for our meeting carrying an oversized box of freshly baked cookies and a note his wife asked him to bring.

"Mr. Ladensack, A special note of thanks just for you," the card read in blue ink and tidy penmanship. "Thank you for having the courage, integrity, and compassion to protect the children and families of Arizona. You are a true hero in my book.

"Best regards, Joe's wife."

The card and the cookies were incredibly thoughtful. And I will treasure Susan's heartfelt note forever. At the same time, I thought how both were indicative of the behavior of so many abuse victims I'd dealt with through the years. They all had a desperate desire to please — to go out of their way to make any gesture to win acceptance. There was a burning need for approval. I understood it and respected it.

About an hour into our meeting, as Joe was only getting started with his stories, I stopped him and leaned over to him, elbows on my knees and hands clasped as if in prayer. The priest in me — the counselor, confidante, mentor, advisor, spiritual guide — took over.

"Joe, you need to understand none of this is your fault," I said, leaning toward him and locking our eyes. "None of this is your fault. You did nothing wrong."

Joe wept yet again. He shook sobbing.

"I don't know how the church has covered this up," he moaned shaking his head. "What is wrong with me? Why can't I get this out of my brain? Why does my brain care about this?"

"Joe," I said again, "none of this is your fault."

Toward the end of our powerful exchange, Joe talked about why he finally found the courage to bring his lawsuit — knowing full well what skeptics of repressed memories would say, knowing full well the bishop would deny everything, and knowing full well most Catholics would scorn his allegations.

"One of my concerns was that he (O'Brien) would die without knowing I was still out there," Joe said. "There was a time when I wanted O'Brien dead. I said that to my doctor. But what I want now is for the jerk to frigging say, 'Yeah, I frigging molested you.'"

"I wish people who commit sexual abuse would know that the two minutes of ejaculation and joy they get ruins a person's life forever."

I don't know what is going to happen with Joe's lawsuit. As I was writing this, Judge Udall threw out the motion to have the Diocese of Phoenix declared a public nuisance. But he allowed the specific allegations against "Perpetrator O'Brien" to go forward.

In November 2017, just as this book was going to the publisher, Joseph W.'s steadfast attorneys beat back an attempt by O'Brien's team to "bifurcate" the case, which would have allowed them to argue repressed memory theory separate from the allegations against the former bishop. Essentially, O'Brien's attorneys were hoping to have the case thrown out before the former bishop could be deposed.

Judge Udall denied that motion, and ordered the two sides to begin the process of discovery—exchanging documents and other information relevant to the case—in early 2018

Despite those two procedural wins, chances are the lawsuit still could be dismissed. I wouldn't be surprised. I learned back in 2003 that the fix was in. O'Brien could probably get away with murder.

For what it's worth, though, I believe Joseph W. I thank him for meeting with me, telling me his story, and allowing me, hopefully, to assist him on the long journey toward healing.

Joseph W. helped bring closure to my mission as Father Ladensack. I gave every bit of my energy to exposing the sins of pedophile and predator priests in the Diocese of Phoenix.

Just as I had done at the battles of An Lộc, Núi Bà Đen, Thunder III — and every other day in Vietnam — I left everything on the field.

Acknowledgments

JOE LADENSACK: My deep appreciation to all the members of Maricopa County Attorney's Office who participated in Operation Broken Oath, especially Richard Romley, Cindi Nannetti, and Rachel Mitchell, who worked so hard to protect the children and give voice to the victims of the shameful acts of pedophile priests.

A special, heartfelt bow to my beautiful wife, Anita C. Ladensack, for her continuous support and her chronicling of my Vietnam stories when I was diagnosed with Hairy Cell Leukemia.

I am supremely indebted to Mark Stribling, an incredible investigator, who patiently allowed me to tell my story and became a good friend and guiding hand through terribly difficult times.

My thanks, too, to Ken Freedman who stood shoulder to shoulder with me until his untimely death; to Richard Treon, a courageous champion of justice who remains a good friend; to Richard Felix, who was with me at the start of my journey, and, last, but not least, to Terry Greene of the Phoenix *New Times,* who was way out in front of the story.

JOSEPH A. REAVES: The word hero gets thrown around too easily. But this project gave me the great honor of getting to know a true hero — an extraordinary man who struggled, suffered, and triumphed for country and faith. Thank you, Joe — and Anita — for letting me join your amazing journey and for giving me a new, joyous mission.

I'm especially grateful to longtime friends Coleen L. Geraghty, Susan B. Hornik, and Richard H. Hornik for their patient, thoughtful, and desperately needed feedback on the many drafts of this effort.

And to Jeff Noble, my neighbor and friend, whose generous offer of his incredible photographic talents helped bring life to this endeavor.

Thanks, too, to our editor and publisher, Harley B. Patrick, who was incredibly supportive and thorough. We couldn't have asked for anyone better to shepherd this venture.

My deep respect to Rick Romley, Mark Stribling, Cindi Nannetti, and Mike Manning — four amazing people; heroes, too — who led the fight for justice. And to Tim Hale and Carlo Mercaldo, who refused to let the pain and suffering of long-ignored victims fade into history.

Finally, my lasting and loving thanks to my son, Kelly P. Reaves, for more than I can say, and to my wife, Lynne Reaves, for a lifetime of friendship and fun — and for agreeing to let me exorcise the "dark spirits" that invaded our lives.

Appendix

JOE LADENSACK'S MEDALS

DEPARTMENT OF THE ARMY
Headquarters, 1st Infantry Division
APO San Francisco 96345

GENERAL ORDERS: 18 September 1969
NUMBER 10914

AWARD OF THE SILVER STAR

1. TC 320. The following AWARD is announced.

LADENSACK, JOSEPH C. SECOND LIEUTENANT United States
Army Company A 2d Battalion (Mechanized) 2d Infantry

Awarded: Silver Star

Date of Action: 24 May 1969

Theater: Republic of Vietnam

Reason: For gallantry in action while engaged in military operations
involving conflict with an armed hostile force in the Republic of Vietnam. On this date, Lieutenant Ladensack was serving as a platoon
leader with his mechanized unit on a battalion-minus reconnaissance
in force operations near the village of Minh Duc. As the friendly force
proceeded through the treacherous region, it was suddenly subjected
to an intense automatic weapons, small arms, and rocket-propelled
grenade fusillade from an undetermined size insurgent unit. Acting
with tactical deliberation, Lieutenant Ladensack immediately deployed
his men into strategic positions and directed their suppressive fire
with devastating effect. Personally leading his men on a determined

assault of the aggressor emplacements, Lieutenant Ladensack maneu-
vered from position to position as he coordinated his platoon's steady
advance into the insurgent strongholds. When a key enemy fortifi-
cation prevented his platoon's forward movement, Lieutenant Ladensack silenced the obstacle with accurate fire from his rocket grenade
weapon. Continuing to expose himself to the hostile fusillade, he led
his platoon to a triumphant rout of the aggressor force. His courageous initiative and exemplary professionalism significantly contributed to the successful outcome of the engagement. Second Lieutenant
Ladensack's unquestionable valor in close combat against numerically
superior hostile forces is in keeping with the finest traditions of the
military service and reflects great credit upon himself, the 1st Infantry
Division, and the United States Army.

Authority: By direction of the President, as established by the Act
of Congress, 9 July 1918, and USARV Message 16695, dated 1 July 1966.

DEPARTMENT OF THE ARMY
Headquarters, 1st Infantry Division
APO San Francisco 96345

GENERAL ORDERS: 5 September 1969
NUMBER 9907

AWARD OF THE SILVER STAR

1. TC 320. The following AWARD is announced.

LADENSACK, JOSEPH SECOND LIEUTENANT INFANTRY United States Army Company A 2d Battalion (Mechanized) 2d Infantry

Awarded: Silver Star

Date of Action: 12 July 1969

Theater: Republic of Vietnam

Reason: For gallantry in action while engaged in military operations involving operations with an armed hostile force in the Republic of Vietnam. On this date, Lieutenant Ladensack was serving as a platoon leader with his mechanized unit on a reconnaissance in force operation along the northeastern edge of the Black Virgin Mountain. As the friendly force proceeded to the base of Nui Cau, the rugged terrain required that the infantry dismount and advance up the hill without tracks. When the ground elements began the initial maneuver, it was suddenly subjected to an intense automatic weapons, small arms, and rocket-propelled grenade fusillade from a well-entrenched insurgent unit. Acting with tactical deliberation, Lieutenant Ladensack immediately organized his men into a strategic withdrawal. Observing a seriously wounded comrade lying in an exposed area, Lieutenant Ladensack ignored the hostile barrage and proceeded to the injured man's location. After applying emergency first aid to the casualty, he carried the disabled soldier to the medical evacuation zone. Although painfully wounded in the right arm, Lieutenant Ladensack assumed command of the entire element when he learned the company commander had been mortally wounded. Immediately organizing the rapid removal of all the casualties to the medical evacuation zone, he then redeployed his men into strategic positions for a determined assault of the aggressor emplacements. His courageous initiative and exemplary professionalism significantly contributed to the successful outcome of the engagement. Second Lieutenant Ladensack's unquestionable valor while engaged in military operations involving conflict with an insurgent force is in keeping with the finest traditions of the military service and reflects great credit upon himself, the 1st Infantry Division, and the United States Army.

Authority: By direction of the President, as established by the Act of Congress, 9 July 1918, and USARV Message 16695, dated 1 July 1966.

DEPARTMENT OF THE ARMY
Headquarters, 1st Infantry Division
APO San Francisco 96345

GENERAL ORDERS: 27 September 1969
NUMBER 11623

AWARD OF THE BRONZE STAR MEDAL

1. TC 320. The following AWARD is announced.

LADENSACK, JOSEPH C. FIRST LIEUTENANT United States Army
Company A 2d Battalion (Mechanized) 2d Infantry

Awarded: Bronze Star Medal with "V" device

Date of Action: 6 June 1969

Theater: Republic of Vietnam

Reason: For heroism not involving participation in aerial flight, in connection with military operations against a hostile force in the Republic of Vietnam. On this date, Lieutenant Ladensack was serving as a platoon leader with his unit on a reconnaissance in force operation northwest of An Loc. While moving to support another friendly force heavily engaged with a battalion-minus North Vietnamese Army base camp, it was suddenly subjected to intense automatic weapons, small arms, and rocket-propelled grenade fusillade from a firmly entrenched enemy emplacement. Undaunted, Lieutenant Ladensack immediately deployed his men into strategic positions and placed devastating suppressive fire upon the aggressor positions. With complete disregard for his personal safety, Lieutenant Ladensack personally led his men on victorious assaults of the enemy bunkers. During a sweep of the area, Lieutenant Ladensack was responsible for the discovery of numerous weapons and vital intelligence information. His courageous initiative and exemplary professionalism significantly contributed to the successful outcome of the encounter. First Lieutenant Ladensack's outstanding display of aggressiveness, devotion to duty, and personal bravery is in keeping with the finest traditions of the military service and reflect great credit upon himself, the 1st Infantry Division, and the United States Army.

Authority: By direction of the President, under the provisions of Executive Order 11046, 24 August 1962.

DEPARTMENT OF THE ARMY
Headquarters, 1st Infantry Division
APO San Francisco 96345

GENERAL ORDERS: 30 September 1969
NUMBER 11623

AWARD OF THE BRONZE STAR MEDAL
(First Oak Leaf Cluster)

1. TC 320. The following AWARD is announced.

LADENSACK, JOSEPH C. FIRST LIEUTENANT United States Army Headquarters and Headquarters Company A 2d Battalion (Mechanized) 2d Infantry

Awarded: Bronze Star Medal (First Oak Leaf Cluster) with "V" device

Date of Action: 14 August 1969

Theater: Republic of Vietnam

Reason: For heroism not involving participation in aerial flight, in connection with military operations against a hostile force in the Republic of Vietnam. On this date, Lieutenant Ladensack was serving as a platoon leader with his mechanized reconnaissance platoon on a counterinsurgency operation along Highway 13, north of Lai Khe. Informed of a friendly convoy under heavy fire near Quan Loi, Lieutenant Ladensack immediately directed his platoon to the aid of the beleaguered element. Approaching the embattled region, the friendly platoon was suddenly subjected to an intense automatic weapons, small arms, and rocket-propelled grenade fusillade from an undetermined size insurgent unit. Acting with tactical proficiency, Lieutenant Ladensack dauntlessly deployed his men into strategic positions and led them on a determined assault of the aggressor emplacements. Maneuvering from track to track, he repeatedly exposed himself to the hostile barrage as he directed his men's suppressive fire on the enemy with devastating effect. Observing a rocket-propelled grenade team preparing to fire on a friendly vehicle, Lieutenant Ladensack immediately silenced the aggressors with a burst from his personal weapon. As the friendly elements forced the insurgents into full retreat, Lieutenant Ladensack observed a lone enemy soldier and advanced on the bewildered aggressor. Quickly overpowering the insurgent, he accounted for the only prisoner of the encounter. His courageous initiative and intrepid determination significantly contributed to the successful outcome of the engagement. First Lieutenant Ladensack's outstanding display of aggressiveness, devotion to duty, and personal bravery is in keeping with the finest traditions of the military service and reflects great credit upon himself, the 1st Infantry Division, and the United States Army.

Authority: By direction of the President, under the provisions of Executive Order 11046, 24 August 1962.

DEPARTMENT OF THE ARMY
Headquarters, 1st Infantry Division
APO San Francisco 96345

GENERAL ORDERS: 31 October 1969
NUMBER 13588

AWARD OF THE BRONZE STAR MEDAL
(Second Oak Leaf Cluster)

1. TC 320. The following AWARD is announced.

LADENSACK, JOSEPH C. FIRST LIEUTENANT United States Army Headquarters and Headquarters Company A 2d Battalion (Mechanized) 2d Infantry

Awarded: Bronze Star Medal (Second Oak Leaf Cluster) with "V" device

Date of Action: 6 September 1969

Theater: Republic of Vietnam

Reason: For heroism not involving participation in aerial flight, in connection with military operations against a hostile force in the Republic of Vietnam. On this date, Lieutenant Ladensack was serving as a platoon leader with his mechanized unit on a convoy escort mission along Highway 13. As the friendly force proceeded through the treacherous region, it was suddenly subjected to an intense automatic weapons, small arms, and rocket-propelled grenade fusillade from an undetermined size insurgent unit. Acting with tactical proficiency, Lieutenant Ladensack immediately deployed his platoon into strategic positions and directed their suppressive fire with devastating effect. With complete disregard for his personal safety, Lieutenant Ladensack repeatedly exposed himself to the hostile barrage to determine the exact location of the enemy targets and effectively silence the insurgent strongholds. His courageous initiative and exemplary professionalism enabled the friendly convoy to proceed safely through the aggressor ambush. First Lieutenant Ladensack's outstanding display of aggressiveness, devotion to duty, and personal bravery is in keeping with the finest traditions of the military service and reflect great credit upon himself, the 1st Infantry Division, and the United States Army.

Authority: By direction of the President, under the provisions of Executive Order 11046, 24 August 1962.

CITATION

BY DIRECTION OF THE PRESIDENT

THE BRONZE STAR MEDAL
THIRD OAK LEAF CLUSTER
IS PRESENTED TO

FIRST LIEUTENANT JOSEPH C. LADENSACK

INFANTRY HEADQUARTERS AND HEADQUARTERS COM-
PANY, 2ND BATTALION (MECHANIZED), 2D INFANTRY, 1ST
INFANTRY DIVISION

who distinguished himself by outstandingly meritorious service in
connection with military operations against a hostile force in the
Republic of Vietnam. During the period

1 November 1968 to 30 November 1969

he consistently manifested exemplary professionalism and initiative
in obtaining outstanding results. His rapid assessment and solution
of numerous problems inherent in a counterinsurgency environment
greatly enhanced the allied effectiveness against a determined and
aggressive enemy. Despite many adversities, he invariably performed
his duties in a resolute and efficient manner. Energetically applying his
sound judgment and extensive knowledge, he has contributed materially to the successful accomplishment of the United States mission in
the Republic of Vietnam. His loyalty, diligence and devotion to duty
were in keeping with the highest traditions of the military service and
reflect great credit upon himself and the United States Army.

CITATION

BY DIRECTION OF THE PRESIDENT

THE BRONZE STAR MEDAL
FOURTH OAK LEAF CLUSTER
IS PRESENTED TO

FIRST LIEUTENANT JOSEPH C. LADENSACK

INFANTRY COMPANY D, 2ND BATTALION (MECHANIZED), 2D INFANTRY, 1ST INFANTRY DIVISION

who distinguished himself by outstandingly meritorious service in connection with military operations against a hostile force in the Republic of Vietnam. During the period

1 December 1969 to 1 February 1970

he consistently manifested exemplary professionalism and initiative in obtaining outstanding results. His rapid assessment and solution of numerous problems inherent in a counterinsurgency environment greatly enhanced the allied effectiveness against a determined and aggressive enemy. Despite many adversities, he invariably performed his duties in a resolute and efficient manner. Energetically applying his sound judgment and extensive knowledge, he has contributed materially to the successful accomplishment of the United States mission in the Republic of Vietnam. His loyalty, diligence and devotion to duty were in keeping with the highest traditions of the military service and reflect great credit upon himself and the United States Army.

CITATION

BY DIRECTION OF THE PRESIDENT

THE BRONZE STAR MEDAL
FIFTH OAK LEAF CLUSTER
IS PRESENTED TO

FIRST LIEUTENANT JOSEPH C. LADENSACK

INFANTRY COMPANY D, 2ND BATTALION (MECHANIZED),
2D INFANTRY, 1ST INFANTRY DIVISION

who distinguished himself by outstandingly meritorious service in connection with military operations against a hostile force in the Republic of Vietnam. During the period April 1969 to April 1970, he consistently manifested exemplary professionalism and initiative in obtaining outstanding results. His rapid assessment and solution of numerous problems inherent in a counterinsurgency environment greatly enhanced the allied effectiveness against a determined and aggressive enemy. Despite many adversities, he invariably performed his duties in a resolute and efficient manner. Energetically applying his sound judgment and extensive knowledge, he has contributed materially to the successful accomplishment of the United States mission in the Republic of Vietnam. His loyalty, diligence and devotion to duty were in keeping with the highest traditions of the military service and reflect great credit upon himself and the United States Army.

THIS FIRST DAY OF MARCH 1970

TIMELINE

1946 (24 October): Joseph Conrad Ladensack born Saint Claire, Michigan

1968 (June): BA History, Arizona State University, Tempe, Arizona

1968 (17 August): Ladensack enters U.S. Army (2LT — Infantry). ROTC Distinguished Military Graduate

May 1969-April 1970: Vietnam Service

1969 (24 May): Battle of An Lộc, Ladensack earns first Silver Star

1969 (06 June): Battle northeast of An Lộc, Ladensack earns first Bronze Star

1969 (12 July): Battle of Black Virgin Mountain; Ladensack awarded second Silver Star & Purple Heart

1969 (20 July): Ladensack given Recon Platoon

1969 (13 August): Ladensack arrives at Thunder III

1969 (14 August): Ladensack captures POW and uses Flame Track in battle for first time

1969 (15 August): Ladensack gets 2nd Bronze Star pinned on him by Gen. Albert "Ernie" Milloy

1969 (17 August): Ladensack promoted to 1LT

1969 (05 September): Battle of Thunder III

1969 (06 September): Ladensack earns third Bronze Star in fighting along Thunder Road

1969 (22 December): Ladensack serves as escort at Bob Hope Christmas show

1969 (26 December): Ladensack awarded fourth Bronze Star for fighting in November

1970 (05 February): Ladensack notified he is chosen to carry 2d Battalion (Mech.), 2d Infantry colors to new 1st Division home at Fort Riley, Kansas, in April

1970 (26 February): Ladensack awarded fifth Bronze Star for fighting in November

1970 (April): Ladensack awarded sixth Bronze Star for fighting in April

1970 (17 August): Ladensack leaves Army active duty, Captain, Company Commander

1970 (01 September): Ladensack Enrolls in St. John's Seminary in Camarillo, California

1970-1976: Ladensack attends St. John's Seminary, Camarillo, California

1971 (28 November): Robert Joseph Ladensack, Joe's brother, killed in Vietnam 24 days after his 24th birthday

1975 (17 February): Fr. Harry R. Morgan arrested for molesting nine-year-old in Fountain Hills, Arizona

1976 (June): Ladensack ordained as priest by Bishop Edward A. McCarthy

1976-1978: Associate pastor, St. Mary's Parish, Chandler, Arizona

1978-1980: Director of Religious Education, Diocese of Phoenix

1978 (23 September): Giandelone ordained over protest of Fr. John Grindel, rector of St. John's Seminary

1978 (15 Oct-24 December): Patrick Colleary molests ten-year-old Mark Kennedy

1979 (01 July) — 1980 (28 February): Indictment puts Giandelone's molestation of Ben Kulina in this time frame

1979 (August): Ladensack first reports a pedophile priest (Giandelone) to Bishop James S. Rausch

1979-1986: Keeps reporting pedophile to bishops

1980 (July): Joins Army Reserves as Chaplain

1981 (October): Giandelone later admits first time he had oral sex with Harry Takata Jr.

1981 (18 May): Bishop James S. Rausch dies of heart attack

1981 (09 November): O'Brien appointed Bishop of Phoenix

1983 (June): Ladensack resigns as Vicar of Christian Formation

1984 (January): O'Brien names Giandelone Campus Minister Bourgade High School

1984 (26 May) Saturday of Memorial Weekend: Harry Takata catches Fr. John Giandelone having oral sex with his son; Ladensack calls Bishop O'Brien's "Bat Phone"

1984 (01 June)-1986 (25 October): Associate pastor, St. Augustine's Parish (gang-infested) West Phoenix

1984 (June-Dec): Giandelone treated at Servants of Paraclete

1984 (29 October): Giandelone pleads guilty to one felony, one misdemeanor sex with a minor

1984 (November): Ladensack resigns Army Reserve Chaplain

1986 (24 October): On Joe's fortieth birthday, O'Brien revokes Ladensack's privileges (faculties) as priest

1986-1994: Practice Manager, Dr. Jim Young, Sierra Vista, Arizona

1989 (18 May): Bredemann pleads to reduced charge of child molestation

1990 (17 November): Deposition in George Bredemann civil case

1991 (14 October): Paul LeBrun has sex with minor Tommy Acosta

1993 (30 June): Dick Teron files suit in Roman Gomez case: defendants, Laurence Florez, Giandelone, Perez, Zubia

1994 (15 January): Ken Freedman severely injured in one-car crash near St. Joseph's Hospital

1994 (18 January): Freedman dies of his injuries in St. Joe's

1994 (07 June): Bishop O'Brien deposed by Dick Treon

1994 (04 July): Treon finds Ladensack in Sierra Vista

1995-2012: Ladensack employed by Sierra Vista United Methodist Church; Hacienda Rehab & Care Center; Dr. Monica Vandivort; Life Care; Valor Hospice

1995 (13 May): Joe Ladensack proposes to Anita Cooper

1995 (05 August): Joe Ladensack marries Anita Cooper

1995 (09 September): Chandler Police Officer Richard Felix found dead in patrol car of heart attack

1996 (15 May-31 August): Karl LeClaire molests minor Justin Mullins

1997 (June): Fr. John Picardi, known sex offender from Boston, placed in Phoenix Diocese

1998 (23 May): John Cooper's death

2002 (30 May): County Attorney Rick Romley announces Operation Broken Oath, a criminal investigation of Diocese of Phoenix

2002 (31 May): Romley's team serves subpoenas for church documents

2002 (June 27): Second set of subpoenas served. The two yield 100,000 docs

2002 (July): Grand jury empaneled to investigate Phoenix Diocese. This grand jury disbanded 06 November 2003 because several jurors dropped out

2002 (03 December): John Giandelone arrested at his home in Fort Myers, Florida, for 1979-80 molestations of Ben Kulina

2002 (04 December): Patrick Colleary arrested for sexually molesting eleven-year-old Mark Kennedy in 1978

2002 (08 December): Michael Manning quits as diocesan attorney after just six months

2002 (11 December) Ladensack located in Sierra Vista, Arizona, by Mark Stribling, chief investigator for Maricopa County Attorney

2002 (12 December): Stribling interviews Ladensack.

2003 (03 January): Joe Ladensack testifies before grand jury, Maricopa County, Phoenix, Arizona

2003 (08 January): Charges against Patrick Colleary dropped after Maricopa County Sheriff's Office finds a police report on the 1978 molestation, meaning statute of limitations expired

2003 (09 January): John Giandelone pleads guilty to sexually abusing Ben Kulina

2003 (10 February): Phoenix Diocese agrees to turn over 2,286 documents it had been fighting to keep

2003 (05 March): John Giandelone sentenced to twenty-two months in prison for rape of Ben Kulina

2003 (25 April): Mark Stribling and Cindi Nannetti give Jordan Green subpoena for O'Brien to grand jury

2003 (03 May) Bishop Thomas J. O'Brien signs a plea agreement admitting he covered up sex abuse by priests under his control for decades. The agreement is kept sealed for a month.

2003 (30 May): Mark Stribling arrests Fr. Paul LeBrun in South Bend, Indiana

2003 (02 June): Joseph A. Reaves breaks news of Romley's agreement with Bishop O'Brien in morning editions of *Arizona Republic.* That afternoon Romley's office publicly releases details of agreement along with indictments of six priests: Joseph Briceno; Patrick Colleary; Paul LeBrun; Karl LeClaire; Lawrence Lovell, and Henry Perez (deceased)

2003 (14 June): Bishop O'Brien kills forty-three-year-old carpenter Jim Reed in a hit-and-run accident.

2003 (16 June): Police arrest Bishop O'Brien at his residence. He is released on forty-five thousand dollar bond hours later.

2003 (17 June): Romley brings felony hit-and-run charges against O'Brien

2004 (17 February): Jury finds Bishop O'Brien guilty in hit-and-run death

2004 (23 March): Treon sues Bishop O'Brien in Harry Takata case

2004 (26 March): O'Brien sentenced to four years of probation and 1,000 hours of community service

2004 (02 September): Cindi Nannetti named Prosecutor of the Year

2005 (17 November): Former Phoenix Diocese priest Paul LeBrun convicted of sexually abusing eleven- to thirteen-year-old boys from 1986-91

2005 (21 November): Monsignor. Dale Fushek arrested on ten charges of sexual misconduct

2005 (12 December): Joseph Briceno, priest indicted in May 2003 on six counts of sexual conduct with a minor, is arrested in Mexico

2006 (13 January): LeBrun sentenced to 111 years in prison

2007 (January): Victim Harry Takata Jr. civil case deposition

2007 (March): Joe diagnosed with Hairy Cell Leukemia

2009 (March): Anita Ladensack diagnosed with breast cancer, treatment, remission

2010 (14 November): Charlie Cooper and Allison Ewing marry

2013 (February) Bone marrow biopsy confirms Hairy Cell leukemia has returned. Ladensack given six weeks to live

2013 (April): Joe and Anita Ladensack move to Tucson

2013 (23 May): Ladensack begins hospice on Memorial Day

2014 (November): Ladensack discharged from hospice

2016 (14 September): Complaint filed in Maricopa County Superior Court alleges former Bishop Thomas O'Brien had oral sex with an altar boy identified as "Joseph W." repeatedly before or during church services from 1977-82.

2017 (10 January): Amended allegations filed against O'Brien in the "Joseph W." case.

2017 (01 August): In oral arguments before Judge David K. Duvall, Phoenix Diocesan attorney John Kelly asks for summary dismissal of major portions of the "Joseph W." case against O'Brien.

2017 (24 August): Joe Ladensack and Joseph A. Reaves meet with Joseph W., a former altar boy who filed suit accusing Bishop Thomas J. O'Brien of sexually molesting him from 1977-82

2017 (20 November) Judge David K. Udall refuses request by former Bishop Thomas J. O'Brien's attorneys to "bifurcate" the civil suit filed in the "Joseph W." case. The ruling denied church attorneys' request that they be allowed to argue against "repressed memory" separately from the allegations against O'Brien. Instead, the case against "Perpetrator O'Brien" was allowed to move forward.

About the Authors

JOE LADENSACK was a highly decorated Infantry officer in Vietnam who came home to become a Roman Catholic Priest, school administrator, medical practice business manager, youth pastor, social worker, and hospice chaplain. He considers each to be a mission from God in his life-long journey. Ladensack lives in retirement with his wife, Anita Dawson Ladensack, in Tucson, Arizona. They are fifteen minutes from their son, Charlie Cooper, and his spouse, Allison Ewing-Cooper.

JOSEPH A. REAVES is a journalist, author, and former Major League Baseball front office executive who has lived and worked on five continents as a correspondent during a forty-year career. He was nominated for the Pulitzer Prize five times by the *Chicago Tribune* and *Arizona Republic.*

This is his fourth non-fiction book. He is also author of chapters on the history of baseball in Korea and China in two other collections.

Reaves received his undergraduate degree in journalism from Louisiana State University, where he is a member of the Manship School of Communication Hall of Fame. He has a Master of Philosophy in historical research from the University of Hong Kong and a Ph.D in Education Leadership and Policy Studies from Arizona State University.

Reaves and his wife, Lynne, live in Scottsdale, Arizona, with their two Labrador retrievers, Harry and Caray.

Index

www.hellgatepress.com